As If an Enemy's Country

PIVOTAL MOMENTS
IN AMERICAN HISTORY

Series Editors

David Hackett Fischer
James M. McPherson
David Greenberg

As If an ENEMY'S Country

The British Occupation of Boston and the Origins of Revolution

RICHARD ARCHER

OXFORD
UNIVERSITY PRESS

OXFORD
UNIVERSITY PRESS

Oxford University Press, Inc., publishes works that further
Oxford University's objective of excellence
in research, scholarship, and education.

Oxford   New York
Auckland   Cape Town   Dar es Salaam   Hong Kong   Karachi
Kuala Lumpur   Madrid   Melbourne   Mexico City   Nairobi
New Delhi   Shanghai   Taipei   Toronto

With offices in
Argentina   Austria   Brazil   Chile   Czech Republic   France   Greece
Guatemala   Hungary   Italy   Japan   Poland   Portugal   Singapore
South Korea   Switzerland   Thailand   Turkey   Ukraine   Vietnam

Copyright © 2010 by Richard Archer

Published by Oxford University Press, Inc.
198 Madison Avenue, New York, New York 10016
www.oup.com

First issued as an Oxford University Press paperback, 2012.

Oxford is a registered trademark of Oxford University Press

Library of Congress Cataloging-in-Publication Data
Archer, Richard, 1941–
As if an enemy's country : the British occupation
of Boston and the origins of revolution / Richard Archer.
p.   cm. — (Pivotal moments in American history)
Includes bibliographical references and index.
ISBN 978-0-19-538247-1 (hardcover); 978-0-19-989577-9 (paperback)
1. United States—History—Revolution, 1775–1783—Causes.
2. Boston (Mass.)—History—Colonial period, ca. 1600–1775.
I. Title.
E210.A73 2010
973.3—dc22   2009039919

1 3 5 7 9 8 6 4 2

Printed in the United States of America
on acid-free paper

For Julie Mayo, Steve Archer, and Steve Mayo

Contents

Illustrations

Editor's Note

Ten generations after the event, Americans still vividly remember their Great Revolution—and in very different ways. As these words were written on September 12, 2009, tens of thousands of angry taxpayers were marching through the streets of Washington. Some wore eighteenth-century dress. They remembered the Revolution as a revolt against taxation, and even against government itself—"Don't Tread on Me!"

Other Americans remember their Revolution as a larger movement, for a government that might actively protect many rights of the people, and serve their vital interests. An empathetic English leader observed in 1775 that the American colonists were moved by a multitude of "moral causes," and they felt deeply threatened by imperial oppression in many ways at once. They sought a strong and effective self-government that would respect rights of conscience, promote security of property, expand liberty of trade, and preserve trial by jury. Seamen in New England demanded protection against impressment. Hunters in North Carolina claimed a natural right to move beyond the mountains. Woodsmen in New Hampshire were outraged when imperial officials branded the King's broad arrow on their biggest trees and seized them for the Royal Navy. Teamsters in Delaware asserted their ancestral right to drive to Pennsylvania without being stopped by British customs officers. And people in many colonies regarded the presence of British troops as an army of occupation. Each of these many conflicts caused outbreaks of explosive violence before 1775.

This new book by Richard Archer reminds us that many Americans most deeply feared and loathed the tyranny of a standing army in their midst. This was specially the case in Boston, where on October 1, 1768, a fleet of British warships anchored in a ring around that unruly seaport, and three regiments of British infantry marched ashore with bayonets fixed. Town-born Bostonians perceived these redcoated regulars as invaders, and saw them as a double threat to liberty from arbitrary power, and freedom to govern themselves as they had always done.

The events that followed in Boston make a story of high drama, which is at the very heart of the American Revolution. No novelist could have invented the first collision. It happened at Boston's Manufactory House, a place of refuge for poor, ill, and homeless townfolk. Officials ordered their removal so that a regiment could be quartered there. The homeless refused to go, and an attempt was made to evict them by force. A "scuffle" followed, with swords and bayonets against tools and brooms. To everyone's amazement the homeless won and the troops retreated—not a good omen for the empire. Other scenes followed, with increasing violence. On the night of March 5, 1770, an angry mob rioted against the British troops. In turn, the angry soldiers rioted against the civilians, fired without orders, and five people died.

Many large themes run through the stories that are told in this book. One of them is about the mobilization of Boston's radical Whigs—not one group but many, and deeply divided in their thoughts and acts. Their leaders struggled to keep the Whig spirit growing, but also to keep it in bounds. Men such as Samuel Adams and John Adams were determined to win, but also mindful of the moderates. It is interesting to watch these very skillful politicians at work.

Another and more poignant theme is about the emergence of American loyalists. In 1765, the colonists had been nearly united against the Stamp Act. After 1766 they began to divide. Some deeply believed that the protection of human rights required both liberty and order. Boston's loyalist clergyman Mather Byles observed that he had less to fear from one tyrant three thousand miles away than three thousand tyrants one mile away. By 1775, New Englanders were speaking of the conflict not as a revolution but as a civil war.

Yet a third theme appeared in the cross-purposes of imperial leaders such as General Thomas Gage. They also thought of themselves as Whigs, and cherished the traditions of the English Revolution of 1688. Many were deeply divided within themselves. And the British troops in Boston were a trial for them as well. Edmund Burke observed that an army of occupation was "fully as difficult to be kept in obedience" as the people of the town. The result was a fatal combination of assertion and hesitation, aggression and retreat. In the pages of this fascinating book, we observe these events as a web of choices that caused the American Revolution, shaped its consequences, and are still evident in our divided purposes.

David Hackett Fischer

Introduction

A Garrisoned Town

Ambivalence about military power is not new to our era. English-speaking people in the eighteenth century supported their military during wartime. That was fortunate, for the British were engaged in combat against the French and their allies throughout a substantial part of the Northern Hemisphere for much of the 1700s. Expanding the British Empire and protecting existing territory seemed a worthy use of armed might. Officers chose (and purchased) military careers, soldiers and sailors enlisted when other options were worse or on occasion were impressed to service against their will, and the general citizenry reluctantly paid taxes, grateful that their involvement went no further.[1]

A standing army during peacetime, on the other hand, was something altogether different. British people had long believed that, rather than protecting the population and promoting imperial interests, its purpose was to enforce the will of those in power. It was a threat to basic British rights. To ensure that the military would be kept in check, Parliament authorized the army for only twelve months at a time by annually renewing the Mutiny Act, a bill that regulated mutinies and desertions and, most important, established the means for quartering and supplying troops, without which an army could not exist. On March 24, 1765, Parliament ominously extended the provisions of the Mutiny Act to its American colonies with the creation of the Quartering Act. Although its apparent rationale was to provision regiments and smaller units that temporarily dwelled in towns as they moved from one place to another, colonists felt threatened by the possibility of standing armies placed in their midst.[2] And they would be proved right.

Bostonians, more than most other Americans, considered themselves especially vulnerable. They were in the forefront of opposition to British revenue bills and enforcement of trade regulations. Following political protests in August 1765, when residents intimidated officials by physical harassment and destruction of private property, the British ministry perceived Boston popular leaders, including James Otis Jr. and Samuel Adams, as emerging rebels who required close monitoring and tightened supervision. Witnesses to recurring conflicts with Crown officials and reinforced by the time-honored fear of standing armies, Boston newspaper editors published articles elaborating on how such power would undermine inherent rights and spread rumors speculating on the imminent arrival of troops. Even the royal appointee, Lieutenant Governor Thomas Hutchinson, warned in October 1767, after the passage of a tax on paper, glass, lead, painters' colors, and tea, "It is impressed in the minds of the people that these Duties are a prelude to many more much heavier and that a Standing Army is to enforce Obedience and the Legislative power of the Colonies to be taken away." And on September 27, 1768, the minister of the New North Church, Andrew Eliot, lamented and prophesized, "To have a standing army! Good God! What can be worse to a people who have tasted the sweets of liberty! Things are come to an unhappy crisis; there will never be that harmony between Great Britain and her colonies, that there hath been; all confidence is at an end; and the moment there is any blood shed, all affection will cease."[3]

A day later, on September 28, six ships of war and two armed schooners sailed into Boston Harbor, augmenting at least six other British naval vessels already present. Onboard were the 14th and 29th Regiments, two companies of the 59th Regiment, and an artillery detachment. Two days later, in preparation for landing the troops, the war ships maneuvered closer to the town and ranged themselves as if for a siege. At about noon on Saturday, October 1, the two armed schooners and boats from the ships docked on the Long Wharf, a pier that jutted nearly two thousand feet out into the harbor, where first the 14th Regiment disembarked. With drums beating, fifes playing, and flags streaming, soldiers marched along the wharf past the shops and warehouses and continued up King Street, stopping at the Town House, the site of the colony's House of Representatives and Council, until the 29th Regiment arrived. The 29th echoed the 14th's pageantry, with the variation that the drummers of all nine companies were Afro-Caribbean, attired in yellow coats with red

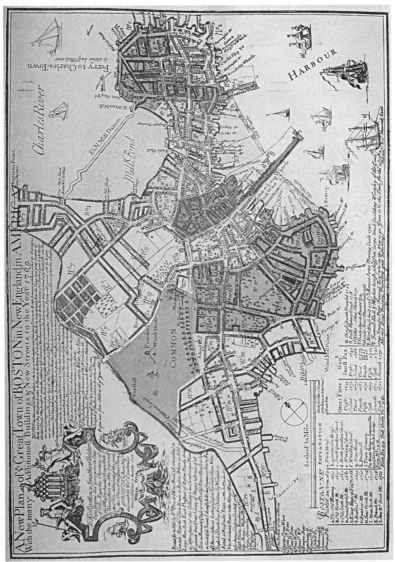

Boston, 1769. William Price's 1769 revision of John Bonner's map of Boston in 1722. Note that north is in the direction of the upper right corner. (Historic Urban Plans, Inc., Ithaca, New York)

facing and lapels. From the Town House, the two regiments paraded up a few short blocks of mixed residences and shops until they reached the Common. By midafternoon the companies of the 59th and the artillery detachment had joined them.[4]

In all, roughly twelve hundred British soldiers and officers had landed in Boston. In November two regiments from Ireland, the 64th and most of the 65th, arrived, increasing the total to approximately two thousand.[5] Wives, children, and hangers-on accompanied the troops and enlarged their impact, as did the crews and officers aboard the ships of war.

Their presence was an overwhelming and often hostile addition to the town. As of the census of 1765, Boston had a total population of 15,520, a number that included slaves, apprentices, and servants, though not the normal transients of a seaport. Within the provincial city, 2,941 were white males above the age of sixteen, and 510 were male "Negroes and Molattoes" of all ages.[6] If we assume that there were as many as five hundred male transients (merely a guess, and a generous one), adult males constituted no more than four thousand persons. In short, during the British occupation of Boston, one man in three was a soldier. Redcoats were everywhere, on duty and off. Theirs was not a casual or unobtrusive presence. In the streets, along the ropewalks, in the taverns, directly outside the Town House where the main guard was located, at checkpoints, on the Common, daytime and night, the people of Boston encountered the representatives of British power. They could not be avoided.

Boston in 1768 was a much smaller city than we know it today. Its entire circumference was merely four miles, and it was less than three miles from the neck that linked the town to the mainland to the northeastern corner, where the Charlestown ferry landing stood. The bulk of the population resided either in the North End or the South End, which together composed two-thirds of the peninsula. Taking a brisk walk, in about an hour a person could see most of Boston, with its three hills, wood buildings and residences, church spires, and wharfs. No sidewalks aided the pedestrian, nor were there streetlamps providing light after dark.[7]

The British troops upon landing may have been pleased with what they saw. Three years earlier Lord Adam Gordon had described Boston as "more like an English Old Town than any in America." But they would have been foolish to assume that familiarity meant welcome.

A South East View of the Great Town of Boston in New England in America, an engraving by John Carwitham between 1730 and 1760. (Library of Congress)

Though they had not experienced the violent confrontation that had been rumored, for the most part they were met with sullen stares and silence. More overt opposition would come soon enough. "All is at present quiet," Andrew Eliot wrote in mid-October, "but there is a general gloom and uneasiness." He portrayed Boston as a garrisoned town, a recurring characterization used by town residents. Over time, the resentment grew. On April 15, 1769, the Massachusetts Council, writing the Earl of Hillsborough, secretary of state for the American colonies, complained that the secrecy and circumstances attending the landing of troops in Boston were "as if in an Enemy's Country."[8] The ministry was treating American colonies, Boston in particular, as alien land, and colonists, Bostonians in particular, recognized the change. Their loyalty to England was shaken. The immediate issue facing them was how to remove the occupying force. The larger issue was the colonies' place within the empire, and indeed whether there should be a place for them within the empire.

Boston remained an occupied town for seventeen months, until the tragic events of the evening of March 5, 1770. A year and a half is not long by planetary standards—barely the beginning of a blink of an eye—but for mere mortals it can be transformative; attitudes can change, new ideas develop, economic conditions alter, love bloom (and die), governments be overthrown, believers convert, and peace sprout and shrivel. So much is possible. Thirty-five years after the occupation, Mercy Otis Warren, a friend or relation of several Massachusetts leaders, wrote in her three-volume 1805 history of the American Revolution that the "American war may be dated from the hostile parade" of October 1, 1768, when "several regiments were landed, and marched sword in hand through the principal streets of their city, then in profound peace."[9] In this book I explore whether Warren's assessment is accurate by examining what decisions and events led to the military occupation of Boston, what transpired while British troops were there, and what the consequences were.

From Warren's distance of slightly more than a quarter of a century, and especially from our perspective of nearly a quarter of a millennium, the revolutionary past appears to be determined. We are so familiar with what occurred that we assume there were no alternatives. But neither the occupation nor the American Revolution was inevitable. Human will may be limited by the context of the time and the passions of the moment, but it still is powerful. Other decisions could have been made; other actions could have been taken. This is the story of the choices that were made and the results that followed.

As If an Enemy's Country

Chapter 1

Grenville's Innovation

When he accepted the position of prime minister on April 16, 1763, George Grenville could reflect on how fortunate and privileged his first fifty years had been. Educated at Eton and Oxford, called to the Bar, and first elected to Parliament at age twenty-nine, he joined his first ministry just three years later. Hard work, honesty, and the ability to master the intricacies of finance contributed to his success, but family connections should not be discounted. He had been elected to Parliament, after all, as the beneficiary of all thirteen votes in his uncle's "pocket borough," and he was the brother-in-law of the charismatic and mercurial William Pitt, the "Great Commoner."

Not inclined to take risks, Grenville labored in the familial trenches until 1760, when he broke with his more powerful older brother, Richard, Earl Temple, and Pitt over what came to be called the Seven Years' War. Seemingly out of character, he boldly chose to join the youthful, new king, George III, and the king's former tutor and ongoing mentor, Lord Bute, in seeking peace. Although the American phase of the world war, called the French and Indian War, concluded in September 1760 and the conflict in India ended soon after, battles in Europe blazed on. When Bute became prime minister in 1762, he rewarded Grenville with the important ministerial position of secretary of state for the Northern Department. Bute, not well liked beyond the king's circle, quickly showed his inexperience and poor judgment by secretly opening preliminary discussions for peace with France without first consulting his cabinet. Grenville, demonstrating a surprising backbone, objected to Bute's unilateral initiative. Needing his parliamentary connections, Bute retained Grenville in the ministry but demoted him to first lord of

The Right Honourable George Grenville, First Lord Commissioner of the Admiralty, circa 1760, a mezzotint by James Watson based on William Hoare's painting. (Emmet Collection, Miriam and Ira D. Wallach Division of Art, Prints and Photographs, The New York Public Library, Astor, Lenox and Tilden Foundations)

the Admiralty. After countering Pitt and Temple on the one hand and objecting to Bute's approach to peace on the other (on top of which, the king considered him tedious), Grenville must have been surprised after Bute's resignation to find himself head of the ministry.[1]

Grenville inherited a complicated political situation. The most favorable circumstance was the official conclusion of the Seven Years' War. The Treaty of Paris, with the accompanying Treaty of San Ildefonso, gave Britain a resounding victory over France and a favorable arrangement with France's ally Spain. All of North America east of the Mississippi River, including Canada and Florida (Florida at the time not only designated the current state but also today's gulf coast Alabama and Mississippi), was now under British rule. France forfeited its territorial claims in India and militarily retreated in Europe. The West Indies retained its European imperial cast, but Britain brought several more islands into its empire. Without a doubt, Great Britain had become the dominant world power. No European nation could equal Britain's hegemony, and only insular China might have been a genuine rival.[2]

As always, such power came at a great cost. To defeat the French and their allies, the British under William Pitt spent as if they had unlimited resources. Near bankruptcy accompanied their triumph. The overall national debt nearly doubled during the war to almost 150 million pounds sterling. Interest on the debt alone required about half of the total annual revenue (9.8 million pounds). Collecting proved a problem as the war's costs mounted. Taxes on beer, tobacco, and other items dear to ordinary citizens supplemented traditional property taxes. When Parliament passed a tax on cider at the war's end and the beginning of a postwar depression, residents of cider-producing counties rose up in public and noisy protest.[3]

Disturbances in the home country were only a part of the disarray that confronted Grenville. Despite occasional ministerial stabs at bringing about administrative oversight and coherent policy, the colonies, for the most part, ran as local enterprises. The Crown appointed governors, lieutenant governors, and sometimes councils, but popularly elected assemblies who paid the officials' salaries and raised revenue for government operations checked the mother country's power. Diverted by warfare, the empire, by default, was more a federation of affiliated states than a centrally organized institution.

In the waning months of Bute's short ministry, he and his colleagues, with strong prompting from George III, decided to retain a substantial portion of the army in the postwar empire. They did not desire to return to the lower troop levels existing prior to the Seven Years' War. The world, their world, had changed. Defeated nations might want to reclaim and expand their territories; non-English residents of Canada, Nova Scotia, East Florida, and West Florida might grow restive; and there was always the possibility that contact between colonial settlers and traders on the one side and Indians of the Ohio Country on the other would lead to violence. There also was the problem of reducing the officer corps. Forced retirement would mean half-pay for many officers who held seats in Parliament or whose relations did, and George III and Bute were well aware of the potential impact on patronage; and the king, like previous Hanoverian monarchs, held a vital interest in the protection of his military.[4] All were good reasons for maintaining a large, permanent army. So much for the peace dividend.

The traditional antipathy to a standing army, the state of the national debt, and the resistance to new taxes in Great Britain together demanded clever solutions by the Bute ministry to gain parliamentary approval. Reducing the number of soldiers by half while retaining nearly all officers had several virtues. Not only would there be a significant financial savings, but it would keep the administrative structure in place. Should there be a military emergency, the return to wartime strength could be rapid, with enlisted men joining existing regiments. The ministry shrewdly decided that there would be somewhat fewer soldiers in Britain, alleviating fears among the home population of military abuse. The increase would be located in Ireland, where six thousand troops would be stationed (still in the British Isles but not in England), and in North America, where ten thousand soldiers and officers, three times the prewar level, would be placed, far exceeding what was required for security. The number of troops there and in Ireland represented the needs of the empire as a whole, for regiments could be transported wherever there was trouble. What was important to the Bute ministry was keeping no more than a normal military profile in the mother country.

But no matter where the army was located, it still would be costly. From the perspective of London, the solution was obvious: find funding elsewhere. When George III disingenuously claimed that the expenses of the postwar military establishment would be a hundred pounds cheaper than in 1749, he meant that they would be cheaper for the taxpayers of England, not that overall costs would be reduced. The Irish Parliament was responsible for paying for the troops in its midst, and American colonists had a similar obligation for their ten thousand. With little debate, Parliament approved the enlarged peacetime army.[5]

Grenville then faced the monumental task of simultaneously achieving financial solvency and establishing imperial order and sovereignty. He began by implementing and improving the administration of existing law. In the previous year, as first lord of the Admiralty, he had pushed for the enactment of a bill authorizing British ships of war to enforce trade laws. He had added the incentive that crews would share half the proceeds from unlawful merchant ships they seized. The objective was to increase revenue from trade duties by preventing smuggling. The unfortunate result, however, was the transformation of part of the Royal Navy from protectors of commerce to predators on colonial merchant ships. Beginning in May 1763, forty-four ships of the line began policing the sea, some behaving like buccaneers. Grenville also sought to improve customs collection at colonial ports. At the time, the expense of the customs service in the colonies far exceeded revenues it obtained. Collectors who never left England constituted part of the problem. They took their salaries and subcontracted the work to someone at the colonial port, who in turn supplemented his income by taking bribes from merchants who therefore did not pay duties. Everyone along the chain except the government benefited. The remedy was to require customs officials to be in residence. The ministry promptly issued the order that customs men had to leave Britain by August 31, 1763, or face dismissal.[6]

Fixing the bits and parts was an advance, but soon Grenville authorized the construction of a more comprehensive plan for raising revenue and instituting sovereignty over Britain's colonies. After half a year of reports, recommendations, and draft resolutions and having prevailed against a vigorous attack on his ministry from opponents in Parliament, he was prepared and confident of success. On March 9, 1764, he submitted a bill to the House of Commons, and again with little debate it passed through both the House and the Lords and was signed by George III in early April.[7]

Thus was born what came to be called the Sugar Act. On its face, it might appear little more than a revision of previous legislation—a tweak here, a twist there. But at its core dwelled a revolutionary change in the relations of the mother country and her colonies. Although a few articles dealt exclusively with the regulation of trade, such as the requirement that lumber and iron "shall not be landed in any part of *Europe* except *Great Britain*," the central focus of the Act was the collection of revenue in the American colonies. There was no mistaking that the Sugar Act was a tax bill. The preamble, declaring its intent to raise funds to help pay for troops in North America, made that clear. Up to this time, Parliament had requisitioned money through colonial legislatures, allowing the constitutional voices of those who were to be taxed to be heard. For the first time, the British government (Crown and all) prepared to tax colonists directly, with no pretense of representation. The Sugar Act delineated taxable commodities and outlined measures for eliminating, or at least significantly reducing, smuggling.[8] It was a tax bill, not a trade bill.

There was an extensive list of taxed items—foreign sugar, indigo, coffee, wine, and textiles of various types—but Grenville's greatest hope for filling His Majesty's coffers was foreign molasses. There was precedent for a duty on molasses. Passed at the instigation of British West Indies sugar growers, the Molasses Act of 1733 had placed a tariff of six cents per gallon on foreign molasses, making it more expensive than domestic. Molasses, the syrupy residue of refined sugar, was used as a low-grade sweetener and was the essential ingredient of rum, whose production was an important industry in the northern colonies.

As it turned out, the Molasses Act was both unnecessary and ill conceived. The British West Indies did not produce enough molasses to satisfy demand, and after their own distilleries had filled their needs there was little left to be sold. They did not need protection or a stimulus for increasing demand. Moreover, from New England's perspective, foreign molasses, particularly from the French West Indies, where there was an abundance, was essential. And there was the additional benefit of the French Caribbean market, a market that provided a favorable trade balance to New Englanders, thus allowing them to purchase other goods elsewhere. The duty of six cents a gallon on molasses made the production of rum unprofitable. New Englanders therefore had the choice of closing their distilleries and significantly reducing business with the French West Indies or avoiding the duty by smuggling. Merchants quickly discovered that a bribe to customs officials between half a cent and one and a half cents per gallon made smuggling profitable. Grenville's hope was that the combination of tougher inspection and a lower duty would make payments on molasses preferable to the dangers of smuggling. After weighing possible tax returns against projected levels of merchant compliance with the law, he settled on the tax of three cents per gallon.[9]

Slightly more than half of the Sugar Act's forty-seven articles involved enforcement, and most of the burden was placed on merchants' shoulders. They had to post substantial bonds. No cargo could be loaded before the posting, and at their destination ship captains had to present a certificate proving that bond had been posted. The government could hold bonds for up to a year after the completion of the voyage. Merchants had to secure affidavits testifying to the provenance of sugar, rum, spirits, and molasses. They also had to provide lists of all cargo before sailing and certificates verifying those lists at the port where the cargo was unloaded. The Sugar Act empowered the Navy to search ships within six miles of shore. Penalties for violations ranged from forfeiting a bond to losing the ship and its cargo and incurring triple damages. Royal Navy ships split the proceeds with the Crown. At ports customs officials could expect a one-third share, the other two-thirds being divided between the governor of the province and the Crown. Should a merchant want to appeal a seizure of his ship and cargo, he had to pay sixty pounds just to go to court, and even then the burden was on him to prove his innocence. If the court determined that there had been probable cause for seizing a ship, though there had been no actual violation of the Act, the customs official faced no liability; the Sugar Act instructed juries to find all persons engaged in enforcing its provisions not guilty. Should the prosecutor choose an admiralty court rather than a common court, there would be no jury, only a Crown-appointed judge.[10]

When Grenville began his tenure as prime minister, the national debt was enormous, and supporting a large military added to the burden. British taxpayers already were taking to the streets and it was politically unwise to increase their obligations. From the vantage point of Whitehall, moreover, colonists were only loosely connected to the empire. Taxing them and cracking down on smugglers would raise revenue and centralize authority, and it seemed reasonable to expect that Americans should contribute to their own defense. It was time to remind colonists that they were colonists. What Grenville may not have realized was that the Sugar Act did not affect all colonists equally or similarly. The region most closely coupled to rum distilleries and trade with the French West Indies, New England, would disproportionately experience the new customs rules. For now, Grenville withdrew the resolution for a stamp tax, at least until he heard reactions from the colonies and what alternatives they might offer.

These new British policies could not have come at a much worse time for the people of Boston. By the mid-eighteenth century, the town no longer was the premier urban center in British North America. Wars, competition from other seaports, epidemics, and limited exportable produce and goods had all taken their toll. The overall population had diminished, while at the same time the number of poor had increased. Such formerly prosperous industries as shipbuilding declined, and unemployment rose. The American phase of the Seven Years' War sporadically energized and enriched merchants supplying the British military, but for many Bostonians the economy remained depressed. Perhaps a patriotic zeal to protect their province from French and Indian attack prompted men to volunteer, but it is equally plausible that they joined the army as an alternative to unemployment. In either case, Massachusetts contributed far more than her share of men, more than New York and Pennsylvania combined. By war's end, a third of eligible Massachusetts men had served, and one-tenth of the provincial soldiers had died.[11]

All of the American colonies experienced a decade-long, postwar depression, but Massachusetts, particularly Boston, was hit hardest. The economic boost from military expenditures disappeared, and unemployment increased as mustered-out soldiers returned. Fewer merchant ships sailed; artisans, shopkeepers, and merchants failed; and the widows and children of fallen soldiers augmented the ranks of the poor.[12]

The costs of poor relief mounted at a steady rate, and the debts accrued from the war were staggering. Despite 350,000 pounds in reimbursements from Great Britain, Massachusetts in 1761 still owed creditors 500,000 pounds for military expenses, a sum five times greater than the annual provincial revenues of roughly 100,000 pounds. By the end of the war, the average Boston taxpayer faced a 60 percent increase in town and province taxes, a levy that was higher than anywhere else in the empire, including England, and unmanageable for many of Boston's citizens. Samuel Adams, a wily politician and perhaps the most compassionate of the town's tax collectors in the early 1760s, gained popularity by his reluctance to press for payment. Yet what could be done? Economic distress made it nearly impossible for substantial segments of the population to meet their obligations, and for several years in succession tax revenue fell short of the town's requisitions.[13]

Compounding Boston's economic miseries were the twin calamities of fire and disease. On March 20, 1760, after three days of small fires, the town suffered its worst conflagration of the entire colonial period. Beginning at two in the morning, flames spread from the house of Mary Jackson on Cornhill Street to adjoining houses and buildings. Five hours later, when townspeople had finally contained the blaze, a large part of the central section of the city had been consumed: 174 houses and tenements (roughly 10 percent of all dwellings) and 175 warehouses, shops, and other commercial buildings had burned to the ground. Home furnishings, artisans' tools, and merchants' goods were destroyed as well. At least 220 families lost their homes, and three-quarters of them were instantly destitute. Damages from the fire totaled at least 100,000 pounds sterling—as we've seen, equivalent to the tax revenues the entire province of Massachusetts raised in a year. The proud citizens of Boston had to look beyond their community for assistance, which came from Massachusetts towns, other colonies, and even from London. The following year, Faneuil Hall, the site of the town meeting with a capacity for a thousand people, town offices, and a general marketplace, disappeared in flames, only its brick walls left standing. Almost miraculously, within a year it was resurrected. And on January 25, 1764, on the other side of the Charles River in Cambridge, Harvard Hall, which contained the College's library, telescopes, and other "valuable treasures," caught fire and was destroyed. The General Court of the colony, having fled from a smallpox epidemic in Boston, had been holding sessions there while students were on vacation, and after the representatives had left for the day a spark from the fireplace ignited a beam over the hearth. The House voted to compensate Harvard for its loss, but at this point every penny was dear.[14]

Apparently no person perished in any of the fires; the smallpox epidemic, which raged through Boston from December 1763 to July 1764, was a different story. By late June 170 people had died: 124 from the disease and 46 from inoculation. At first, the disease worked stealthily, and it took nearly a month before Bostonians became cognizant of the danger. By January 17, members of the House learned that smallpox had spread to seven or eight houses, and hence when they formally requested that Governor Francis Bernard "adjourn them to Cambridge," Bernard readily approved. The ensuing month, Boston physicians agreed to establish a hospital for inoculation. Recipients of the vaccine could stay at the hospital or some other quarantined dwelling, but in either case they had to remain isolated during recovery, a period typically ranging from three to six weeks. The *Boston Gazette* reported that "near 2500 People" were inoculated in the first week "since Liberty was granted" to administer it.[15]

Other protective measures soon were taken. Assuming that the contagion had come from merchant ships, authorities kept cargoes from being unloaded and crews from coming ashore. The *Gazette* assured readers that its paper had arrived six months earlier, but "if any are timerous, and chuse to discontinue, they are requested to send their Pay for what may be due."[16]

Many who were able left town. "Philip Freeman, Hereby gives Notice to his Country Customers, That on Account of the Small Pox being likely to spread in Boston, he has open'd a Shop of Goods at Medfield, at the House of Mr. Nathan Plimpton's, very near the Meeting House, where they may be accommodated the same as at Boston," read one of five similar merchants' ads on February 27. More followed.[17] With trade at a standstill, few residents escaped the impact of the disease.

It was at this devastating moment that Bostonians received word of the impending Sugar Act. Nearly everyone determined that it was an ill-conceived piece of legislation that would do more harm than good, yet few comprehended the degree of popular consensus on the subject, Governor Francis Bernard among them. Before arriving in Massachusetts in 1760, Bernard had been governor of New Jersey, where he had been reasonably successful. Massachusetts, however, offered the possibility of a greater income that would help support his large family and a more prestigious position that would help feed his ambitions. Like other royal governors, he was responsible for representing the Crown's interests and enforcing parliamentary law, and yet his salary came from the colonial legislature and he lived among colonists. His public role was clear, even though he might play it in as accommodating a way as possible. He might have reservations, even serious disagreements, about British policy, but they had to remain private. Confidentially—and only confidentially—he was concerned about the tightening trade restrictions. In a series of letters to friends and officials in England prior to the passage of the Sugar Act, Bernard argued for a relaxation of trade laws, particularly in relation to the West Indies. In his estimation, both Britain and America would benefit by lowering the duty on molasses to a penny per gallon. "I am all this while arguing against my own interest," he asserted in a letter to the lord commissioners for trade and plantations. "Laws that are like to be productive of Forfeitures ought to be acceptable to Governors. But, for my own part, I should be glad, at the expence of all such Profits, to see the Laws of Trade in America so regulated, as to be effectually executed, chearfully submitted to, and most conducive to the advantage of Great Britain." A year later he secretly backed a petition from the Massachusetts House and Council requesting the rescinding (or at least a major modification) of the Sugar Act and opposing the imposition of a stamp tax.[18]

The lieutenant governor, Thomas Hutchinson, found himself in an even more complex situation. Unlike the English-born Bernard, Hutchinson was a native son of Massachusetts and a direct descendent of Anne Hutchinson. Born into wealth, bright, tall and handsome, ambitious, a devotee of fashion who instructed his London tailor on the smallest details of his clothing, and an elitist, he promoted himself, his family and kin, his empire, his colony, and his town—more or less in that order. He quickly showed an aptitude for augmenting his riches as a merchant and acquiring power as a politician. In 1737, when just twenty-six years of age, Hutchinson first was elected as one of Boston's representatives to the House of Representatives. Nine years later he rose to speaker of the house. As a consequence of leading the victorious fight to restore Massachusetts's currency to a hard-money standard, he alienated Boston's consumers and debtors—the bulk of the population—and never won another popular election. His political alliance of family and friends, fellow merchants, and rural conservatives (often referred to as the Hutchinson-Oliver faction, or the court faction) ensured that he still would hold office. At the time of the Sugar Act, he was, simultaneously, lieutenant governor, chief justice of Massachusetts's highest court, a member of the Council, and a judge of probate in Suffolk County.[19]

As a merchant and citizen of Boston and Massachusetts, Hutchinson found fault with the new British policies. As a royal officeholder with ambitions and as a guardian of the standing order, he defended the prerogative of the Crown and the sovereignty of Parliament. His dilemma was how to reconcile the two. His solution was to protest the economic consequences of the Sugar Act but to avoid publicly challenging Parliament's right to tax the colonies. Hutchinson was able to finesse this position through the legislature, but not without adding to his growing list of detractors.[20]

At the head of the list was James Otis Jr. The Otis family had been rivals of Hutchinson and his faction since the late 1750s, and in the early 1760s James Otis took the lead. As a young man, he had left the comforts of the family home in Barnstable (on Cape Cod) for the lure of Boston. Smart, articulate, even eloquent, and seeking advancement, he quickly established a thriving law practice and married a wealthy heiress. He maintained a strong bond with his family while forging

Thomas Hutchinson, eighteenth century, oil on canvas by unidentified artist, after Edward Truman's portrait of Hutchinson. (Courtesy of the Massachusetts Historical Society)

his own path. His father being Barnstable's representative and speaker of the Massachusetts House and a man with extensive financial ties assisted the son's progress, but James Jr. was so obviously capable that he readily attracted attention from Boston's elite. Bernard's predecessor, Thomas Pownall, appointed him deputy advocate general of the vice admiralty court in 1757, a lucrative post that augmented his legal fees by two hundred pounds per year. When the chief justice position opened as a result of Samuel Sewall's death in 1760, Otis became the point man for his father's aspirations. Apparently, two governors, William Shirley and Pownall, had promised James Sr. the office upon the next vacancy. Bernard, new to the Massachusetts governorship, faced his first critical political decision. He could appoint Otis Sr., but in doing so he would alienate his lieutenant governor and his faction. Another option was to elevate one of the other Superior Court justices (all allies, if not relations, of Hutchinson) to chief justice and offer Otis a Superior Court judgeship. Instead, he offered the chief justice position to Hutchinson, a person

The Hon. James Otis, jun. Esq, circa 1770, a woodcut on the cover of *Bickerstaff's Boston Almanack*. To the left Hercules stomps on a snake, and to the right Minerva holds a staff with a liberty cap on top. (Library of Congress)

with administrative experience but no legal training. The Otis family was outraged, and James Jr. soon thereafter became the leading voice of the opposition faction.[21]

The event that catapulted Otis into public attention was the writs of assistance case. In 1755 the Superior Court began issuing writs of assistance—general search warrants that required no specific indication of illegal activity and authorized the holder to inspect any house or warehouse during the day—to customs officials. George II died in 1760, and the writs issued during his reign expired six months later. Charles Paxton, the Boston collector of customs, most likely requested a revival of the writs. A large group of merchants countered with their own petition to the Superior Court, opposing the renewal. The court hearing opened in February 1761 before an influential audience in the Council chamber of the Town House. All five justices, including Chief

Justice Thomas Hutchinson, who presided, sat in traditional judicial garb, and all the lawyers of Boston and Middlesex County, dressed in their legal finery, attended. Jeremiah Gridley, representing the Crown, argued that Parliament had granted the exchequer the right to issue writs of assistance and that subsequent statutes had given colonial courts, including the Massachusetts Superior Court, similar power. Extensive precedent, he continued, supported him.

The merchants' lawyers, Oxenbridge Thacher and James Otis, in turn offered their counterarguments. Thacher's response was straightforward and simple: the writs were illegal because the Superior Court did not have authority to originate them; the Court of Exchequer had powers that colonial courts lacked. When Otis's turn came, he opted against narrow legal arguments and instead raised fundamental principles. General writs were wrong and illegal, he argued passionately, because they violated the basic right of domestic security. Unless there was specific cause for government intrusion, a man's home was sacrosanct. There were rights greater than parliamentary law.[22]

Otis must have been delighted to help place Hutchinson in the predicament of having to decide between the Crown and customs service on the one hand and a substantial segment of Boston's merchant community on the other. Hutchinson, for his part, did what any skilled politician would do: he postponed making a decision. Avoiding the great principles Otis had espoused, he adjourned the court until word could be received from England on the narrow question of what types of writs the exchequer was authorizing. Nine months later, with all information in, Hutchinson and the Superior Court determined that they could provide writs to Boston's customs officers.[23]

The decision, coming on top of Hutchinson's role in Massachusetts's currency debate and his relentless accumulation of political offices, diminished further his standing with the Boston community, while the writs case elevated Otis's esteem in the eyes of merchants, shopkeepers, and artisans connected to trade, indeed anyone alienated from established power. In May 1761 Otis's fellow citizens elected him one of Boston's four representatives to the Massachusetts legislature, and he remained one of the town's most influential leaders throughout the decade.

How much Otis believed the principles of his writs argument and how much he was using the case to attack Hutchinson is difficult to know with certainty. During the years he served as deputy advocate general of the vice admiralty court, with the responsibility of prosecuting smugglers, he did not once object to writs of assistance. After the writs hearing he often reiterated and elaborated on his natural rights discourse, but he also contradicted himself. His 1764 pamphlet, *The Rights of the British Colonies,* asserted that there were laws higher than parliamentary acts, that Parliament had no right to tax colonies without their consent, and that the American colonies should have their own representatives in Parliament; his 1765 tract, *A Vindication of the British Colonies,* proclaimed the sovereignty of Parliament. He took pleasure in verbally attacking Thomas Hutchinson, but on occasion he vacillated so much as to break with his allies and even vote for Hutchinson's chief justice salary.[24]

Otis was a complex and erratic man. Bernard described him as possessing a violent temperament and capable of confounding his friends with his inconstancy. Similarly, John Adams, in the privacy of his diary, characterized him as "fiery and fev'rous. His Imagination flames, his Passions blaze. He is liable to great Inequalities of Temper—sometimes in Despondency, sometimes in a Rage."[25] Eloquence, energy, and charisma were his strengths; inconsistency and instability were his disabilities.

As the Grenville ministry created the Sugar Act and moved it through Parliament, then, Boston was divided between two political factions that fought over the distribution of power and their self-interest but that often unknowingly agreed in their concern over emerging British trade and tax policies. The court faction, headed by Hutchinson, consisted of a group of men connected by patronage, family, friendship, and an elitist worldview. They were a small but powerful minority within Boston, where they were able to capture only one of the four representative slots in the early 1760s and none after 1765. Were it not for alliances with representatives from the countryside, with their conservative and deferential traditions, the court faction would have had little influence in the legislature. Their power resided in the Council, the courts, and appointive offices.

The popular faction combined a loose-knit band of men who for one reason or another were disaffected with Bernard or the customs service or Hutchinson or the court faction or anyone seemingly responsible for the hard times. Otis was the most important public face of the faction, but he was not *the* leader. He was far too mercurial, too apt to chart his own course. The popular faction was strongest in the House, well represented in the Council, but was absent from most appointed positions. It also had a significant, often controlling presence in the Boston town meeting.

The two factions countered each other much as segments of Massachusetts's government checked and balanced power. The royally appointed governor with the advice of the Council administered the province. He could make judicial appointments and request the support of British troops, for example, but only with the Council's concurrence. Members of the House of Representatives were popularly elected by towns (each town had at least one representative, some had two, and Boston had four) and, with the Council serving as an upper house, had broad legislative powers, the most important being the raising of revenue. The governor could not authorize expenditures, not even the paying of his own salary, without legislative approval, but he could veto any bill he chose. He was obligated by charter to call elections for the House and Council each May (the twenty-eight members of the next year's Council were nominated by the House and the current Council but required the governor's consent to be seated), but was empowered to adjourn or prorogue the House at his discretion. The governor, Council, and House together formed the General Court, which on occasion functioned as a court, such as resolving disputes between towns over boundaries.[26] Within this convoluted structure, the court faction and the popular faction vied for power.

Perhaps because of the distracting heat of political rivalries, the trauma of a smallpox epidemic, or the hope that the ministry and Parliament would recognize their mistakes and rectify them on their own, the more vigorous enforcement of trade laws and the enactment of the Sugar Act prompted only a tepid response. Not a single Massachusetts institution even bothered to instruct its agent in London to oppose such action. The reaction was local and scattered: individuals wrote letters, newspapers printed critical articles, and the Boston Merchants Club, which reconstituted itself as a permanent organization, contacted fellow merchants in other colonies and England for their support.[27]

In October 1763 one of Boston's representatives, Thomas Cushing, had presciently informed Jasper Mauduit, the colony's agent, of the economic consequences of tightening trade restrictions. The basic problem, in Cushing's estimation, was that the British West Indies did not have sufficient molasses for the northern colonies' distillery needs or an adequate market for their lower-quality fish, an important part of the catch that had no purchasers in Europe. Without the French and Dutch West Indies trade, the fishing industry would be severely reduced, and New Englanders would have no funds with which to purchase British goods in current quantities. British manufacturers and their employees would be hurt, and "Great Britain will be deprived of an nursery for Seamen." Foreign colonies could satisfy both supply and market issues, but only if the duty on molasses was low enough to make New Englanders a profit. Two weeks later, in another letter to Mauduit, Cushing asserted that with the molasses duty at six pence per gallon (the rate prior to the Sugar Act), traders would have the option of desisting or smuggling. "In either case the Crown will receive no revenue," he concluded. Cushing recommended the duty be set at "an half penny or a penny per gallon." His was the typical response at the time, the primary focus being on the economic consequences of British policy rather than on its philosophical assumptions. Only rarely did someone challenge Parliament's right to tax the colonies without their having representatives. That would come before long.[28]

An extract of the Sugar Act first appeared in Boston newspapers on May 7, 1764. Townspeople might have been relieved that a stamp tax had been postponed, but they could no longer ignore the reality that a threshold had been crossed. Britain's new law jeopardized their trade and fisheries as well as undermined their rights as Englishmen. Acquiescence no longer was an option. Shortly before the annual election, "Nov-Anglicanus" in the *Boston Gazette*, the town's most radical newspaper, demanded that passive representatives be replaced by a House that would stand up for Massachusetts's interests and rights. "Let them account for their neglect or be neglected themselves," he cajoled his readers. After the election, Boston instructed its representatives—Royall Tyler, James Otis Jr., Thomas Cushing, and Oxenbridge Thacher—"to support our Commerce in all its Just Rights, to vindicate it from all unreasonable Impositions and promote its prosperity."[29]

When the House met in June, despite the growing fervor among its constituents, it accomplished little more than finally sending instructions to Jasper Mauduit and rebuking him with the weak charge that "the Silence of the Province should have been imputed to any Cause, even to Dispair, rather than be construed into a tacit Cession of their Rights, or an Acknowledgment of a Right in the Parliament of Great-Britain to impose Duties and Taxes upon a People, who are not represented in the House of Commons." As disjointed as any communication written by committee, the letter jumped from topic to topic, but it provided a number of arguing points for Mauduit and made clear that he should attempt "to obtain a Repeal of the Sugar-Act, and prevent the Imposition of any further Duties or Taxes on these Colonies." Along with its letter, the House sent a copy of Otis's *Rights of the British Colonies*.[30]

Soon thereafter Bernard prorogued the legislature and did not call it back into session until October. The governor hoped to hinder more radical statements, in particular a petition to Parliament denying its right to tax the colonies. He also wished to impress his London masters and to flaunt his authority, even when it needlessly antagonized the opposition.[31]

Newspapers continued to print articles critical of British taxation policy, although there was little new content to them, simply variations of the economic and rights arguments. However, a new tactic arose in September, when Bostonians conspired to limit their purchases of British-made clothing. Rather than acquiring new mourning clothes, for example, men limited the symbol of their grief to a mourning band and women forsook full funeral regalia for "black Bonnet, Gloves, Ribbons, and Handkerchiefs." Many tradesmen resolved to wear only leather garments rather than British broadcloth. (Leather dressers, of course, saw an opportunity, and within a week Adam Colson, "near the Great-Trees at the South End," advertised that he "dresse[d] all Sorts of Skins . . . in the neatest and genteelest manner.") In coming months and years, nonconsumption would expand the boycott to include most British manufactured goods, but for the time being even this modest initiative gave ordinary citizens as well as legislators a means to protest British trade restrictions and taxes and develop solidarity with one another.[32]

Exasperated by Bernard's delays, the House resumed its meetings on October 18. In less than a week, it drew up and approved a petition to the king, proclaiming that the colonies alone had the right to tax themselves and calling on the monarch to defend them against the depredations of Parliament. The Council, led by Thomas Hutchinson, strenuously disagreed with the tactic of attacking parliamentary sovereignty and refused to support the petition. It preferred an address to the House of Commons that skirted any issues involving sovereignty or rights. Hutchinson and the rest of the Council believed their best approach was a reasoned statement of the deleterious impact taxes would have on the colonies' trade with the mother country. A direct attack, they thought, would merely anger Parliament. Surely British leaders would recognize that the empire would prosper from growing commerce and decline if taxes and trade restrictions reduced the colonies' ability to purchase British goods. The House was left with the choice of a confined appeal with broad legislative support (and the approval of the governor, as it turned out) or sending on its own petition focusing on controversial principles. Because it already had made the fundamental argument in its instructions to the colony's agent and because it appreciated the value of consensus, the House reluctantly concurred with the Council.[33]

Whether he intended to or not, Hutchinson had made a huge gamble. Everyone knew that he was at the center of the legislative tussle. The final draft of the petition represented his strategy for seeking emendation of the Sugar Act and preventing a stamp tax: no confrontation, reiteration of the mutual self-interest between Britain and her colonies, and recommendations of alterations of current policies for reciprocal trade benefits and cessation of taxes imposed from London. Should Parliament be persuaded by his approach, Hutchinson would be lauded in Boston and positioned for promotion from the Crown. Should Parliament ignore the petition, he would be further denigrated as a self-promoting tool of British authorities and an enemy to his own people.

Chapter 2

On the Brink

Thomas Hutchinson was accurate in his assessment that challenges to Parliament's authority to tax the colonies without representation would be counterproductive. As he predicted, they hardened the resolve of the Grenville ministry and the vast majority of the House of Commons to preserve the Sugar Act as it was and to pass a stamp tax. But Hutchinson was wrong that a more moderate approach would be more effective. British authorities were just as immune to meek petitions warning of the potentially dire economic consequences of their current and impending trade and tax policies. Despite Grenville's carefully constructed assurance that he would weigh proposed alternatives before imposing a stamp tax, he intended nothing of the kind. It was all a sham. He needed to raise revenue, and he had little sympathy for colonial objections. To his mind, a stamp tax similar to the one in England would be the easiest to administer and enforce. His deceit gave him time to assemble a bill while mollifying would-be opponents.[1]

By February 1765, when Grenville presented the Stamp Act for parliamentary approval, many members of Parliament were so angered as to support the bill purely from spite. The colonists were ungrateful dependents who had been nurtured by the mother country and now shirked their responsibilities. Offended that Parliament's sovereignty had been disputed, the members expected the Stamp Act to raise funds and command respect. They would demonstrate where power rested. Disdaining all pretence that the colonies were represented in the decision, they officially refused to read any of the colonial petitions. To be sure, a few members questioned the wisdom of the legislation and defended the colonists, but even they supported Parliament's authority. After three readings the bill was overwhelming approved, and with the concurrence of the House of Lords and George III it became law on March 22.[2]

The Stamp Act would go into effect on November 1, and few colonists could escape its reach. Most legal documents, newspapers, pamphlets, college degrees, clearance papers for merchant ships leaving port, appointments to office, land deeds, admission of lawyers to practice law, wine and liquor licenses, playing cards, and even dice required the purchase of stamps.[3] To marry, you paid a stamp tax. To write a will or inherit property, you paid a stamp tax. To sell or buy land, you paid a stamp tax. And so on. With the Sugar Act, a colonist could avoid taxable transactions; the Stamp Act touched the daily lives of almost everyone.

While the Grenville ministry was completing the stamp tax bill for submission to Parliament, Boston was sinking deeper into economic misery. In January 1765 several prominent merchants declared bankruptcy, and their failures compounded the difficulties of their creditors. The most devastating was the collapse of Nathaniel Wheelwright's enterprises, a debacle that brought down the businesses of John Scollay and Joseph Scott, among others. James Otis claimed the events were comparable to England's calamitous "South Sea bubble," and John Hancock warned his English partners, "Be carefull who you trust, times are very bad & precarious here & take my word, my good Friends, the times will be worse here, in short such is the situation of things here that we do not know who is and who not safe."[4]

The times indeed grew worse. In the spring Bostonians learned exactly how ineffective their province's petition to the House of Commons had been. As early as April, they received word that a stamp tax was impending. A month later newspapers reported that there would be no changes to the Sugar Act, that the provisions of the Mutiny Act concerning the quartering of troops had been extended to the colonies, and that the Stamp Act would take effect on November 1. More details soon became known. Alleged violations of the Act could be tried in admiralty courts without juries, and Thomas Hutchinson's brother-in-law Andrew Oliver had been appointed commissioner of the stamp duties for Massachusetts.[5]

Not always the best bellwether of Boston's mood, Hutchinson wrote the colony's agent in London on June 4 that the "Stamp Act is received among us with as much decency as could be expected." His assessment and his townspeople's behavior soon changed dramatically. Objections to the Stamp Act were similar to those against the Sugar Act: the tax burden already was heavy and new taxes would make it unbearable; the economic consequences to the colonies and to Great Britain would be disastrous; and Parliament violated a constitutional right when they taxed people who were not represented in the decision. What was different was the emphasis. Where earlier the economic argument had been primary, now the rights argument was ascendant. This shift in part reflected the fact that the Sugar Act, on its surface, resembled a trade regulation, whereas the Stamp Act was indisputably a tax. Opposition based on broad principles also appealed to a larger cross-section of the population than did resistance to laws jeopardizing the economic self-interest of only a part, though substantial, of the citizenry. Perhaps most important of all, the focus on rights asserted Bostonians' identity as fellow British citizens deserving of the same constitutional protections as those living in England. In short, they should be treated as subjects, not as colonists—as equals, not as subordinates. The corollary, of course, was that there were limits to Parliament's authority.[6] Here was the rub. Colonists demanded equality under the constitution, and Parliament required recognition of its imperial sovereignty. The preservation of the British empire, as it then existed, depended on finding an accommodation satisfactory to all.

Enlarged participation in protest and the use of extralegal tactics accompanied the change of emphasis. With the exception of those engaged in the nonconsumption of British goods, opponents of the Sugar Act were almost entirely merchants, legislators, and writers of newspaper articles. Because the Stamp Act affected almost all Bostonians, residents from all levels of society took part in attempts to stop its implementation. The refusal of the ministry and Parliament to take colonists' views seriously, or even to read petitions from provincial assemblies, prompted alternative measures outside the traditional and normal political process.[7] Parliament had taken its stand; Bostonians would respond however they were able.

Though well aware that something was expected of them, the Massachusetts House of Representatives began prudently, much as Thomas Hutchinson had anticipated. Their minutes for June 6 read, "The Committee appointed to consider what dutiful, loyal and humble Address may be proper to make to our gracious Sovereign and his Parliament, in relation to the several Acts lately passed, for levying Duties and Taxes on the Colonies, have attended that Service, and are humbly of opinion." Having obsequiously cloaked themselves in cautious and deferential language, they dared to suggest that all the colonies send representatives to a joint conference at New York beginning on the first Tuesday in October. Together they would send a petition to the king and Parliament "to implore Relief."[8] Individual petitions had been ignored before. Perhaps a joint resolution would be more effective.

Here was a start, but one that paled by comparison to the resolves issued by the Virginia House of Burgesses or, more accurately, to what Bostonians believed to have passed in Virginia. As the House of Burgesses was winding down its affairs in late May, Patrick Henry, a new young legislator, proposed a series of resolutions to a reduced assembly. They declared that colonists, in this case, Virginians, were entitled to the same rights as those living in Great Britain and that only legislative bodies that represented them may tax its citizens. So far, this was fairly standard fare, but the fifth resolution went a step further by insisting that the House of Burgesses, with the consent of the Crown, had the "Sole Right and Authority to lay Taxes and Impositions upon It's Inhabitants." That was such a direct affront to Parliament that on the following day more conservative burgesses hastened back and rescinded the last of the five resolves. On June 24 the *Newport Mercury* printed six resolves, including the revoked fifth resolution and two that were never passed or, possibly, even discussed. One asserted that inhabitants of Virginia were not obligated to obey any tax law other than those emanating from their own legislature, and the other charged that anyone "speaking or writing" to the contrary "shall be deemed an Enemy to his Majesty's Colony."[9]

The *Boston Gazette* reprinted the *Mercury*'s article on July 1, emboldening Bostonians to take more dramatic action. Praise for Virginians and condemnation of the authors of Massachusetts's "tame, pusilanimous, daub'd, insipid" petition came in the next issue of the *Gazette*. Few readers would have been unaware that Thomas Hutchinson was the target of the writer's lashing words. "We have been told with an Insolence the more intolerable, because disguis'd with a Veil of public Care," he wrote, "that it is not prudence for us to assert our Rights in plain and manly Terms: Nay, we have been told that the Word RIGHTS must not be once named among us! Curs'd Prudence of interested designing Politicians! who have done their utmost to have the Liberties of Millions of honest and loyal, and let me add, brave and free-born American Subjects,— brave because free born,—sacrificed to their own Ambition and Lust of

Dominion and Wealth."[10] The anger of people caught in an economic depression, victimized by fire and disease, plagued by taxes from an arrogant, unsympathetic, and distant Parliament, and compromised by some of their own, seeming, self-serving leaders was about to explode.

Acutely aware that petitions alone would not stop the implementation of the Stamp Act, the citizens of Boston decided to prevent the selling and distribution of stamps by coercing the stamp agent to resign and creating an environment in which no one else would accept appointment. Early on the morning of August 14, an effigy of the stamp collector of Massachusetts, Andrew Oliver, dangled from Deacon Elliot's tree along the main road in the south side of town. Hanging beside it was a boot, representing the purported author of the revenue bills, Lord Bute, with a "Greenvile Sole" and a devil peeping out. Oliver's initials were on the right arm of the effigy, and on the left were the lines "What greater Joy did ever New England see / Than a Stampman hanging on a Tree." So many people had gathered around the soon-to-be-called "Liberty Tree" by 5 a.m. that Elliot attempted to take the display down, but he prudently yielded to the crowd's dissent. When the sheriff appeared to cut down the effigy later in the day, he met with similar discouragement and left the site.

Macabre as this was, it was not a grim political demonstration. Throughout the day, there was a festive quality in the activities, a joy in the camaraderie, a rejoicing that they were acting, not merely complaining. People from the countryside had to stop and have their goods and produce "stamp'd by the Effigy" before they could proceed to the Boston market. At nightfall, several thousand people of all strata of society gathered around the hanging effigies while several of their number cut them down and placed them on a mock bier. The "funeral" procession then paraded down the main street to the Town House, where the governor and Council were convening.

Having shown the authorities their force and contempt, the crowd marched down to Oliver's Dock, where Andrew Oliver recently had constructed a building, reputedly for stamp distribution. They soon demolished the structure and continued on to Fort Hill. The would-be stamp agent's house was nearby, and they paused there to decapitate the Oliver effigy before climbing to the summit and building a bonfire with timber and lumber from the destroyed building. They threw the effigies into the blaze and might have concluded the pageantry were it

View of the Year 1765, an engraving by Paul Revere. In this political cartoon, Revere adapted a British print of the Stamp Act in the form of a dragon trampling traditional rights, and added the Liberty Tree, an emerging icon of Boston's resistance. (Courtesy of the American Antiquarian Society)

not for the proximity of Oliver's house. Friends had warned Oliver and his family to flee just before the crowd began its ascent up the hill, and a few remained in his house for protection. As the multitude came to the residence, some of them pulled down the fence and threw stones, breaking panes in the kitchen windows. Oliver's friends shouted from the house, antagonizing the throng more. What had been an orderly demonstration then became a riot. The crowd stripped trees in the garden, stormed the house, destroyed furniture, including a mirror "said to be the largest in North America," and raided the liquor supply in the cellar. Around 11 p.m., Hutchinson and the sheriff arrived. Whether from arrogance, or the belief that people still would defer to his command, or from being out of touch with popular sentiment— probably all of the above—he demanded that the crowd disperse. His words and his body were met with stones, and he and the sheriff wisely fled. By midnight all agreed that their point had been made, and people went home.[11]

The following day, a chastened Oliver sent a card to several reputable citizens, informing them that he had resigned the office of stamp commissioner. Despite the notice being read publicly, a large gathering of men and women formed that night. They erected a few tar barrel pyramids for a bonfire and placed a "Flag Staff, and a Union Flag" in the middle. As matters seemed to be growing more threatening, Oliver sent a letter repeating his renunciation of the office. That quelled the crowd, but before dispersing they marched to Hutchinson's house, ostensibly to have a talk. He was not at home, so after cheering the stamp master's resignation the assemblage disbanded for the time being.[12]

The town remained quiet until August 26, when rumors circulated that there would be an attack on the houses of various customs and admiralty officers that evening. Governor Bernard took no chances and departed for the safety of Castle William, a fort situated on an island at the entrance of Boston Harbor. Lieutenant Governor Hutchinson was more confident, having been assured by friends that "the rabble was satisfied with the insult I had received & that I was become rather popular." Events that night would disabuse him of such optimistic notions. As nightfall approached, a rapidly growing crowd constructed a bonfire on King Street. Unlike the assemblage of August 14, which was a cross-section of the town's population, the participants of the 26th came almost exclusively from the lower class of laborers, artisans, and sailors—at least that was what all reports agreed. Persuaded by "some Gentlemen" to extinguish the fire, the throng set out toward the house of William Story, deputy-register of the vice admiralty court. There they destroyed Story's and the court's papers as well as much of his furniture. The home of Benjamin Hallowell, Comptroller of Customs for Boston, was next. The crowd broke his fence and windows and forced their way into the dwelling. They then damaged wainscoting and furniture, drank liquor from his cellar, and stole clothing, papers, and about thirty pounds in cash.

All the while, Hutchinson, a widower, was dining with his children. When word arrived that a mob was headed his way, he sent the children to a safe location, secured the house, and prepared to face the angry populace. To his dismay, his eldest daughter returned and refused to leave without him. Reluctantly he rushed with her to a neighbor's house. And then the onslaught began. By dawn, when the multitude finally quit the premises, only the shell of the house and a damaged roof remained. Furniture, room partitions, the cupola, which took several hours to dismantle, clothing, jewelry, wine and liquor, paintings, books and papers he had been collecting for thirty years in preparation for his history of Massachusetts, trees on the property, and about nine hundred pounds sterling were either destroyed or stolen. Hutchinson placed the total value at three thousand pounds, not including the missing money.[13]

When the Superior Court met the following day, the distraught and tearful chief justice appeared, dressed not in the robes of his office but in remnants from the preceding night and borrowed clothes, "Destitute of Everything," Hutchinson stated, "no other Shirt—no other Garment, but what I have on." He claimed the public had been deluded into believing he had anything to do with "aiding, assisting or supporting, or in the least promoting or incouraging what is commonly called the Stamp Act," and he hoped his experience would open people's eyes to how they might be manipulated. With that the court adjourned until October 15.[14]

Hutchinson had endured a terrible loss, but he overdramatized his plight. Despite the extensive damage to his Boston home and possessions, he still had his Milton country estate and his belongings there. And though he truthfully said he had not supported the ratification of the Stamp Act and in fact had opposed it, once it was passed he informed at least one correspondent three months before the assault on his house, "It is now become my duty as an executive officer to promote the execution of the act & to prevent every evasion." Nonetheless Hutchinson struggled to understand why he had been the target of so much animosity. At one point he attributed it to his role in changing over the province to a hard currency fifteen years before, in supporting writs of assistance, and in the widespread belief that he had written letters in favor of the Stamp Act. Later he concluded that a group of merchant smugglers had "contrived a riot" to destroy depositions that might implicate them. There may be some truth in his analyses, but he never recognized that his wealth at a time of widespread economic malaise, his multiple offices and sinecures at a time of unemployment and political rivalries, his refusal to respect the colonial demand for equal rights as British citizens at a time of Parliament's insistence on its sovereignty, and his arrogance at a time when deference toward authority was breaking down made him a contemptible figure to many.[15]

The events of August 14 and August 26 presented problems and opportunities for the political elite of both sides. The stamp commissioner had resigned, royal officials had been intimidated, extralegal tactics had produced change and disorder, the lowest strata of society had taken to the streets and refused to be ignored, political power had shifted, and it was unclear whether the ports and courts would be open after November 1, were no stamps issued.

From the governor's perspective, the immediate goal was to regain control as quickly as possible and, at the very least, to provide security for officers of the Crown, including himself. After each episode, Bernard had issued a reward for information leading to the conviction of offenders, but no one had come forward. Even when one of the leaders, perhaps the leader, of the destruction of Hutchinson's house, Ebenezer Mackintosh, was apprehended, he was released for fear of retribution. Not a single participant was convicted, let alone brought to trial. Order returned only when the town's militia, with energetic commanding officers, patrolled for a few nights.[16]

An anxious and shaken Governor Francis Bernard, wanting a stronger military presence, sought royal troops. Thus he began his peculiar dance—prancing here, tiptoeing there—that would not cease until British regiments entered Boston three years later. He knew that he could request soldiers only with the concurrence of the Council, and that body adamantly opposed the suggestion. The initiative had to come from elsewhere, preferably England, without a trace of his own involvement. As obliquely as possible, he detailed the necessity for military force but avoided making a direct request. In a letter to the commanding general for North America, Thomas Gage, Bernard related the Council's resistance, adding, "Nor can I with Safety declare my own thoughts on this Occasion." He feared for the security of the stamped paper when it arrived and was stored at Castle William. With the agreement of the Council, he intended to double the provincial garrison of sixty men stationed at the castle. But those reinforcements might well be insufficient. "If the Assailants are numerous and desperate they must take it," he coyly reasoned, "for the outworks must be left undefended: but I hope they will not arrive to that Pitch of desperation."[17]

Gage, of course, caught the hint and devised a plan to fulfill Bernard's wishes for soldiers and anonymity. Although troops were "scattered over the Continent," Gage proposed sending one hundred men from the 29th Regiment and twelve artillerists, all from Halifax. He provided one letter ordering the transfer and a second for Lord Colville of the Navy requesting transportation. Should Bernard agree, he could forward the letters bearing Gage's signature, and the troops would arrive shortly to bolster Castle William.[18]

Sir Francis Bernard, Bart, attributed to John Singleton
Copley. (By permission of the Governing Body of
Christ Church, Oxford)

By the time the communication arrived, Bernard had changed his
mind. Word had leaked that sixty men were to be raised from the
province and that they might be joined by royal troops. Between three
hundred and four hundred people approached the house of Richard
Salstonstall, a provincial colonel and chief recruiter for the supplemental
soldiers as well as a representative for the town of Haverhill, and
demanded "to know by what Authority he was raising Men, and for
what Service." After he admitted that the recruitment was for defending
stamp paper, the crowd persuaded him to disavow his efforts and have
"nothing further to do in the Afffair." Bernard in the meantime concluded that the behavior of Bostonians had returned to tranquil pur-
suits and devised a plan to shift responsibility for the protection of the
stamp paper from himself to the Massachusetts legislature. The presence of British soldiers would antagonize representatives just when he
wanted their cooperation. Crown regiments might be needed eventually
(he certainly did not dismiss that possibility), but for the time being

he was willing to risk a less aggressive approach. "Indeed the Power & Authority of Government is really at an end," he lamented to Gage, "but I am willing to content my self with the form of it, in hopes that in time the peoples Eyes may be opened & their passions subside before the application of external force shall become necessary."[19]

Popular leaders uniformly praised the events of August 14, when the effigies were burned. The citizens of Boston had stopped the distribution of stamps in their city. They had stood up to the local agent of an unconstitutional parliamentary law and forced him to resign. Like the Liberty Tree, that date became a symbol of their assertion of rights, and they annually celebrated it as a political ritual until it was displaced by even more significant dates. August 26 was a different matter. Publicly the popular elite criticized the destruction of property and the disorder and disavowed any connection to it, blaming the disruption on the "lower sort" and outside agitators. There was a practical side to this stance: they sought to influence Parliament and the ministry, but they did not want to antagonize those powerful bodies by showing sympathy to people who had so devastatingly attacked the houses of servants of the Crown. As important, distancing themselves from the events of August 26 protected them, the town, and the province from claims for restitution. Privately they were more ambivalent. Anyone might be the target of the crowd's wrath, yet they knew that royal officials and customs agents felt particularly vulnerable, and this gave the popular leaders leverage in their political and economic maneuverings.[20] While Bernard danced, they walked a tightrope.

When the House of Representatives returned to session on September 25, the recent news that the Grenville ministry had been removed and replaced by one led by Lord Rockingham bolstered their expectations for relief. Two days later Boston held an election to replace one of their representatives, the prominent lawyer Oxenbridge Thacher, who had died. It required a second round of voting for one candidate to receive a majority, but finally Samuel Adams emerged victorious.[21]

From the start, Adams was a leader of the emerging, popular party. James Otis might have had charisma and oratorical brilliance, but he was erratic. Adams was not eloquent, yet he possessed organizational and writing skills that could make a political movement successful. Born in 1722 into a prosperous Boston family, he graduated from Harvard College with the class of 1740. Choosing not to enter the ministry, merely flirting with a legal career, and incompetent at business, he eventually found his abilities and interests joined in politics. Adams was much more motivated by power and principle than by wealth. Austere in many ways, he still enjoyed music, having a fine voice himself, and hosting friends. "He affects to despize Riches, and not to dread Poverty," assessed his cousin John Adams. "But no man is more ambitious of entertaining his Friends handsomely, or of making a decent, an elegant Appearance than he." He was of medium height, slightly portly, and bore himself very erect, not an imposing figure like Thomas Hutchinson and John Hancock, but with an intense personality that made him formidable nonetheless. Until he became a representative in the legislature, from 1756 to 1764 Adams was a prominent town politician with an influential position as one of the four tax collectors. Perhaps because he was using that office to further his own ambitions, or perhaps because Boston's economic plight hindered collection, as he claimed, he owed the town eight thousand pounds in uncollected taxes at the end of his term. Although no one charged him with stealing the funds, few believed him innocent of dereliction of duty.[22]

In his address to the Council and House of Representatives on the first day of the session, Bernard tried to recapture his jeopardized authority. He attempted to regain trust by expressing his devotion to Massachusetts, then began to lecture his captive audience on the difference between opposing Parliament's "right" to tax and the expediency of a particular tax. That was old ground and, most likely, attracted little attention. What was new was his elaboration on the consequences of not complying with the stamp tax. Without stamps, the courts would shut, debts would remain unpaid, and injuries would not be compensated. Persons and property would be threatened. Outlawry might prevail. Without stamps, the ports would close. Unemployed sailors might make mischief, particularly if they ran short of necessities. People directly connected to trade and others who were dependent on it would suffer. Could the province be certain there would be adequate provisions to get them through the winter? "This Province seems to me to be upon the Brink of a Precipice," the governor warned, "and that it depends upon you to prevent its falling." At the end of the address, he slipped in the demand that compensation should be paid to the "Sufferers of the late Disturbances." In a second message later in the day, he mentioned that the stamped papers had arrived, and he requested the House's "Advice and Assistance" in keeping them safe.

When the House refused to offer any help, Bernard adjourned them before they could respond further.[23]

In other times, Bernard's words would have aroused the legislators, but with three representatives shortly to leave for the Stamp Act Congress in New York and others wishing to consult constituents about compliance with the soon-to-be-instituted stamp tax the adjournment was little more than an irritation. The governor's depiction of the effects of noncompliance, however, intensified concerns about closed courts and ports and raised critical questions.[24] What alternatives were there to submitting to the tax? How dire would be the consequences of disobedience? What risks of losing control did the popular leadership take? Despite their protests, would they be compelled by necessity to comply?

Even before the governor's address, the *Boston Gazette* had tried to alleviate townspeople's fears. "Some People among us affect to be mightily concern'd, least the want of Employ for Seamen, after the first of November, should be the Occasion of great Uneasiness and Tumult," stated an article on September 23; "and the Detention of them among us thro' the ensuing Winter should cause a Famine: They may be assured, that an Expedient will be attempted to keep this valuable Set of People honestly employ'd; but in Case of Failure, there is no such great Danger of Scarcity of Provisions, while Muscles, Clams and Tom Cods are so plenty in this Harbour, and are of late become in so high Repute, as to make favorite Dishes, upon special Entertainments, at Tables of Persons of highest Rank."[25] It is hard to imagine that many readers thought the months ahead would be so easy. The leadership of the popular party, particularly those who resided in Boston, faced a significant problem. Should they and their fellow citizens choose not to use stamps, they had to discover a way quickly to reopen the ports—their top priority—and also the courts. Otherwise they risked the bitter alternatives of capitulation or chaos.

In late October, when the legislative session resumed, the House responded to Bernard's September address. The legislators denied that anarchy would arise if stamps weren't purchased, for criminal cases were exempt from the Stamp Act and the executive branch still had power to enforce the law. As for compensating the victims of the August attacks, they asserted that the province had no responsibility for the behavior of a few and rejected the governor's request. Central to their response, they reasserted their argument that Parliament had no right to tax them. The Magna Carta, the Massachusetts's charter, and the traditional rights of British citizens protected them from such unconstitutional laws. Most important, they drew a line between their obligations to obey Parliament and their allegiance to the king. The people of Massachusetts retained "the strongest affection for his Majesty, under whose happy government they have felt all the blessings of liberty," but they would not comply with an act that would deprive them of "those inestimable rights which are derived to all men from nature, and are happily interwoven in the British constitution."[26]

A recalcitrant and defiant House was trouble enough for Bernard, but earlier in the month Westminster had placed him in charge of distributing stamps until a new agent for Massachusetts was appointed. As November 1 approached, a genuinely frightened governor wrote of his "difficult and perilous situation": distrusted by the populace, lacking the support of the Council, and "without a force to protect my person." Despite the occasion of the anniversary of the king's ascension to the throne on October 25 and the traditional public celebration, Bernard left town by noon. In his absence, the Company of Cadets mustered, cannon fired from Castle William, and representatives and Council members joined together that evening at the British Coffee House to drink to the king's health.[27]

November 1, the official beginning of the Stamp Act, finally arrived, bringing with it uncertainty, apprehension, and two effigies dangling from Liberty Tree at the south part of Boston. Several measures had been taken to prevent disorder and pageantry, including a curfew after 9 p.m. for "Molatto and Negro Servants" without permits, but nothing could stop protests. The question was whether they could be controlled, not whether they would occur. A conch shell's "melancholy blast" accompanied by the pealing of church bells awakened the funeral day. Ships' flags flew at half-mast, and many shops remained closed. By 3:00 in the afternoon several thousand people "of all Ranks" had congregated around the representations of George Grenville and John Huske, the perceived perpetrators of the Stamp Act. The ritual followed steps similar to those of August 14: people cut down the effigies and placed them in a cart; then the procession began, first stopping at the Town House, where the House was meeting; the demonstration proceeded to the North End of town, then reversed itself until it reached the gallows at Boston Neck, isolated from residences and other buildings; there the effigies were strung up and, after an appropriate pause, were yanked down and torn into fragments that were thrown about. The sun was still up at this carefully choreographed event, when the multitude gave three cheers and good-humoredly left for their homes.[28] The August disturbances had not repeated.

Popular leaders must have sighed in relief. Even news on that same day of the Stamp Act Congress's petitions denying Parliament's authority to tax unrepresented colonies created little stir. The importance of that assemblage was its united political voice—an accomplishment with long-term ramifications—but for the short term the residents of Boston had other priorities and concerns. In the past, November 5 had produced a melee. Called Pope's Day (rather than Guy Fawkes Day) it supposedly commemorated the foiling of a plot by a group of Catholics to blow up Parliament in 1605, but had become an organized tumult primarily between working-class adolescent boys and young men of the North End and the South End of town. It was the one day of the year when apprentices, journeymen, and others could flout ordinary authority and escape the usual subordination of their lives. Each side constructed a platform secured to wheels and pulled by horses. Atop were figures of the pope and the devil, and often below were boys with poles reaching into the heads of the figures so that they might turn and appear even more macabre. During the day the carts paraded through the streets, but as night fell the two rowdy groups met at Union Street, the middle ground between their sections of Boston, and attempted to capture each other's pope. In the process, blood flowed, bruises swelled, and occasionally bones broke. The victors took both popes to the town gallows and hanged them. The festivities concluded with celebratory food and drink, paid for by earlier solicitations. In 1764 the North End's cart had run over and killed a child.[29]

Town officials sought to prevent a repetition of the previous year's tragedy, but more important they worried that Pope's Day might unleash a mob whose objects would be greater than competing popes. Some Boston residents petitioned the town to stop the event altogether, but after a heated debate in town meeting they withdrew their request. More successful were "several gentlemen" who brought together Ebenezer Mackintosh of the South End and Samuel Swift of the North End. They negotiated a reconciliation and a "Union" ceremony instead of the traditional Pope's Day brawl. On the appointed day, at about noon, Mackintosh and Swift, both garbed in military apparel, led their respective cohorts with their usual carts loaded with popes and devils to King Street in the center of town. Following a "Union" ritual, each side marched to the other's section of the city and then met once again before the Town House. Together they proceeded to the Liberty Tree, where they "refreshed themselves for a while." Just before 6 p.m. they all gathered at Copp's Hill, and there they burned the effigies. As two of Boston's newspapers reported, "Not a Club was seen among the whole, nor was any Negro allowed to approach near the Stages." With their mission accomplished, all departed peacefully. Because everything went as planned, "a number of Gentlemen" arranged and paid for "a very grand Supper, denominated the UNION FEAST," at the Royal Exchange Tavern. Merchants and other gentlemen entertained themselves in one room, while Pope's Day rivals raised glasses in another.[30]

How long such order could be maintained was questionable; for if the port stayed largely shut for many months and unemployment and underemployment grew, turmoil was merely postponed. Ships could enter Boston Harbor and unload their cargoes, but without stamps (either because there was no stamp distributor or because no one was willing to purchase them), ship owners risked confiscation of the violating ship and cargo. Something had to be done to change British policy, and so far petitions and protests hadn't been successful.

A strategy came from New York: coercion through nonimportation. If British merchants and manufacturers and their employees lost business, they might lobby Parliament to rescind the Stamp Act. Merchants in New York City held a general meeting on October 31, and roughly two hundred of them signed a nonimportation agreement. Until the Stamp Act was repealed, they would send no orders for British goods. Because of the difficulties of transatlantic communication, they made exceptions; ships that already were returning were exempted. But they agreed they would not sell any goods imported from Great Britain after January 1, 1766. By November 14 the merchants of Philadelphia subscribed to the same agreement.[31]

The people of Boston might have been in the forefront of opposition to taxation, but the city's merchants dragged behind their counterparts to the south. To be sure, several merchants and shopkeepers had independently begun their own nonimportation policy. As early as October 14, for example, the wealthy merchant John Hancock informed his British business associates that until the Stamp Act were repealed he would not send out any ships after the end of the month. "This letter I propose to remain in my Letter Book as a Standing monument to posterity & my children in particular," he proudly added in a postscript, "that I by no means consented to a Submission to this Cruel Act, & that my best Representations were not wantg. in the matter." For the most part, prodding still was necessary. "Y. Z." in the *Boston Evening-Post* gently coaxed Massachusetts merchants to join the "worthy merchants and traders of New-York," and a writer for the *Boston Gazette* more pointedly warned that the Boston citizenry would take matters into their own hands by not purchasing British goods if merchants continued to import them.[32]

By December 9 Boston's commercial community finally chiseled out a set of resolutions. For the most part, it was identical to the nonimportation agreements of New York and Philadelphia. The chief difference was a list of exempted items essential to fishing and local manufacturing. Two hundred and twenty "principal Merchants," signed immediately. Others, such as the future Loyalist James Murray, may not have subscribed but complied nonetheless. Murray's sugar business was so bad he was closing his warehouses. Fortunately for him, an inheritance from his wife's deceased mother made his retirement all the easier.[33]

The drawback of nonimportation was that it would take time to be successful, and in the meantime the port would stay closed. The opportunity for direct action to convince customs officials that they could provide clearance for ships without stamps came in an "anonymous tip" to the editors of the *Boston Gazette*, Benjamin Edes and John Gill. The informant claimed that despite Andrew Oliver's public resignation in August as Massachusetts's stamp agent, he recently had received the commission from England. Before publishing the tip, the editors asked Oliver whether the rumor were true. Oliver acknowledged the deputation, but as Edes and Gill conveyed to their readers on December 16, "He had taken no Measure to qualify himself for the Office, nor had he any Thoughts of doing it; and gave us Liberty to assure the Public that he would not."[34]

The Loyal Nine (also called the Sons of Liberty) were dissatisfied with Oliver's response, and they realized that a large public demonstration could send a far-reaching message. Acting quickly that evening, they concocted a letter for Oliver, informing him of their displeasure and requesting his presence at the Liberty Tree "to make a public Resignation" the following noon. By morning they had posted a hundred advertisements of the upcoming spectacle throughout the town. Attempting to diminish his humiliation, Oliver proposed that he resign at the Town House. But the Sons of Liberty and two thousand eager townspeople insisted he go to the Liberty Tree. Escorted by Ebenezer Mackintosh, Oliver trudged forlornly to resign before his fellow citizens. When he unequivocally renounced the office, the multitude gave him three cheers. He responded that "he had an utter Detestation of the Stamp Act, and would do all that lay in his Power to serve this Town or Province; and desired that they would no longer look on him as an Enemy, but as another Man." The crowd gave three more cheers and dispersed within ten minutes.[35]

That afternoon the customs office, with full knowledge of what might befall them, resumed service with the announcement that ships could clear port without stamps. Within the limits of the nonimportation agreement, Boston wharves and commerce were back in business. John Hancock modified his earlier stance and rushed his ship, *Boston Packet*, filled with whale oil off to London. "Should there be any Difficulty in London," he wrote his English agents, "You will please to represent the circumstances that no stamps could be obtained and we cannot obtain a more Regular clearance." And on the evening of that momentous December 17, the Loyal Nine, joined by Samuel Adams and a few other friends, privately had a "very Genteel Supper" to celebrate their accomplishment.[36]

Still to be resolved was the issue of the closed courts, though that task didn't have the same urgency for many Bostonians. No one wanted the vice admiralty courts reopened, and debtors, a group that ranged from the poor to wealthy merchants, relished their temporary immunity from lawsuits. Criminal cases, moreover, didn't require stamps for prosecution. Still, law-abiding residents demanded the restoration of their legal system. Lawyers particularly sought a return to full employment. On December 18 John Adams lamented in his diary that he had "not drawn a Writ since 1st. Novr." As was often the case throughout his long life, Adams took adversity personally. Just as he was overcoming obstacles to his success, just as he was gaining "a small degree of Reputation," the Stamp Act, "this execrable Project," was "set on foot for my Ruin as well as that of America in General, and of Great Britain." On the following day, the mercurial Adams had reason to rejoice. The town meeting had shifted its attention to the courts and had created a role for him to play.[37]

Now energized by the humiliation of Oliver and by the newfound willingness of the customs office to clear ships without stamps, the town designated Adams, as well as the more experienced and prominent Jeremiah Gridley and James Otis, to argue before the governor and Council that, like the ports, the courts should be permitted to operate without stamps. Never one to underestimate his own abilities, Adams nonetheless was perplexed at why the townspeople had selected him. His cousin Samuel Adams, who obviously was central to his appointment, later told him he hoped it would boost his legal practice in Boston and Braintree and tie him closer to the opposition.[38] It did both.

The trio of town representatives met with Bernard and the Council late on December 20. They presented constitutional principles and practical reasons why they believed the Stamp Act invalid and the courts needed to hear cases. Bernard made no judgment that night, but soon thereafter the judicial system was resuscitated. Once again Thomas Hutchinson entered the story. Not only was he the chief justice of the Superior Court, but he was judge of the Suffolk County Probate Court, the probate court for Boston, and he refused to activate either in violation of the Stamp Act. Warned by friends that his adamancy endangered his well-being and still recovering from the August 26 traumas, he agreed to resign from the probate court and have his brother Foster Hutchinson, who, the *Boston Gazette* chortled, "had no Scruples about the Matter," replace him for a year. Bernard leaped at the opportunity to reduce tensions between him and townspeople; despite the requirement that stamps were needed for all Crown appointments, he convinced himself that temporary positions were exempt and he appointed the replacement.[39]

Judges of the Inferior Court of Common Pleas for Suffolk County quickly grasped the situation, and by early January were hearing cases again. All that remained was the Superior Court, over which Thomas Hutchinson presided. When the court's regular term began on March 11, Hutchinson, who continued to joust with the House of Representatives, decided to absent himself. Under the leadership of Justice Benjamin Lynde, the court heard a case that had been initiated before the Stamp Act went into effect. Then, with lawyers and judges agreeing not to take a greater gamble of breaking parliamentary law, the court adjourned until April, by which time all hoped Parliament would have rescinded the Stamp Act.[40]

Chapter 3

Power and the Opposition

Resistance to the Stamp Act transformed the political dynamics of Boston. No longer satisfied with petitions and resolutions from their legislature to a nonresponsive Parliament, Bostonians resorted to extralegal measures. The nonimportation agreement, the nonconsumption of certain British goods, and, most dramatic of all, thousands of people taking to the streets on six occasions between August 14, 1765, and the end of February 1766—all were indications of widespread political involvement. This revealed more than the expansion in the power and influence of the popular party; it marked the beginning of an opposition movement.

There has long been speculation about the organization and leadership of the protesters. Many believed that a few masterminds manipulated the multitude. As early as March 1766, for example, Thomas Hutchinson concluded that there was a hierarchy of control. The "rabble of the town of Boston" led by the shoemaker Ebenezer Mackintosh were at the bottom; they were the group "employed" to hang effigies and pull down houses. Their masters were the "superior set" of skilled artisans. The top leadership, according to Hutchinson, consisted of an economic wing of merchants headed by John Rowe and a political wing working through the town meeting, where James Otis prevailed.[1]

Had Hutchinson had access to John Adams's diary, he would have found testimony that partially corroborated his perception. The twenty-seven-year-old lawyer confided to his private pages in 1763 that a group of men called the Caucus Club had prepared a slate of candidates for town offices "before they are chosen in the Town." Meeting in the smoke-filled garret of Tom Dawes, Samuel Adams and others decided on selectmen and representatives to the legislature as well as lesser posts.

They conferred with members of the Merchants Club, negotiating the list that representatives of each club presented at the town meeting. John Adams, apparently astonished that such maneuverings went on, leaped to the assumption that ordinary Bostonians, knowingly or not, rubber-stamped those candidates. But he exaggerated the clubs' power. Although they influenced town elections and were often successful, the Caucus and the Merchants were not completely cohesive, nor were they the only groups with political aims.[2]

The election for town representative in September 1765 demonstrates how uncertain and complicated such contests could be. Samuel Adams of the Caucus won the seat with 265 votes, but it required two rounds for him to secure a majority. His opponents were John Rowe, ostensibly the head of the Merchants Club; John Ruddock, another member of the Caucus; and the wealthy merchant John Hancock. Merchants, if unified, represented the largest bloc at the town meeting; the 250 signatories to the nonimportation agreement constituted roughly a third of qualified voters. They might agree on opposition to trade restrictions, but beyond that their interests often diverged, and they were competitors as well as allies.[3] And so it went from group to group, from individual to individual. Backroom politics were at work, but the townspeople of Boston wouldn't always find common ground.

More compelling evidence in support of Hutchinson's contention of secret controllers is a letter written by Henry Bass just two days after the humiliation of Andrew Oliver at the Liberty Tree. Bass, a twenty-six-year-old merchant, revealed that the Loyal Nine had orchestrated the whole affair, from drafting and delivering the letter to Oliver demanding his appearance for a public resignation to advertising the event to its satisfactory conclusion. Their celebratory dinner the evening of December 17 with Samuel Adams and three or four additional guests suggests that Adams and others may have helped coordinate the demonstrations, or it might simply indicate that the Nine wanted to rejoice with older and more prominent allies. Despite Bass's request to Samuel Savage to "keep this a profound Secret," Thomas Crafts and Thomas Chase, two of the Nine, visited John Adams and regaled him with news of their triumph.[4] It is unlikely that Savage and Adams were the only people entrusted with the "Secret." By week's end probably most of Boston knew the story. Such self-promotion, even if clandestine, confirmed Hutchinson's vision of the opposition: that behind the scenes

Samuel Adams, circa 1772, an oil on canvas portrait
by John Singleton Copley. Deposited by the City
of Boston. (Photograph courtesy of the Museum
of Fine Arts, Boston)

a small cadre manipulated thousands of Bostonians to act out their
play.

But who were the Loyal Nine, and did they have the power they
claimed to have? These were young men in their twenties and thirties
who, for the most part, fit Hutchinson's category of a "superior set"
of skilled artisans. Stephen Cleverly and John Smith were braziers,
Benjamin Edes a printer, Thomas Crafts a painter, and George Trott
a jeweler; Thomas Chase was a distiller, John Avery and Bass rising
merchants, and Henry Welles a shipowner. They were well connected
in the town. The thirty-three-year-old Edes was co-owner and coeditor
of the *Boston Gazette*, and twenty-six-year-old Avery was a third-
generation graduate of Harvard College and the son of a prosperous
merchant. Three of them were members of the North End Caucus,
a political club with a wide reach, and one other was a Mason at St.
Andrew's Lodge.[5]

The key to whatever influence the Loyal Nine had lay with their affiliation with other segments of Massachusetts's capital city. Boston was a heavily networked town, and it is hard to imagine Samuel Adams, the lenient tax collector and skilled politician, more than three degrees of separation away from anyone else. Clubs and fraternal organizations abounded; besides the Merchants Club, the Caucus Club, and the Loyal Nine, there were the Possi Club, the Fire Club, the Number Five Club, the Ancient and Honorable Artillery Company (a social rather than a military organization), the Massachusetts Charitable Society, and the Wednesday Night Club. Many men belonged to several of these organizations at once and dined and drank with a regular set of friends at any of the many taverns throughout the town. In addition, there were two Masonic lodges representing the two branches of masonry, St. John's and St. Andrew's. St. John's was a part of Modern Masons; its more conservative members were primarily merchants and professionals. John Rowe was proud to be grand master of the lodge. St. Andrew's was associated with Ancient Masons, the preferred lodge for skilled artisans and many members of the opposition movement, including Joseph Warren, John Hancock, Thomas Crafts, William Molineux, Paul Revere, and William Palfrey. Occasionally the contrarian, Samuel Adams disapproved of secret societies and their elaborate rituals and never joined, nor did his cousin John. A separate but related type of close-knit fraternity was the Boston bar, an essential professional association for attorneys. Without its support a lawyer could not practice, and its members, though rivals before the bench, provided convivial company both in town and while riding the circuit.[6]

Clubs, fraternal societies, and professional organizations connected the middle class and elite, but they didn't cross the economic and social divide to the laboring class and poor. Less formally joined than its social superiors, the lower order, at least its young men and adolescent males, identified with the North End and the South End, and its older men and women met as neighbors, working colleagues, and social companions. But here, too, the chasm remained.

Business along the waterfront connected diverse people engaged in maritime trade, however, and several town institutions did cut across class lines. The town meeting was open to all, even if fewer than half of Boston's males over the age of sixteen were eligible to participate in formal decisions and the elite and middle class dominated its proceedings. Still, there would have been opportunities for interaction at various levels. The Boston militia, with its many companies, was another. It consisted of all males between the ages of sixteen and sixty (with a few exemptions, such as clergy, firefighters, and the disabled). Within each company men of varying social strata drilled and socialized together.

The most broadly based institution was the Congregational Church, where merchants, artisans, and laborers, men and women, worshipped together. Their contact may have been limited, yet a certain rubbing of elbows occurred. At least three ministers (Charles Chauncy of the First or Old Brick Church, Samuel Cooper of the Brattle Street Church, and Jonathan Mayhew of the West Church) steered their congregations toward the resistance movement. All of them gave highly political sermons. On at least one occasion, Mayhew feared he might have gone too far. The day after the attack on Hutchinson's house, he rushed to offer the lieutenant governor his condolences and to dispel rumors that he had encouraged the event in his sermon of the previous Sunday. The West Church minister acknowledged that he had spoken strongly in favor of liberty and had criticized the Stamp Act as "a great grievance." But he implored Hutchinson, "In truth, Sir, I had rather lost my hand, than be an encourager of such outrages as were committed last night."[7]

At least one of the Loyal Nine was an active member of a Congregational Church, and several must have employed workers from the laboring class, but whether that enabled them to influence thousands of people to do their bidding remains unclear. Thomas Hutchinson pointed to twenty-eight-year-old shoemaker Ebenezer Mackintosh as the leader of the South End and the link between the "rabble" and their social superiors. There is evidence of Mackintosh's presence and even leadership at no fewer than four of the massive demonstrations in 1765. On August 14 he reputedly hanged the effigies of Oliver and Bute. On August 26 he led the assaults on the houses of Story, Hallowell, and Hutchinson; the sheriff detained him the next day but released him without a charge. On November 5 with his North End counterpart he led the procession through the town and presided over the festivities. On December 17 he escorted Andrew Oliver to the Liberty Tree for his public resignation. These were heady, but perhaps not unexpected experiences for a shoemaker whom Hutchinson described as "a bold fellow & as likely for a Massianello as you can well conceive." Hutchinson's relation Peter Oliver portrayed Mackintosh as "sensible & manly" and possessed of enormous power.

When Mackintosh marched at the head of two thousand men, Oliver grudgingly marveled that "if a Whisper was heard among his Followers, the holding up his Finger hushed it in a Moment."[8]

Born in Boston to a poor family on June 20, 1737, Mackintosh was fourteen when his mother died. Two years later his father was warned out of town, but Ebenezer remained, probably as an apprentice to his uncle, learning the trade of shoemaker. By seventeen he was a private in the militia and living in the South End. He enlisted in the army in 1758 and fought in several battles in the French and Indian War before the expiration of his term later in the year. After the great fire in 1760 Stephen Greenleaf, the head of one of the fire engine companies and later the sheriff who detained Mackintosh following the Hutchinson episode, asked the Boston selectmen to appoint the shoemaker to his engine brigade. They complied. By Pope's Day 1764, if not earlier, Mackintosh was the leader of the South End contingent in the annual skirmish, and people took notice.[9]

What extended Mackintosh's influence from the rambunctious Pope's Day to the August 14 political protest against Andrew Oliver is a matter of conjecture. There is the cynical view that he was bribed and coerced. Three months after the November brawl, he and a few others were brought before the court to answer for the melee. No record exists, but apparently he was discharged outright or after paying a minor fine. In either case, the judges gave him no more than a gentle rebuke. The next month the town selected him as one of the four sealers of leather, a position of authority and importance. Tanners and curriers could not sell leather without the official seal of approval, and being an officer who affixed the seal would have been a huge benefit to a consumer of leather such as a shoemaker.[10]

On August 12, two days before the first political demonstration, Samuel Adams took out a warrant against Mackintosh and Benjamin Bass (probably his partner in making and selling shoes) for back taxes. They were required to pay up or face confiscation of property or imprisonment. Somewhat miraculously, Adams ordered the warrant to be returned to the court, though the two shoemakers had not paid a cent. Less than forty-eight hours later, Mackintosh was hanging effigies. The evidence of collusion is spotty and circumstantial, but intriguing nonetheless. A more charitable interpretation would be that Mackintosh, like other Bostonians, was struggling financially and that the Stamp Act could compound his troubles. He had cause to oppose British policy and its agents. Moreover Mackintosh need not be relegated to a false dichotomy of motives. He very well could have sought his self-interest, the pleasure of recognition, and the belief in the rightness of the opposition.[11]

The Loyal Nine with their key allies—in particular, Samuel Adams—and Ebenezer Mackintosh played prominent, even indispensable, roles in the Stamp Act demonstrations. Should we agree with Thomas Hutchinson and Peter Oliver, that's all we need to know. The multitudes participated solely because their superiors commanded it. They were rabble, a senseless mass, hooligans, and blind followers who could be silenced by a raised finger. That, of course, is an explanation that echoes to the present. Effigies and bonfires were unquestionably magnets to the curious and mischievous, diversions and entertainments for those bored with routine. Some may have seen them as cover for illegal acts, for there is no denying the plundering that occurred on August 26. Mackintosh on his own could draw a crowd of South Enders.

But none of this fully explains why so many people throughout Boston rallied. Except on the Pope's Day march of solidarity, few from the North End would have joined on Mackintosh's account. All six mass demonstrations were political events with the clear intent of halting the implementation of the Stamp Act. They were not random acts. A large cross-section of Boston society participated. Although laboring people swelled the crowds, wealthy merchants, well-to-do lawyers, and middle-class skilled artisans and shopkeepers marched beside them. Had British policy been different, there would have been no public protests. By the time newspapers announced the impending Stamp Act, Bostonians had suffered through five years of a depressed economy and calamity. The Seven Years' War had left a large provincial debt as well as widows and fatherless children. Fire and smallpox had produced individual tragedies and inflicted additional blows to an already faltering financial system. Merchants went bankrupt; sailors, laborers, and artisans struggled to maintain a living. The ranks of the poor swelled. The ministry and Parliament had ignored the plight of colonists and declined even to read their petitions; instead they had passed two acts that would restrict trade, extract revenue by new taxes, further depress the economy, and undermine the colonists' rights as equal British citizens under the Crown. These were not mindless mobs; they were people with a purpose.[12]

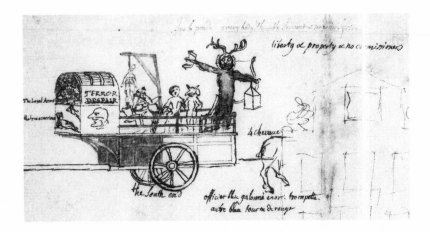

Boston Affairs, 1767, details depicting a South End wagon (top) and a North End wagon (bottom) on Pope's Day, from sketches by Pierre Eugène Du Simitière. (The Library Company of Philadelphia)

Thomas Hutchinson was simply wrong. He may have wished to see a tightly organized, top-down opposition, but the reality was far more complex and diffused. The Loyal Nine were excellent orchestrators of public events, well connected, and among their number was the coeditor of the *Boston Gazette*; yet they were but a part of a larger resistance movement. Ebenezer Mackintosh was a charismatic leader with strong ties to the laboring class and to the poor and a representative of their rising voice; yet he alone could not have organized the Stamp Act protests. So many others were involved: merchants formed a nonimportation agreement; town officials and representatives to the legislature constructed resolves and strategies; Congregational ministers implored their congregations to resist British policy; consumers of all classes and both sexes attempted to reduce their purchases of British goods; writers of newspaper articles and broadsides provoked their readers to resist; rope makers and shopkeepers joined other Bostonians in the streets. Yet none of these groups on its own constituted the opposition movement. Clubs and fraternal organizations met to discuss the issues of the day and to enjoy each other's company. Glasses were raised, rituals were performed, networks were utilized, and ideas were debated. People gossiped at the market, visited each other's homes, shouted on the wharfs, fought in the alleys, rode circuit together, and some of the time conversed about politics. Not all Bostonians opposed the Stamp Act, though most disagreed with it, but the authors of the Act unintentionally brought disparate Bostonians together, giving them a common cause and an emerging identity.

Chapter 4

An Accommodation of Sorts

Bostonians anticipated that a change of ministry would remove the source of their grievances and improve relations with the mother country, but were not fully aware of the political dynamics in the empire's capital. Succeeding Grenville in the summer of 1765, the Rockingham ministry was supposed to be a stopgap until William Pitt could be convinced to take the helm, but for whatever reason the Great Commoner stayed aloof. Without an experienced and well-connected prime minister, Rockingham and his colleagues in the ministry viewed the growing Stamp Act crisis with alarm, anger, and uncertainty. As news reached England of the Virginia Resolves, as well as resolutions from other colonial assemblies denying Parliament's right to tax them, street demonstrations, and coerced resignations of stamp agents, the ministry realized that the status quo was unacceptable. However, they were too perplexed to find an alternative. Increasing the military stationed in America to enforce the Stamp Act was too costly, yet repealing the Act would appear to acknowledge that the colonies were outside Parliament's authority. To make matters worse, the ministry's alliances within the House of Commons were so precarious that even had it found a compromise there was no guarantee that it could muster a majority to pass the legislation to enact it. And failure to do so would drive it from office.[1]

Pitt, though no friend of the Rockingham ministry, offered a direction. On January 14, 1766, in one of his greatest speeches, he condemned the Stamp Act as a violation of basic British principles and called for its repeal, while simultaneously declaring Parliament's sovereignty over the colonies in all matters other than taxation. When Grenville, now the leader of the opposition in the Commons, defended his legislative program, arguing that America owed England obedience for the protection it received, and questioned when had the colonies been "emancipated" from their obligations, Pitt thundered back, "I desire to know when they were made slaves?" The Great Commoner's eloquence made him a hero to colonists and provided wonderful theater for spectators. Yet anger at Americans' refusal to accept Parliament's sovereignty undercut members' enthusiasm for complying with colonial wishes, and few agreed with Pitt that Parliament lacked the constitutional power to tax the colonies.[2]

The Rockingham ministry now had a formula to resolve the crisis: repeal the Stamp Act *and* assert Parliament's right to tax throughout the empire. But it needed to modify Pitt's position and to construct political alliances to forge the necessary majority for passage. They accomplished the first task by shifting the argument for repeal from constitutional principles to economic necessity. As a result of nonimportation agreements, the American desire to postpone paying off debts to British creditors, and colonial merchants' reluctance to risk commerce without stamps, British merchants and manufacturers were losing considerable business. Their financial plight trickled down to their employees, who could produce serious unrest should they be laid off. Enlisting the assistance of those interest groups to pressure their representatives, the ministry hoped it could build an effective coalition.[3]

Petitions from mercantile constituents and testimonies before the House of Commons produced support, but merely altering the justification for repeal was not enough to satisfy sufficient numbers of antagonized legislators. To salve their irritation, Rockingham and his associates applied the balm of asserting parliamentary power. Countering colonial claims that their legislatures alone could tax Americans, the Declaratory Act affirmed that the king, with the advice and consent of Parliament, had "full power and authority to make laws and statutes of sufficient force and validity to bind the colonies and people of *America*, subjects of the crown of Great Britain, in all cases whatsoever." The Act did not explicitly state the power to tax, but debate in the Commons clarified that the phrase "in all cases whatsoever" included taxation. Pitt, making a fine distinction between Parliament's power to legislate and its power to tax, was one of the few to vote against the bill. It otherwise swept through Parliament along with the less popular legislation to repeal the

Stamp Act. On March 18 George III approved both, and they became law.[4]

Rumors of repeal reached Boston as early as January 15, when the Loyal Nine met to begin planning a public celebration with "such Illuminations, Bonfires, Piramids, Obelisks, such grand Exhibitions, and such Fireworks, as were never before seen in America." John Adams, who was a guest at the meeting and temperamentally cautious, confided in his diary afterward, "I wish they mayn't be disappointed." A report of the Stamp Act's repeal arrived from Philadelphia two and a half months later, and a large crowd gathered around the Liberty Tree, a short distance southeast of Boston Common, where they fired two cannon and gave three cheers. Later in April, ships from England laden with goods delayed by the nonimportation agreement appeared in Boston Harbor. All of these were good signs but still not definitive word of the detested Act's demise. Town officials nonetheless prepared for a controlled and decorous general rejoicing. They ordered that when official news justified a formal jubilation all inhabitants should illuminate their windows to celebrate the repeal and to honor the king, the ministry, Pitt, and parliamentary supporters. Those who were unable to comply because of poverty, illness, or religious scruple "ought to be protected from all Injury." Troublemakers who broke windows or created other disturbances would be prosecuted.[5]

Finally in mid-May the selectmen of Boston received "certain Intelligence," and they chose May 19 as the long-awaited day of rejoicing. At 1 o'clock in the morning the bells of the church closest to the Liberty Tree began to ring, soon to be joined by others throughout the town. As the day progressed, guns fired, drums beat, and there was music everywhere. Ships displayed colors, flags and streamers draped from the Liberty Tree, and banners hung from rooftops. Even Governor Bernard joined the festivities by ordering the firing of cannon at Castle William and the town batteries and inviting the Council to join him that afternoon to drink to the king's health. Libations flowed, John Hancock alone donating a pipe (a cask holding approximately 105 gallons) of Madeira to the populace, and just as the Loyal Nine intended, an obelisk "covered with various Hiereglyphics, and Poetical Lines" was constructed on the Common. Fireworks filled the evening sky until 11 o'clock, ending a perfect day of "utmost Decency and good Order."[6]

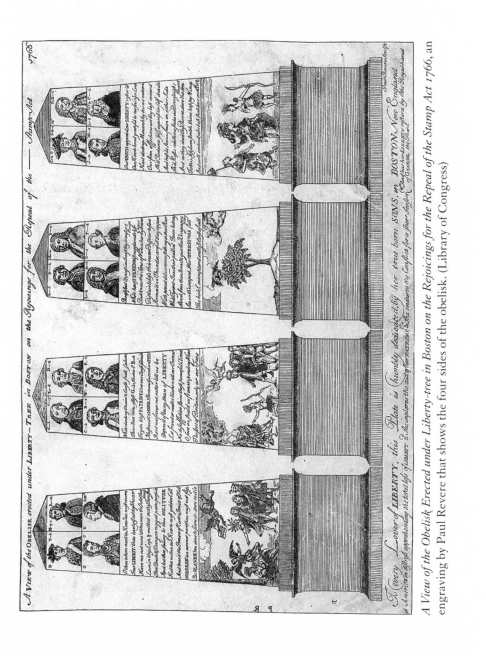

A View of the Obelisk Erected under Liberty-tree in Boston on the Rejoicings for the Repeal of the Stamp Act 1766, an engraving by Paul Revere that shows the four sides of the obelisk. (Library of Congress)

As festive and harmonious as May 19 was, there remained lingering distrust of Parliament and of the Crown's representatives in Boston. The town would not return to its pre–Stamp Act self. Power had shifted. New voices had emerged. Political positions had hardened. Confidence had arisen as people concluded that it had been their efforts, often extralegal efforts, that had changed British policy. They had led; Parliament, reluctantly, had followed. Nor had all irritants disappeared. Despite rumors of modification, the Sugar Act was still in place, and customs officials enforced the law as aggressively as they could.

If relations with the British government improved somewhat, partisan rivalries within Boston grew more heated. Newspaper attacks on James Otis throughout the spring kept tensions high and posed obstacles to reconciliation. As usual, Otis in part brought the verbal assaults upon himself. In response to Otis's lengthy and personal criticisms of Thomas Hutchinson in the *Boston Gazette*, an anonymous writer in the March 31 edition of the *Boston Evening-Post* fired back. Making no attempt to dispute issues, he reviewed the life of "Bluster" (a thinly disguised reference to Otis) in the most derogatory fashion. In four full-length columns he repeatedly portrayed Otis as a madman or an incompetent attack dog. "Bluster had always some oddities in his behavior which gave apprehensions that his head was not as it should be," he wrote in one section, and as scurrilously in another penned, "Bluster has a mortal aversion to *tall men* [almost certainly a reference that included Hutchinson], and will run after them in the street, snapping at their heels, and barking like a dog; while they taking him for some puppy, seldom look behind them, or take any notice of his noise." The ridicule was repeated a few months later in a twelve-sentence parody, each sentence beginning "O —'tis." "O —'tis you that have lost all degree of modesty to presume to defile (by mentioning) the respectable words: Spirit, Resolution, and Fortitude" is a good example of the level of discourse. A constant theme in these and other articles was Otis's grasping for public support to fulfill private and sinister goals.[7]

None of this worked. In April Boston's citizens selected Otis as moderator of the town meeting, and in May they reelected him as one of Boston's representatives to the General Court. The court in turn chose him as speaker.[8]

The emerging popular party could be equally vicious in print and oratory when they saw fit, but that spring they focused on tactics designed to elect friends and defeat the court faction. Raising topics of provincial concern rather than of British policy, Benjamin Edes's newspaper published an article with instructions for would-be representatives. The corrupt practice of holding multiple offices and setting self-interested fees should be stopped; freedom of the press should be preserved; the proceedings of the legislature should be open to the public; and no funds should be paid to those who had lost property "in the late tumults" without constituents' approval—all issues directed at Hutchinson and his friends and family. The author of the piece requested that at each town meeting his advice be read aloud before votes were cast. To help voters further, the *Boston Gazette* printed the names of thirty-two sitting representatives who didn't meet its standards. Throughout Massachusetts voters responded and gave the popular party a majority in the House of Representatives. Nineteen of those on the *Gazette*'s hit list failed to be reelected.[9]

When the General Court met in late May, the "political warfare" (to use Governor Bernard's phrase) intensified. The House selected James Otis as its speaker, and Bernard immediately rejected him. Otis's ally and fellow Boston representative Thomas Cushing replaced him, and Bernard in this one instance acquiesced and allowed the more moderate Cushing to become speaker. Before the bitter day was out, a majority of the combined House and departing Council refused to renominate Thomas Hutchinson, Andrew Oliver, Peter Oliver, and Edmond Trowbridge for the new Council; Benjamin Lynde, a member of the court faction, resigned after twenty-eight years of service rather than be publicly rejected. Bernard retaliated by denying seats to six nominees, including James Otis Sr. and Nathaniel Sparhawk, who previously had been on the Council.[10] The political carnage was considerable, and it would spread.

On the following day, in front of an increasingly hostile House and Council, the governor made perhaps the most vitriolic speech of his career. Beginning mildly enough, Bernard congratulated all present on the repeal of the Stamp Act and expressed the wish that Massachusetts would now return to better times. But then, apparently no longer able to contain his pent-up anger, he issued a charge that everyone in the room must have known was directed at Otis and his colleagues. "In Times of public Calamity," he snarled, "it is not unusual for private Interests and Resentments to intermix themselves with popular Discontent, and execute their Purposes under the borrowed Mask of patriotic Zeal. This has been the primary Cause of that unlimited Abuse which has been cast upon the most respectable Characters in this Province." The outcry against the Stamp Act in its many forms had resulted from the self-interested manipulation of the few upon the many. Most in the audience must have been aghast at this reductionist interpretation. They cringed even more when the governor wished that "a Veil could be drawn over the late disgraceful Scenes" but lamented that this was not possible until "a better Temper and Understanding shall prevail." Shock turned to outrage when Bernard then suggested that "some Proceedings" would both reinforce the judgment of those in England who opposed the repeal and alienate the colonists' friends. Those "Proceedings" were the removal from the Council of the government's "best and most able Servants, whose only Crime is their Fidelity to the Crown." In Bernard's view, those acts constituted an attack on the government and a sign of an ungrateful people, and he made clear that was how they would be depicted in reports to London.[11]

It took the House nearly a week to respond to the governor's address, and by then it was able to cool its collective temper and craft a politically effective reply. All was surprise and innocent hurt feelings. It joined Bernard in celebrating the repeal of the Stamp Act and professed its "Loyalty and Gratitude" to the sovereign and to "those illustrious Patriots who have distinguished themselves in our Cause." The members of the House welcomed drawing a veil over past disruptions and a return to harmony, but they were astonished by the tenor of the governor's remarks and inserted a detailed, textual analysis of the speech.

When it came to the Hutchinson episode, they proved as disingenuous as their opponents, declaring that it was unfair and inaccurate to charge "the People" for the destruction. There were valid reasons for widespread discontent, but that by itself was not evidence of the involvement of the general population. "Under Cover of the Night," they patiently explained, apparently with straight faces, "a few Villains may do much Mischief." In a sentence, the House took the interpretation of a few being responsible and turned it upside down. The culprits were not an elite cabal but rascals from the bottom of society. Above all, the people of Boston should not be held accountable. Bernard was simply mistaken, and the House hoped he would not publicly convey such erroneous judgments. He probably had been "misinformed by Persons not well affected to this People, and who would be glad to have it thought that we were turbulent and factious, and perpetually murmuring, even after every Cause of Complaint is removed."

As to the transformation of the Council, the House was perfectly within its rights to choose whomever it determined best for the job, and former councilors with other administrative responsibilities, such as judges of the Superior Court, would have more time to devote themselves to those tasks. The House finally noted Bernard's declaration that whenever an opportunity arose to "restore Harmony and Union to the Provincial Councils" he would "most cordially embrace it." "The Time, Sir," it announced, "is already come." In short, should antagonism continue between Bernard and the legislature, the fault was the governor's.[12]

Having each fired their opening salvos, the governor and the House proceeded to their own separate agenda. The representatives fulfilled one of the planks of their preelection platform and approved the construction of a gallery. Not only would an audience make government seem more transparent, but it would reinforce popular positions and discourage supporters of the administration. To make sure it would get the the desired political impact from the presence of spectators, the House ordered "That no Person be admitted to a Seat in the Gallery without applying to and being introduced by a Member of the House."[13]

On the very day of the House response, Bernard notified both chambers that he had received a communication from Secretary of State Henry Conway, enclosing the repeal of the Stamp Act and the Declaratory Act as well as a resolution from Parliament calling for compensation "to the late Sufferers by the Madness of the People." It was impolitic enough to refer to Bostonians in such a way, but the governor, still incensed, could not restrain himself from once again scolding the House for excluding the four Crown officers from the Council. It should have shown its gratitude to king and Parliament instead of snubbing them and, deservedly, should now expect the displeasure of British authorities. The assembly had a choice: it could allow itself to be seduced by the self-serving interests of a few, or it could win the approval and the forbearance of the British government by offering restitution to the recipients of the crowd's discontent.[14] Blinded by resentment at the shift of power and caught in a debate where winning points seemed more important than persuading the legislature, Bernard did little more than further antagonize the representatives.

Town House as of 1785. In *Re-dedication of the Old State House* (Boston, 1882), opp. 95. From the cover of *Boston Magazine*. (Reproduced by permission of The Huntington Library, San Marino, California)

Not able to resist besting an argument themselves, the legislators explained, as if to a slow schoolboy, that they would not relinquish their charter right to choose whomever they wished for the Council. Moreover there was no suggestion in Conway's letter that they should. That sentiment required nearly five pages in the *Journals of the House*. Almost as an afterthought, they conveyed that they would entertain the question of compensation at their first convenient opportunity.[15]

And so it went. Charge and countercharge, feisty insult and scathing retort. A week after the exchange, the House raised the issue of restitution and decided to postpone a decision until the next session of the General Court. After Andrew Oliver, as secretary of the province, transmitted estimates of the losses sustained by Thomas Hutchinson and others in the August riots, the House informed the governor—now fully three weeks after his request—that responsibility for compensation fell to the perpetrators of the acts, not to the province as a whole. Should the legislature incur the expense, it should do so "not as an act of Justice, but rather of Generosity." The House would attempt to identify the offenders but would need to consult with its constituents before agreeing to the requested act of charity. No judgment, therefore, could be made until later in the year. Faced with an impasse over compensation and a disagreement over troop levels at Castle William and Fort Pownall, an exasperated Francis Bernard adjourned the session.[16]

The partisan press, of course, joined the fray. One writer raised the alarm that should the legislature lose its liberty to choose Council members, worse violations of rights—the possibility of a standing army in their midst being the most dire—would ensue. In fact, it was more than a possibility. Two regiments were already stationed in New York City, though the author of the article was unaware of this.[17]

The buildup had begun gradually, almost unnoticeably. The previous August, anticipating protests against the Stamp Act, the acting governor of New York, Cadwallader Colden, had appealed to the commander of the British Army in North America, Thomas Gage, to transfer some soldiers from the backcountry to New York City. Gage, himself wary of the popular movement, happily complied, and forty-six men were stationed in the city by late in the month. Although they arrived as a potential police force, Gage pretended that they were simple soldiers doing regular duty at Fort George, a small fortress within the town where arms were stored. Under the same guise, two artillery companies joined their comrades in early September, bringing the combined total to 130 men. Colden wanted an even larger force, but royal regulations required that the Council join him in any request for military aid, and it demurred against taking such provocative action.[18]

Equally stymied was Gage, who hungered to supply a military solution to the problem of growing colonial unrest and resented the restraints placed on him. The general was convinced that the "disturbances" in Boston and elsewhere were more like the "forerunners of open Rebellion" than mere riots. He longed for a pretence to bring substantial troops to a single locale—it apparently didn't matter which—to show would-be revolutionaries what they could expect. His immediate concern was how long it would take to bring widely dispersed troops together.[19]

That spring Gage got his wish. In early June 1766 two regiments (approximately one thousand men) reported for duty in New York City. Clashes between soldiers and townspeople occurred within a month. Bostonians were regularly regaled and horrified by newspaper accounts of events that could just as easily be erupting in their own city. In late

July they learned of a brawl initiated by four drunken British officers. Weaving out of a tavern, the four amused themselves by breaking street lamps along their way back to the barracks. Reproached by a publican leaning against his door, they assaulted him with their swords, wounding him in the arm. The officers then dashed inside the public house and "terrified the family and lodgers, some of whom they pulled from their beds." Finally they tired of that and, accompanied by two more soldiers, went back to demolishing lamps, eventually destroying thirty-four before they encountered four town watchmen. In the ensuing skirmish, several watchmen were stabbed, two officers "knock'd down," and another officer captured. The officers who escaped gathered a dozen soldiers and stormed the city hall to liberate their jailed comrade. The next day two of the officers were arrested but freed after posting bail.[20]

More overtly political in nature was an attack on New York City's Liberty Pole. On the occasion of the king's birthday in June, townspeople erected a pole on their common to celebrate the repeal of the Stamp Act and inscribed it with the names of George III, William Pitt, and Liberty. In mid-August some soldiers from the 28th Regiment cut down the pole. New Yorkers perceived the action as an "insult to the town" and replaced the pole the next day. A drummer from one of the regiments chose the wrong time to saunter by. When the assemblage noticed his presence, "they fell upon him and afterwards upon a corporal who came to his Assistance and pursued both to the Barrack Gate," where the first of several melees between groups of soldiers and townspeople began. The newspaper account nonetheless asserted that based on many affidavits "the soldiers were entirely the aggressors." Moreover, went the account, "the people are in general very uneasy that such a number of armed men, without any visible occasion for them, are station'd among us, & suffer'd to patrol the streets, as in a military or conquer'd town." Gage had a different assessment; he concluded that the general populace believed their newfound power was challenged by the military and therefore opposed their presence, while the "better Sort" wished to see order restored and supported the troops.[21]

Within a week Bostonians read of a soldier who received "500 Lashes for assaulting a Gentleman in the Street." Despite commanders' attempts to rein in their men, citizens still complained that soldiers on their rounds made it difficult to pass on the narrow New York streets. Such stories peppered the papers throughout the occupation.[22] This was not the social order Gage hoped to achieve nor the lesson he wished to convey to prospective "revolutionaries."

Nearly lost in all the partisan turmoil in Massachusetts and in the tales of the standing army in New York City was news about revisions to the Sugar Act. Rumors of a reduction of the tax on molasses had circulated since early spring, and finally on September 8 Bostonians learned that the modification would go into effect on November 1. On the second page of the *Boston Gazette*, stuck between short items on a woman's death and a ship's foundering, was the simple announcement "The Duties of *One Penny* per Gallon (Wine Measure) on Molasses, takes Place the First of November next."[23] That was the only news provided about the altered Act, and nothing further appeared in subsequent issues.

The revisions of the revenue measure had other, important consequences, but all that seemed to matter to merchants who shipped molasses, rum manufacturers, and everyone connected to those enterprises was that the duty had been lowered to a level that made the risky business of smuggling unnecessary. Duties on both British and foreign sugar put American merchants at a competitive disadvantage, but no nonimportation agreement appeared. New restrictions on coffee and pimento lowered profits for American merchants, but no resolutions demanding repeal emerged from colonial legislatures. New requirements blocked trade between the British colonies and northern Europe, yet no one took to the streets.

The people of Boston appeared to have abandoned important principles when the tax was lowered. The Molasses Act of 1733 had placed a duty on foreign molasses but not on British molasses; it was a trade bill, not a tax. The Sugar Act of 1764 kept the distinction between place of origin and lowered the duty. Though it looked like a regulation of commerce, it was passed by Parliament to raise taxes, not to protect British West Indian growers. In the summer of 1766 the bill dropped the duty even further, but it also discarded any distinction between foreign molasses and British molasses. It placed a tax on all molasses, whatever its provenance. There was no pretence of its being a trade act. It was intended to produce revenue. And yet there were no cries of "no taxation without representation."[24]

Were the people of Boston therefore hypocrites, raising principles about their rights as British citizens only when imperial policies undercut their economic interests but otherwise remaining silent? There is no simple answer to that question, and no explanation covers the full range of townspeople's behavior and motives. Whatever their disposition, Bostonians were not abstract political philosophers, protesting (or not) in a social vacuum. They were sailors and shopkeepers, merchants and artisans, lawyers and laborers, consumers and manufacturers, men and women, employers and employees, pious and profane, politicians and constituents, citizens and slaves, who responded to the world they experienced. Simultaneously self-interested and civic-minded, they looked to heaven and worried about the bottom line. Their principles intersected with the demands of their lives, making it far more compelling to fight for a political right that was connected to their day-to-day existence than to struggle for a theoretical doctrine. "No taxation without representation," "equal rights of British citizens," "Liberty," and "Charter rights and privileges" were inherited values, battle cries, markers of personal and collective worth, and tools for power that resonated most when they overlapped other aspects of people's lives. Bostonians were complicated beings, and sometimes they settled for what was favorable rather than what was optimal. There is no reason for us to come to an either/or conclusion regarding their motivation. The residents of Boston were principled and pragmatic. Perhaps in the late summer of 1766 most of them merely hoped for a return to normality.

Such hopes soon were dashed. At about 8 o'clock in the morning on September 24, the sea captain and trader Daniel Malcom was in his bedroom, when he heard people entering his house in the North End of Boston. Descending to his parlor, he found the intruders to be William Sheaffe, deputy collector of customs; Benjamin Hallowell, comptroller of the port; two minor customs officials; and Benjamin Cudworth, deputy sheriff of Suffolk County. Trying to be gracious, Malcom invited them to sit down, but Hallowell brusquely replied that he wanted Malcom to get his keys and show them around the residence. An informer had told them that the sea captain had undocumented brandy, wine, and other liquors in his possession. Unfazed, Malcom gave his visitors a house tour, including his outbuildings, the kitchen cellar, and a second cellar—all places where illegal goods might be hidden. Hallowell inquired whether there was an additional cellar behind a partition. Malcom acknowledged there was; but when the comptroller asked to have that cellar opened, he refused. He explained that he had let out that space to William Mackay, also a sea captain and a business associate, and that the cellar was under his colleague's control. Hoping to head off a crisis, Sheaffe went to Mackay's residence and asked for the key to the cellar. Mackay said that he didn't have it but accompanied Sheaffe back to Malcom's dwelling.[25]

The whole business had all the makings of a second-rate farce, except for the ever-present possibility of violence. Upon the return of Sheaffe and Mackay, Malcom still rebuffed all requests to open the locked cellar. An increasingly irate Hallowell threatened to break into the cellar. He asked Malcom if he knew who he was dealing with. Just as angry, Malcom answered, yes, a "dirty fellow." He would "blow the brains out of the person" who tried to force his way in. Mackay joined the fray with the taunt that he "always understood a Man's House was his Castle, and that it could not be broke open unless for Murder, Treason and Theft." While tears streamed down Mrs. Malcom's blanched face and their children scurried through the rooms in fright, Hallowell warned that he could have Malcom "tried for life." After two hours of this bickering, Malcom grabbed two pistols (at the time, only he knew they were unloaded), strapped on his sword, and ordered the customs officials out of his house. Before departing, Cudworth, well aware of his precarious predicament, pulled the sea captain aside and confided, "Capt. Malcom I hope you are not angry with me." Denying knowledge of why he was there, he then hastened away. For the moment, the participants put the controversy aside.

At midday Malcom and Mackay went for a walk into the center of town, where they unexpectedly encountered Hallowell. The comptroller had calmed down and tried to work out a compromise. No harm would come to Malcom should he allow customs officials to enter the locked cellar. Again the sea captain refused, and again Hallowell made a threat, informing him that this time a regiment of soldiers would be brought in to assist the customs officers. At that they went their separate ways.

By 2 o'clock Malcom was back home, and he immediately locked the doors and shuttered the windows. Hallowell went to the governor for assistance, and Bernard summoned Sheriff Stephen Greenleaf, directing him to solicit justices of the peace for help. Justice Stoddard claimed he was too ill. Judge Ruddock begged off with the excuse that he was so heavy he couldn't walk the distance and would have to be carried in a chaise. Judge Tudor agreed personally to survey the scene but promised no more.

About 3 o'clock in the afternoon customs officials returned to Malcom's residence, only to find it tightly secured. After calling for Malcom for nearly half an hour, Hallowell sent a minor official to the adjoining backyard. Coaxing a Mr. Brown to pull himself up the high fence to observe Malcom's house from the rear, the customs officer had no greater success and abandoned the effort.

By late afternoon a large crowd had gathered (estimates ranged from fifty to four hundred people, with Malcom's supporters seeing a small and orderly assembly and customs officials perceiving a large and unruly mob). Captain William Wimble warned Hallowell not to break into the cellar. Were customs officers to make such an attempt, they were certain to be "insulted and ill used." A signal would be given to ring the bells of the Old North Church, as if there were a fire, and a much larger crowd would form. Hallowell, one of the "sufferers" on August 26, 1765, was reminded that the incident could be repeated and that there might be "fatal Consequences." As the sun began to set, the Crown officers ended their vigil. Malcom left the sanctity of his house and offered the group of supporters several buckets of wine, then advised them to go home.

Later, under oath, both Malcom and Mackay denied that they held illegal goods. Malcom had without protest shown his house, outbuildings, and two cellars to the customs officers, but had drawn the line at one locked cellar. No one had shown him a writ of assistance or other legal orders, and therefore he was under no legal obligation to open any of his house. Still, it is highly suspicious that he would refuse to unlock one small part of his house after revealing the contents of all the rest. In a deposition dated September 25, Hallowell and Sheaffe claimed that they had brought a writ of assistance with them, but they never stated that they had shown it to Malcom. Accepting Bernard's advice, they had sought the assistance of several judges, but what more the justices could achieve was unclear. For the time being, Malcom had successfully resisted His Majesty's customs officers.

That was the message that Bernard would communicate to London, along with a packet of evidence. Within a week, he had obtained depositions from Hallowell and Sheaffe, some of the justices, High Sheriff Greenleaf, and a few bystanders. Conspicuously missing were the testimonies of Malcom and Mackay. Bernard's packet bolstered his claim that he and other royal officials had lost control of the town; although he avoided directly requesting troops, he continued to hint at the necessity of their presence. When Boston leaders learned what the governor had done, they asked for copies of the depositions and then deposed their own witnesses, including Malcom, Mackay, and nearly twenty others. They sent their own packet to the colony's British agent Dennys De Berdt and hoped he could control the damage.[26]

When the House met in late October, it, too, wanted to see the depositions, but its main issue—its only issue, according to Bernard—was compensation for the victims of the August 1765 demonstrations. In response to previous disclaimers that the legislature couldn't act until the "sufferers" made appeals, Hutchinson, Hallowell, Story, and Oliver petitioned the House for restitution of their losses. Story, the former deputy register of the vice admiralty court, expressed sympathy with the people's sentiment that the court had deprived defendants of trial by jury and their argument that most Boston residents were not responsible for the destruction of his property. However, neither Story's attempts to win goodwill nor the plight of the others convinced the House that compensation was appropriate, and it promptly denied the petitions.

This didn't settle the matter, of course. If Massachusetts's representatives did nothing, they would antagonize the king, the ministry, Parliament, and some of their own British allies. And the Boston town meeting had instructed its legislative members to find some way to compensate the "sufferers" without also jeopardizing constitutional rights. But compensation was a bitter pill for the popular party to swallow. They wanted to avoid the appearance of capitulating to a parliamentary resolution that required Massachusetts to raise revenue and were repulsed by the thought of using provincial funds to restore Hutchinson's wealth. They had a difficult enough task simply ratifying the salaries for his multiple offices. In the end, the best the House could do was engineer a bill that both provided funds to those who had lost property and offered amnesty to all participants in the riots. Seeking the cover of constituent support, they requested a recess so that they could discuss the matter with citizens of their various towns.[27]

Upon their return in early December and after some legislative maneuvering, the House passed the dual-purpose act and sent it to the governor. It was a pragmatic compromise, reflecting the divided powers of Massachusetts government. Only the legislature could initiate money bills, and only the governor could grant pardons. Recognizing that it was the best arrangement possible, Bernard approved the statute and dispatched it to England. Years later the Privy Council reviewed the act and rejected it, but by then it didn't matter.[28]

The repeal of the Stamp Act reduced animosity between the British government and Boston, but it didn't restore the relationship that had existed prior to the Act. Too much had happened. Parliament had rescinded the legislation angrily and reluctantly, and only with the accompanying Declaratory Act, declaring its sovereignty and its right to tax. In Massachusetts, and Boston in particular, political positions hardened. There was increased estrangement from the governor and his allies. Bernard, realizing his power had diminished, responded with threats and impatience rather than with diplomacy. At the end of 1766, John Adams believed that "almost all the People, whether better or worse, are of one Mind about the Governor and absolutely hate him and despize him."[29] Customs officials were disliked even more, and the Malcom episode demonstrated that they could be successfully resisted.

Had the British government and its representatives been willing to allow that situation to remain uncontested, had they been willing to maintain only a loose political relationship and close economic ties with few regulations, their association with Bostonians under the Crown could have continued indefinitely. But the year after the repeal of the Stamp Act proved to be only a moratorium.

Chapter 5

The Townshend Blunder

Spring came to Boston. The long winter was over. Trees were leafing. The Stamp Act crisis was more or less resolved. And yet Speaker of the House Thomas Cushing was worried. On May 9, 1767, he wrote the colony's agent in England that his fellow citizens greatly desire "a strict union and harmony" with the mother country but that persons "on both sides of the water" were trying to produce "hostilities with one another." Some on the British side were depicting colonists as disloyal subjects preparing for rebellion, while some on the American side claimed that they were victims of a plot to deprive them of their "most invaluable rights and privileges." In this tenuous situation, the worst mistake would be to send troops to "enforce acts of Parliament." Nearly as bad would be new taxes. Colonists could accept trade regulations, Cushing reasoned, but duties to raise revenue, particularly if those taxes were used to pay the salaries of officials such as the governor and judges, would be met with stiff resistance.[1]

Cushing had good instincts and gave sound advice, but warnings such as his would go unheeded in the halls and chambers of the British government. With William Pitt then nominally head of the ministry, Bostonians were under the impression that their protector would continue to defend the rights of all British citizens. They believed that Pitt's opponents, led by Grenville and Bute, were the threats to their well-being. As usual, the situation wasn't that clear-cut. Pitt had been in power since the previous summer, when he had replaced Rockingham, and had immediately made a monumental mistake: he had accepted appointment to the peerage as the Earl of Chatham. The Great Commoner no longer could orate in the House of Commons. In the streets and in the newspapers former admirers denounced his betrayal.

The Right Honble. William Pitt, Earl of Chatham, 1770, an engraving by Richard Houston based on a portrait by William Hoare. (Emmet Collection, Miriam and Ira D. Wallach Division of Art, Prints and Photographs, The New York Public Library, Astor, Lenox and Tilden Foundations)

Soon after taking office Pitt's ministry had to resolve a crisis brought on by a bad grain harvest and had lost popularity, sending soldiers to quell bread rioters and violating the law by prohibiting grain exportation. Political rivalries, reports of restless colonists, and domestic concerns further undercut Pitt's hopes for imperial reform. Never captivated by the details of governing, in December 1766 a frustrated and fatigued Pitt retreated to Bath, where he remained for most of the next two years.[2]

At this critical moment, Chancellor of the Exchequer Charles Townshend stepped into the power vacuum. The forty-one-year-old second son of Viscount Townshend was experienced, bright, a persuasive orator, and erratic. Since his early days as a member of the Board of Trade, he had advocated that royal officials be freed from their financial

The Right Honble. Charles Townshend Esq.,
late Chancellor of the Exchequer . . . , 1770,
a mezzotint by John Dixon after a portrait
by Joshua Reynolds. (Emmet Collection,
Miriam and Ira D. Wallach Division of Art,
Prints and Photographs, The New York
Public Library, Astor, Lenox and Tilden
Foundations)

dependency on colonial legislatures. In Pitt's absence, Townshend had
argued that the colonies should contribute to the support of troops
in their midst. When Parliament cut the land tax in Great Britain,
thereby reducing revenue by £500,000, pressure for colonial assistance
intensified. Under those circumstances, it required little to convince the
House of Commons that their North American colonies be taxed. The
reluctance of the Massachusetts General Court to compensate victims of
crowd violence and the refusal of the New York legislature to provide
full provisions for troops stationed in New York City—a violation of the
Quartering Act—fueled lingering animosities. Parliament hungered for
an excuse to demonstrate its sovereignty, and here it came.[3]

In the same month as Cushing's premonitory letter, Townshend presented his program to Parliament. It consisted of three major components.

Under the delusion that colonists would not object to taxes in the form of duties, he recommended that taxes be levied on four commodities manufactured in England—glass, lead, painters' colors, and paper—and on tea that was re-exported from the mother country. The projected annual revenue was merely forty thousand pounds, and it was specifically earmarked for defraying salaries of royal officials in the colonies and for reducing troop expenses. Townshend was well aware that the funds were inadequate, but he viewed the duties as a pilot program. Should colonists accept them, more would follow.

The second component was the establishment of an American Board of Customs Commissioners. Being located in America, it could more closely supervise customs operations in the mainland colonies and make the collection of duties more efficient, more honest, and more profitable. The city selected for its headquarters was Boston.

The final component was to punish the New York legislature for its failure to satisfy all the requirements of the Quartering Act. Parliament would disqualify that assembly from passing acts beginning on October 1, 1767. Once the legislature fulfilled its responsibility to house and provision the regiments in New York City, its authority would be restored.[4]

At the end of June 1767 Parliament approved the Townshend program. Once again the British government asserted its sovereignty over its American colonies. Whether the colonies would accept the arrangement as they had after the revision of the Sugar Act in 1766 or would challenge parliamentary dominance as they had in reaction to the Stamp Act was an open question.

Bostonians received their first whiff of the Townshend Acts in early July, and other hints drifted in during the course of the summer, but confirmation of their passage and full details of their contents weren't known until October. Their reaction was tepid, possibly disheartened. An occasional piece appeared in the newspapers, declaiming taxation without representation or raising concerns about Crown officials becoming financially independent of colonial legislatures. And there were fears expressed that the new duties were merely a prelude to more taxes. But there was no passion, no fire. Had the New York legislature not capitulated and fully funded the troops residing in their major city, thereby avoiding suspension, there might have been a broad outcry. Instead there was a wait-and-watch attitude toward the commissioners who landed in Boston on November 5, nothing more demonstrative than the now-moderated Pope's Day activities. On December 10 the minister Andrew Eliot observed, "The present burthens may possibly be borne without any great opposition; I believe they will; but it is easy to see that the people are sullen, and think themselves ill-treated."[5] Perhaps the vigorous resistance to the Stamp Act had been an anomaly.

Boston was divided and weary of internal dissension. "What do we mean by Country and by Court, / What is it to oppose, what to support?," rhymed one writer in the *Boston Evening-Post*. "The only diff'rence after all their rout, / Is that the one is *in* the other *out*." Eliot despaired that the "managers of our public affairs . . . are governed by private views and the spirit of a party," but nonetheless he believed that the opposition, whatever its motives, checked the "conduct of men in power."[6]

However effective popular leaders might have been, they were hindered by Samuel Adams's financial predicament. As one of the town's tax collectors earlier in the decade, Adams had been personally responsible for the amounts people owed. His leniency may have gained him gratitude, but it did not reduce his obligations. When he left office in 1765, he had neglected to pursue or failed to acquire eight thousand pounds. By 1767 neither Adams's political prominence nor the goodwill he had earned over the years could shield him from scrutiny and possible prosecution. The sorry state of the town treasury demanded no less. As news of the Townshend Acts traveled across the Atlantic, Boston officials demanded that Adams produce a list of debts due him and the names of the individuals in arrears. They called a special town meeting to judge the suit brought against him. Adams temporarily dodged criminal prosecution when the town granted him an extension for collecting the missing taxes. Despite misgivings, even among Adams's sometime allies, such as the merchant John Rowe, the town renewed the extension for an additional six months the following March.[7] Throughout his travail, Adams remained politically active, but his standing in Boston and beyond suffered.

To make matters worse for those who opposed the Townshend program, Governor Bernard skillfully neutralized the House by not calling it back into session during the fall and early winter of 1767. Thus there were no resolutions to challenge Parliament's sovereignty and to energize the population; there were no conflicts with the governor or lieutenant governor to remind everyone how power had shifted. Bernard also may have contributed to blunting one of the popular movement's chief weapons: the threat of an unleashed mob. His letters to the ministry, depicting Boston as unruly and rebellious and indirectly pleading for troops to enforce British policy and his authority, were well known and aroused anxious suspicions. Rumors of the impending arrival of British regiments became as prevalent as concerns about parliamentary violations of colonial rights.[8] The fall of 1767 witnessed a balancing of countervailing threats—troops versus mobs—that moderated the behavior of all Boston residents, for the short term at least.

When "scandalous and threatning Papers . . . tending to excite Tumults & Disorders" appeared in parts of Boston in November, the town immediately convened a meeting and unanimously voted "to assist the Selectmen and Majestrates in the suppression of all Disorders." The mercurial James Otis took the lead in passing the resolution, and for a change columns in the often unfriendly *Boston Evening-Post* bestowed praise on him, though without quite mentioning his name. The selectmen of Boston worried about the town's reputation and possible consequences. "We detest Mobs and riotous assemblies," they proclaimed, "therefore, our Fellow-Townsmen, give us Leave to persuade you to keep your Tempers and study Moderation when you meet with incitements artfully thrown out to beguile you into illegal measures." [9] In the face of new taxes that would be used to pay the salaries of royal officials and of strengthened enforcement of customs acts, the town had lost its nerve. It was on the defensive.

Under these circumstances, popular leaders could not generate support for nonimportation, one of their most effective tools against the Stamp Act. When one writer advocated the legal tactic of limiting imports from Britain to items essential for the fisheries or for protection against inclement weather rather than resorting to illegal "tumult and disorder," a critic promptly countered his suggestion. "Why are you enraged at the measures taken by the mother country to enslave her children," he questioned, "and at the same time propose, as the best method of redress, the enslaving your brethren?" This was a query that resounded with many Bostonians. Some well-stocked merchants might be able to weather a cessation of imports, but the livelihoods of lesser merchants, shopkeepers, sailors, artisans, and laborers, all dependent on maritime trade, would be jeopardized.[10] There must be a better option.

With the House prorogued, Samuel Adams under threat of prosecution, James Otis as unreliable as ever, people disenchanted with partisan strife, the threat of large-scale demonstrations neutralized by the risk of provoking British authorities to send troops, and nonimportation discredited, those who opposed the Townshend Acts had few choices. As New England entered its annual autumnal transformation, however, a tactic gradually emerged. It wasn't new or perfect, but it was a beginning. According to one contributor to the *Boston Gazette*, the city had an unequal balance of trade with Britain. More gold and silver was leaving town than coming in. It was already difficult to afford British goods, and the taxes on glass, paper, lead, painters' colors, and tea compounded the problem. As a matter of necessity, he argued, Bostonians should reduce purchases of "foreign manufactures" and "encourage, by every means, the manufacturing those articles, on the importation of which heavy taxes are laid." Glass was a prime example of a viable industry, but there were others as well. The result would be employment of the poor, "public affluence and felicity," and the preservation of freedom. "I will venture to foretell," he optimistically concluded, "that Great-Britain will soon be convinced that Americans were not made to be her slaves."[11]

By the end of October Boston had endorsed the proposal of non-consumption and manufacturing. Not going so far as advocating an outright boycott, the town meeting identified a long list of items, including clothing, furniture, fire engines, and snuff—leaving out any products taxed by Townshend—and recommended that people sign a subscription "to lessen the use of Superfluities" and the "enumerated Articles Imported from abroad." It also voted to encourage manufacturing in the province, particularly of glass and paper.[12]

Tales of the thirty thousand yards of cloth produced in the town of Dartmouth the previous year and the forty thousand pairs of women's shoes coming out of Lynn soon appeared. Writers exhorted women to be economical and everyone to be frugal and industrious.[13]

There were scoffers as well. "A True Patriot" doubted that domestic manufacturers had the means to replace British producers and challenged whether they were as prevalent as reports indicated. "Can any man of common sense help smiling at the multiplicity of (News-Paper) manufactures that have sprung up within these few weeks," he questioned, "especially when they come to know that all these different branches have little or no existence but in newspapers." Such skepticism may have been politically motivated to discourage the citizenry, as rivals would suggest, but it nonetheless contained some truth. A unified nonconsumption movement might have had some impact on British policy, were a large segment of the population willing to do without. But people had grown accustomed to goods that earlier generations viewed as luxuries. Andrew Eliot, for one, believed that some of the articles on the subscription list were "quite necessary, at least which custom hath made so," and he noted that "few of the trading part have subscribed." Had manufacturing in the colonies, particularly in New England, been more extensive, Bostonians might have been more enthusiastic in promoting boycotts.[14] As a political tactic nonconsumption, or in this case reduced consumption, was a useful companion to nonimportation and may have helped raise the morale of frustrated and despairing town residents, but it was a weak counter to the Townshend program.

Unexpectedly, gentle breezes coming from Pennsylvania nudged slack-sailed Boston out of its doldrums. They came in the form of twelve *Letters from a Farmer in Pennsylvania*. Their author, John Dickinson, may have been born and raised on plantations in Maryland and Delaware (the only justification for his occupational reference), but as a young man he had studied law in London. Urbane, politically astute, and temperamentally conservative, the wealthy Philadelphia lawyer was outraged at the inept colonial response to the Townshend Acts. His central complaint was the legislation's unconstitutional assault on colonial rights.

The first *Letter* examined the suspension of the New York legislature. Although he thought the assembly had acted "imprudently," Dickinson considered the threat of punishment an affront to freedom. The legislature had no choice but to provision the troops, meaning that the people of New York were in effect paying a tax to which they had not consented. By suspending the assembly until it conformed, Parliament had asserted its sovereignty and deprived New Yorkers of their constitutional rights, and an attack on any one colony was an attack on them all.

Succeeding *Letters* differentiated between taxes, which were for raising revenue, and duties, which were for regulating trade. No matter what a bill was called, however, if its purpose was to generate income for the state, it was a tax. Townshend "duties" were essentially taxes, levied without the consent of the colonists and therefore an abridgment of their liberty. In similar fashion, Dickinson challenged the legitimacy of writs of assistance and of salaries of royal officials in the colonies being paid by the Crown rather than by legislatures. He believed that the times were as perilous as during the Stamp Act crisis and wanted to provoke as serious a response, but without violence. Dickinson's remedies were moderate and fitting for a veteran of the Stamp Act Congress, in which he had played a prominent role as a Pennsylvania delegate. Colonies should petition for the rescinding of the Townshend Acts, and they should reduce their consumption of British goods through frugality and their own production of necessities.[15]

The Farmer's *Letters* were not original in their philosophy or criticisms, but they were reasonable, penetrating, and timely. They argued for resolve and fought against lethargy. Above all, they were read and discussed. After their publication in the *Pennsylvania Chronicle*, newspapers throughout the colonies reprinted them one by one, week after week. Their cumulative effect sparked renewed efforts among the colonists to be recognized as equal citizens within the empire and to resist parliamentary arrogance. Three of Boston's weekly newspapers— the *Boston Chronicle*, the *Boston Evening-Post*, and the *Boston Gazette*— published at least eight of the *Letters* over a ten-week period. (The *Boston Post Boy* and the *Massachusetts Gazette*, the voice of the court faction, declined.) By March 1768 only comatose Bostonians were unaware of the *Letters*.

The House resumed operations with reinvigorated resolve almost at the same moment as the *Letters'* first appearance in Boston. From Bernard's perspective the session seemed to begin cordially, but he soon resented the House for employing its own agent and sending letters to the king and various ministers as if it were an independent governmental body.[16] From the House's perspective, letters and petitions were its chief means of seeking a redress of grievances. It was well aware that Bernard would provide no assistance.

Its first letter went to its agent, Dennys De Berdt. The most comprehensive of all the letters the legislature sent that winter, it offered him a wide range of explanations as to why the Townshend Acts were bad policy. Every bit as much a revenue measure as the Sugar Act and the Stamp Act, the bills were an affront to the constitutional principle that taxes could be enacted only with the consent of the governed. Colonists had not been represented, and yet the burden was exclusively theirs. Using those revenues to pay governors and judges destroyed the checks and balances among the executive, judicial, and legislative branches and opened the colonies to corruption and arbitrary rule. The litany continued, as months of pent-up resentment poured out. The suspension of the New York assembly, a terrible precedent in its own right, would be reversed only when the legislature had paid what amounted to a tax for the purpose of supporting a standing army. The newly appointed commissioners of customs were unnecessary. Restraints on trade benefited British manufacturers at the expense of colonial consumers. The colonies had always helped secure and defend the empire but were receiving no share of the recent conquest. All of these harmful measures, the House believed, grew from the fact that "the nation has been grossly misinformed with respect to the temper and behavior of the Colonists: and it is to be feared that some men will not cease to sow the seeds of jealousy and discord, till they shall have done irreparable mischief."[17] As much as an effort to repeal the Townshend Acts, the aim of the letters to De Berdt and others was to combat what the House interpreted as willful misrepresentations that led to disastrous imperial policy.

In quick succession, the Massachusetts legislature sent letters or petitions to the Earl of Shelburne, secretary of state for the Southern Department; King George III; the marquis of Rockingham, former prime minister; Henry Seymour Conway, secretary of state for the Northern Department; and the lords commissioners of the Treasury. None was as thorough as the letter to De Berdt, but each underlined the same point—colonists were being denied the rights to which they were entitled as Englishmen. The recent acts of Parliament violated their civil liberties and represented a misunderstanding of their loyalty to the Crown and empire.[18]

There was a weak link in their argument. Parliament could counter their constitutional argument about no taxation without representation by granting some seats in the House of Commons to the colonies. That was Bernard's recommendation to Lord Barrington. To preempt that possibility, the Massachusetts House, beginning in its letter to the king and repeated in other letters, made a case for its impracticality. The three-thousand-mile ocean that separated the colonies from the mother country made it impossible that "they should be equally represented there." Left unsaid was the obvious drawback that they would be numerically overwhelmed. "All that is desired by the people of this Province, is, that they may be restored to their original standing," the House wrote to Henry Conway. The key word was "original," which referred to the initial charter of the colony, drawn up more than a century earlier. The representatives of the Bay Colony were calling for authority over all legislation, with the only constraints being the prohibition to violate English law and the king's power to annul offending law.[19] Parliament may have been the supreme legislature, but the Massachusetts House had begun to challenge Parliament's authority to legislate the colonies, not simply to tax. Its vision had become that of autonomous colonial governments under the Crown.

Recognizing that coordinating with other colonies would strengthen the force of its petitions and letters, the House sent a circular letter to the other legislatures politely recommending that their addresses to the king and ministry "should harmonize with each other." It cautiously prefaced its objections to the Townshend Acts with the acknowledgment that "his Majesty's high Court of Parliament is the supreme legislative power over the whole empire." Then it laid out its well-rehearsed objections to taxes, salaries for officials, commissioners, and—with the New York legislature back in session—the hardships created by the Quartering Act. The letter concluded with the humble assurance that the Massachusetts House wasn't trying to dictate their affairs to other colonies and expressed confidence in the king's favorably accepting "the united and dutiful supplications of his distressed American subjects."[20]

The usual bickering between the governor and the House—on this occasion focusing on whether Bernard had portrayed the legislature unflatteringly to the Earl of Shelburne—provoked Bernard to prorogue the session on March 4. By then, Boston's attention was on the commissioners of customs: John Robinson, Charles Paxton, John Temple, Henry Hulton, and William Burch. From the vantage point of London, they had selected well. Robinson, Paxton, and Temple had all previously held customs posts in New England. Hulton had served as a customs official in the West Indies and prior to his appointment had been plantation clerk to the original commissioners in London. Burch's background is unknown, but he proved to be a loyal servant to the Crown. Bostonians, predisposed to loathe anyone employed to enforce customs laws, weren't so sanguine. Paxton and Robinson had battled merchants and their allies for years and were roundly disliked. Temple, by comparison, had been more accommodating, and his marriage to the daughter of the wealthy popular leader James Bowdoin improved his standing with the citizenry. Trying to reconcile his friendships in the town with his responsibilities as commissioner was nearly impossible, and Temple's disappointment at becoming one of a board of five (when he had been surveyor general, with no local master) alienated him from his colleagues.[21] Whether Hulton and Burch would side with Paxton and Robinson would determine how well Boston residents received the group.

The commissioners unfortunately arrived from England on Pope's Day, though even with the typical commotion all began uneventfully enough. When Hulton observed people carrying "twenty Devils, Popes, & Pretenders, thro the Streets" with affixed labels proclaiming "Liberty & Property & no Commissioners," he laughed. James Otis returned the cordiality two weeks later. As moderator of the town meeting, Otis extended an olive branch by separating the onus of duties on imports from the office of commissioners and recommended "quiet and proper behavior." On February 10, 1768, the commissioners broke the dreariness of winter by hosting an assembly, a dance attended by about a hundred people, a mix of royal officials and townspeople.[22]

Two days later the board sent a report to the lords of Treasury, and it was evident that the period of affability shortly would rip apart. The commissioners complained that smuggling was extensive in New England, but there had been only six seizures in the previous two and a half years. Of those, only one had been prosecuted successfully; two had been acquitted as a result of intimidation; and mobs had rescued the other three. They also cited the Malcom episode as an example of general resistance to customs officers. Although officials had already voiced all this to the commissioners of customs in London (this was prior to the creation of the American board), no action either to punish offenders or to strengthen the customs service had been taken. Thus far, no one had committed an "act of violence" against a commissioner, though an effigy of Paxton had been hanged. Nonetheless, the commissioners were convinced they needed military protection to enforce the revenue laws. The closest troops were in New York City, and there wasn't a single naval ship in the province.[23]

The commissioners' sense of powerlessness and foreboding escalated rapidly. One reason was the irascible trader Daniel Malcom. Anticipating a shipment of contraband goods, Malcom inquired of a customs agent what "indulgence" was required. The official, at least as described by Bernard, responded that he wouldn't accept a bribe and that Malcom would have to pay the duty. Malcom, happy to know where matters stood, anchored his schooner five miles from Boston and had sixty casks of wine unloaded at night. Guarded by "a Party of Men with Clubs," the hardworking smugglers distributed the wine in various cellars. It was a noisy process, and townspeople were well aware of what had transpired. When the ship entered Boston Harbor, it rode a full yard above its waterline. The ship captain nonetheless declared that he had unloaded no cargo since leaving the port of Surinam.[24] For the time being, the commissioners could only answer such violations with bitter resignation.

A pattern of harassment began as well. Rumors spread that the houses of the commissioners and their assistants would be "pulled down." On one evening "a number of Lads about 100," beating drums and blowing horns, marched through town on their way to Charles Paxton's house, where they serenaded him well into the evening, and another night a group of "at least 60 lusty Fellows" made such a commotion at William Burch's house as to scare away his wife and children. Unemployed and underemployed young men needed little prompting for such diversions as taunting the customs officials who appeared to be causes of their hardships. Popular leaders shrugged off the events as a "Diversion of a few Boys" and a "Joke," but more was at stake. As Hutchinson acknowledged, "It has been a hard winter & many poor creatures suffered for want of work."[25]

The commissioners were not the only ones who sought more effective action. Governor Bernard reinforced their concerns when he described the demonstrations to Lord Barrington. He took the opportunity to tell of the commissioners' apprehensions of future insurrections and their wish that the governor would apply for troops. Caught by the Council's refusal to support any request and his own fears of retaliation from the Sons of Liberty should he do so unilaterally, Bernard informed the commissioners of his inability to comply and beseeched Barrington not to consider his letter "as such an Application."[26]

When ninety-eight Boston merchants met on March 1 in the midst of mounting opposition to the Townshend Acts, it appeared that the ghost of the Stamp Act crisis had returned to haunt the town. They formed a committee consisting of John Rowe, William Phillips, John Hancock, Arnold Wells, Edward Payne, Thomas Boylston, John Erving Jr., Melatiah Bourne, and Henderson Inches—a veritable who's who of Boston smugglers—to draft a nonimportation agreement. The central stipulation of the document, which was approved on March 4, was that for one year subscribers would not import "any European commodities" except those needed for fishing. It also called for encouraging colonial manufacturers. The logic behind the agreement was that economic pressure on British manufactures and merchants would lead to the termination of the Townshend duties. Despite the ongoing tax on molasses, there was no reference made to boycotting or in any way limiting the West Indies trade. Nor were any obstacles raised to shipping any commodity; the restriction applied only to ordering goods. A subscriber to the nonimportation agreement could ship a proscribed article from Great Britain to any port, even Boston; as long as he was not the importer, he would not have broken his pledge. The biggest loophole was the understanding that nonimportation would go into effect only after other towns in Massachusetts as well as in other colonies, particularly Philadelphia and New York, had endorsed the agreement.[27] Many Boston merchants joined the opposition on the condition that their interests not be sacrificed to the advantage of their competitors.

Within a week, a majority of merchants had subscribed to the nonimportation agreement, though with great hesitation. According to Bernard, initial attempts to enlist members of the mercantile community "met with no great success," but threats of mobs tearing down houses and assaulting persons and of opposition leaders damaging trade and wrecking credit worked where appeals for cooperation failed. Even so, there still were "enough of the most respectable merchants in the Town, Non-Subscribers, to defeat this Scheme."[28] Bernard was often guilty of projecting his wishes as reality, but in this case he was accurate. There was a serious split between merchants.

Thomas Cushing offered a more benign explanation of merchant behavior. The reduction of consumer purchases of British goods was working. If people were not buying imported articles in high enough numbers for sellers to pay off British creditors or to earn sufficient profits, there was no reason to order more. The document itself relied more on economic self-interest than political principle, although it embraced both. The scarcity of hard money had presented difficulties for several years, but it had grown worse as a result of the Townshend duties. There simply weren't adequate amounts of gold and silver in Boston to maintain trade at previous levels or to pay the new taxes, and debts to British creditors had accumulated to such a degree that it would be foolhardy to increase them further through new imports. Almost as an aside, the document acknowledged that further consideration had revealed the danger of losing constitutional rights.[29]

Merchants who were associated with the court faction, who were Anglican, who were born outside of New England, or who temperamentally disliked being restricted in their trading practices, whether by British policy or by the popular movement, were reluctant to subscribe to the nonimportation agreement. Those sympathetic to the opposition had a more difficult decision. If they were well stocked in British merchandise, they found nonimportation a boon. They could maintain business without interruption; and as other sellers' shelves became bare, they could raise prices on their stock. If they were small-time merchants or shopkeepers, however, the nonimportation agreement jeopardized their livelihood. Their best hope was that it would take a while before the agreement went into effect and that soon thereafter Parliament, recognizing its mistake, would rescind the hated taxes. As it was, Philadelphia merchants refused to comply, New York merchants followed their lead, and Boston merchants were unwilling to risk losing their trade to other ports. By summer all knew this nonimportation agreement was stillborn.[30]

But there were other tools in the opposition's bag. For years the British had turned the occasion of the monarch's birthday, and often the anniversary of his coronation, into political rituals. In Boston on each June 4, the date of George III's birth, the troop of guards, the town's militia, and the train of artillery mustered. Cannon were fired from Castle William and the batteries, politicians drank to the king's health, and "the day was spent in other Demonstrations of Loyalty and Joy." The pageantry was an attempt to tie the population closer to the empire. When there was unhappiness with Parliament and the ministry, people made an even greater effort to express their affection for the king and prove their patriotism. Opposition leaders learned from these examples, endowing particular dates with political significance. By 1768, March 18 (the day Parliament repealed the Stamp Act) and August 14 (the day of the uprising against the stamp agent Andrew Oliver) were prominent on the popular party's calendar.[31] These were days for self-congratulation and heightened political awareness as well as for celebrating their emerging identity as a separate people. They were reminders of their rights and a means to bond Bostonians with the opposition.

Reminiscent of the Stamp Act crisis, the morning of March 18, 1768, dawned with drums beating, guns firing in most of the major streets, flags streaming from houses, *and* two effigies hanging from the Liberty Tree. They bore the initials "C. P." for Charles Paxton and "J. W." for John Williams, the inspector general of customs. Some Sons of Liberty not wanting more exuberant activity quickly removed them, but Bernard was furious. Having heard rumors of effigies, the governor had negotiated on the previous day to prevent them and had been assured that they wouldn't appear. The commissioners were alarmed, for they had been told that the effigies were merely a prelude to a mob escorting them to the Liberty Tree and compelling them to renounce their offices. They sent a letter to Bernard asking for his protection. When Bernard met with the Council that morning, he conveyed his concerns and presented the commissioners' letter to them. The Council dismissed their apprehension. In the afternoon, the governor asked the Council to reconsider, but again it denied that any government response was necessary.[32]

While Bernard and the commissioners stewed, the celebration flourished. Town leaders had convinced residents to combine St. Patrick's Day and the commemoration of the Stamp Act repeal into a single festive day. St. Patrick therefore joined George III as the subject of toasts in taverns throughout Boston. There were several other changes from the previous year's toasts. Still basking in the glow of the Stamp Act's demise, Bostonians in 1767 had raised their glasses to the king, the queen and royal family, the Parliament, the ministry, and one British figure or group after another. Not until the twenty-first toast had Massachusetts been mentioned. The Sons of Liberty and the town of Boston had been the last two objects of (by that time) inebriated admiration. In 1768 goodwill toward the British had shrunk under the shadow of the Townshend program. The first toast honored the king, queen, and royal family, and the second favored British political leaders, including Pitt and Rockingham. More pointed were healths drunk to the Farmer, the *Boston Gazette*, "Unanimity, Oeconomy, Patriotism and Perseverance, throughout the Colonies," the Corsican rebel Pascal Paoli, and "Halters to Parasites."[33]

By nightfall most of the celebrants had left the taverns. One group of "Gentlemen," however, lingered at the Exchange Coffee House, overlooking the crowd on King Street below the Town House. As "young fellows & negroes . . . made great Noise & Hallooing" through the darkened streets, a gathering of about eight hundred people "of all

Kinds, Sexes, and Ages" assembled. Each time there was an attempt to ignite a bonfire—for warmth on that winter evening, conviviality, and as a magnet to draw more participants—the "gentlemen," fearing a riot, rushed from the coffee house to prevent its being lighted. Deterred, the crowd, banging drums, trailing streamers, and tailed by a cart holding "four swivel Guns," marched to the Liberty Tree. After firing the guns, with loud shouts and other "hideous" noises they paraded through Boston's streets, past the governor's house (perhaps glancing up at the Indian statue and cupola perched above the three-story brick structure), past some of the commissioners' houses, until about 9 o'clock when they arrived at John Williams's house and taunted him. That was the extent of the day's entertainment. No one was assaulted, no houses invaded, no gardens destroyed.[34] But the people had sent a message.

The commissioners and the governor understood it. In a letter to the secretary of state Bernard acknowledged that no one had been harmed and no property had been damaged. What galled him was his limited power. "I am allowed to proceed in the Ordinary Business of the Government without Interruption," he explained; "in the business of a popular Opposition to the Laws of Great-Britain founded upon the Pretentions of rights and Priviledges, I have not the Shadow of Authority or Power." The popular movement controlled the streets. His hands were tied, for without the Council's consent he couldn't order troops to enforce the law and his commands. He expected a repetition of the 1765 violence, should Parliament not respond positively to the House's petitions for repeal of the Townshend Acts. The shaken commissioners echoed Bernard's alarming analysis. Should the Acts not be rescinded or should troops not be sent, their lives and property were in danger. "In the mean Time," they fearfully lamented, "we must depend on the favour of the Leaders of the Mob for our protection."[35]

Neither side had the rights or power it demanded. The colonists had to pay taxes without their consent and had to live as subordinates to citizens of Great Britain. Government officials had to enforce the law without police powers and remain subordinate to the crowd. Authorities in England could remove the source of colonial complaint or they could muster the military. Their choice soon would follow.

Chapter 6

A Momentous Decision

Early in the afternoon of April 8, while John Hancock's recently arrived ship *Lydia* was docked at Hancock's wharf, two tidesmen (customs officials who boarded ships), Owen Richards and Robert Jackson, clambered on. Aware that the brig carried a cargo of "Tea, Paper, and other Customable Goods," the collector and the controller of the port had ordered the tidesmen to ensure that the freight be properly landed and not smuggled away. Later that afternoon Hancock, accompanied by a large though unarmed retinue, appeared and asked Richards his purpose. Learning that the officials' assignment was to observe, Hancock ordered the ship's captain, James Scott, and the mate not to allow the tidesmen or any other customs officers to go below deck. He warned them that they would be fired for noncompliance.

For the remainder of the day and most of the next all went well, but at about 7 o'clock in the evening of April 9 Richard and, apparently, Jackson went below into the steerage. Within ten minutes the captain grabbed the men by the shoulders, telling them they were risking his job unless they returned to the deck. The tidesmen obeyed, but by 8 o'clock Richards was back down in steerage. As midnight approached, Hancock and "eight or ten people, all unarmed," reboarded his ship and confronted the customs agent. Richards refused to leave the steerage. Hancock demanded to see his orders and his commission. After noting that the commission had no date, Hancock asked the official whether he had a writ of assistance. He did not, and immediately Hancock commanded the mate and boatswain to eject Richards from the ship's hold. While the tidesman was being hauled bodily on deck, the ubiquitous Daniel Malcom shouted, "Damn him hand him up, if it was my Vessel I would knock him down."

With Richards back topside and with the companionway secured, Hancock inquired whether he wanted to search the ship. The customs officer maintained that he didn't. Nonetheless Hancock magnanimously granted that he might search aboveboard but not below.[1]

As might be expected, the commissioners of customs were furious with the treatment of their agent and petitioned the province's attorney general, Jonathan Sewall, to prosecute. Sewall was a friend of John Hancock and had been especially close to John Adams. Born into a well-connected Boston family in 1728, Sewall became an orphan just three years later. Family and friends supervised his upbringing and helped him attend Harvard, where he completed both bachelor's and master's degrees. His first career was as a schoolmaster in Salem, but with the assistance of friends he began studying law. His legal mentors had alliances with Frances Bernard, and Sewall soon became a beneficiary of the governor's patronage. A capable and honorable man, certainly no sycophant, he became a member of the court faction and the recipient of important offices, including the position of attorney general. Viewing the conflicts in the 1760s as no more than rivalries between competing political groups, Sewall attempted to reconcile his principles and his ambitions as best he could. Adams thought he had been duped and "deeply regretted an irreconcileable difference in Judgment in public Opinions."[2]

Although Sewall believed "Mr. Hancock may not have conducted so prudently or courteously as might be wished," he concluded that he had violated no laws. Nothing worse than the employment of rough language and the manhandling of Richards had occurred. Hancock and his crew had only attempted to prevent the tidesmen from venturing below deck and used no weapons. Because the customs officers had no search warrant and no admitted intent to explore the ship, Sewall reasoned that the only possible offense could be an infringement of the officers' right "freely to go and remain on Board until the Vessel is discharged of her Lading." He interpreted that the common meaning of "on Board" was to be on deck and not below, and therefore he found no grounds on which to charge Hancock.[3]

If Hancock had not been a special target of the commissioners before the *Lydia* episode, he certainly was afterward. He was one of the wealthiest men in Boston, if not all of New England, and he was the owner of a number of ships engaged in international trade. As one of

John Hancock, 1765, an oil on canvas portrait by
John Singleton Copley. Deposited by the City of
Boston. (Photograph courtesy of the Museum of
Fine Arts, Boston)

the town's selectmen in May 1768, he had informed the governor and
Council that Faneuil Hall would not be available for the annual election
day celebration should the commissioners or their "Attendants" be present. Since 1766 he had been one of Boston's four representatives to the
Massachusetts legislature. The prosecution and conviction for customs
violations of such a prominent figure would serve as a powerful warning
to Boston's merchant community and constitute sweet revenge.[4]

At the time of Hancock's birth in 1737, few would have predicted
such stature so soon as the spring of 1768. He came from the small town
of Braintree, where his father, a Harvard graduate, was the minister, a
position that made him a substantial citizen of the community but did
not generate great wealth or renown beyond its borders. Hancock was
seven when his father died, and his mother with her three children
was forced to take refuge in Lexington with her husband's father.
John was the fortunate one of the children, for his wealthy and childless
uncle and aunt, Thomas and Lydia Hancock, brought him to Boston

and prepared him for a life of affluence and power. After graduating from Harvard in 1754, he joined his uncle's thriving business. Merchants depended on reliable associates in the ports where they traded, and in 1760 Hancock left for England to establish personal relationships with the firm's partners and to gain a broader understanding of the world. After nearly a year he returned to Boston and with his uncle ailing took increasingly greater responsibility for the business. Three years later Thomas Hancock died, and John made his fortune the old-fashioned way: he inherited it.

By the age of twenty-seven, Hancock was a man of distinction. Thin, with wig-covered, dark brown hair, and fastidious in his dress, like Hutchinson he was a bit of a dandy. Well-educated but no intellectual, accustomed to luxury, a member of Boston's elite by virtue of his wealth, he was ready to lead. Important town offices soon were his, and he increased his popularity by offering employment through the building of his many ships, the construction of wharfs and warehouses, and the conduct of his international trade. The stagnant economy and British regulations and taxation slowed Hancock's ascendancy, and his business suffered. At the time he wasn't a rebel; he was a political moderate and an advocate of a more open economic policy. He moved to the popular movement by degrees.[5]

The next opportunity for the commissioners to apprehend Hancock came on May 9, when his ship *Liberty* docked at his wharf. The sloop had sailed from Madeira and reputedly was laden with wine, a commodity for which duties must be paid. Two customs agents promptly went onboard the vessel to determine the extent of the cargo while it was unloaded. The following day the ship's master, Nathaniel Barnard, listed the goods as only twenty-five casks of wine. There were broad suspicions of underreporting, fostered by Hancock's alleged statement that he would smuggle the cargo on shore, but the tidesman confirmed the master's account and the commissioners were temporarily stymied.[6]

A month later customs officials seized the *Liberty*, in part because of the presence in Boston Harbor of the British frigate *Romney*. As early as February 12, 1768, the commissioners had beseeched Commodore Samuel Hood for naval support, but Hood did not respond until May 2, when he ordered Captain John Corner to sail the fifty-gun man-of-war to Boston. The assignment was to assist the commissioners in enforcing trade laws. The *Romney*'s arrival on May 17 marked the initial installation of a British military police force.[7]

Hood warned Corner to guard "against the Mischievous humour of the populace, as well as to prevent Desertion." No boat was to leave the ship without two petty officers, one to oversee the mission and the other to supervise the sailors. Whenever an officer went ashore, the boat that took him was to return immediately to the *Romney*, thus reducing the possibility of wayward mariners. The *Romney*'s crew may have been understaffed, or despite the precautions there may have been desertions. Whatever the cause, the ship began stopping incoming vessels and impressing seamen. Not only was such action a threat to the freedom of sailors, it was a significant blow to Boston's economy. Rather than risk the menacing British frigate impressing their crews, many merchant ships refused to enter Boston Harbor. Even local residents sailing their boats in the harbor "upon their lawful Business or Recreation" were subjected to gunfire and impressment.[8]

As the *Romney* made its presence known and the frustration and anger of Bostonians rose, one of the tidesmen, Thomas Kirk, had a change of heart and a miraculously restored memory. On June 10, a month after the "underreporting" event, he claimed that one of Hancock's captains, John Marshall, had offered him a bribe to allow several casks of wine to be taken off the *Liberty* before its list of cargo was given to the customs office. When he "peremptorily refused," Marshall, with five or six others, forced him into a cabin below deck and "nailed the Cover down." Kirk broke a door into steerage and was attempting to regain the deck when he was overwhelmed and confined for three hours. During that time, he said, he heard the sounds of many hands hoisting goods out of the ship. After it became quiet, Marshall came below deck and released Kirk with a threat on his life and property should he divulge what had transpired that evening. Kirk reputedly gained his courage after Marshall died (a month before, on May 10) and then testified under oath.[9] Why he waited until June 10 is unclear. Perhaps the might of the *Romney* encouraged him, or possibly there were other inducements.

As it stood, the case against Hancock for landing goods without listing them or paying customs duties rested on the testimony of a single questionable witness. Smuggling most likely had happened, but the evidence was entirely the interpretation of noises in the night and circumstances as reported by a tidesman in testimony that was in contradiction to his earlier statement and offered a month after the event. The only other possible witness was the customs agent who had accompanied Kirk, but he, drunken, had quit the scene before the alleged smuggling had occurred. Nonetheless Joseph Harrison, the collector of the port, took the flimsy case to the commissioners, who, on the advice of their solicitor, ordered that the *Liberty* be seized.[10] This was retaliation for their earlier rebuke, an example to would-be smugglers, and a blow to the rabble who had had the audacity to taunt them. It was an attempt to reassert the authority of the British government. It was not justice.

The responsibility for seizing the *Liberty* fell on Harrison's shoulders. Apprehensive of what might befall him and barely well enough to leave home, he was satisfied merely to place the king's mark on the ship's main mast and to wait for legal proceedings. Benjamin Hallowell, the comptroller, volunteered to accompany Harrison and "share the danger" with him, and convinced the collector that more vigorous action was necessary.

In the early evening of the very day Kirk had made his deposition, the two customs officials, accompanied by Harrison's eighteen-year-old son, warily walked down Hancock's wharf to where the *Liberty* was docked. Waiting until they saw two boats filled with armed sailors and marines depart from the *Romney*, moored a scant quarter-mile away, they then boarded the ship and marked the mast. Others along the wharf and waterfront, including Daniel Malcom, also spotted the approaching boats. Some were loyal employees of Hancock, and they were joined by men fearful of impressment. Quickly a resentful crowd formed. Malcom and five or six cohorts marched onboard prepared to protect the vessel. The naval force drove them off and attempted to release the ship's lines. The crowd along the wharf pulled on the ropes, trying to keep the sloop secured. Eventually the commodore's men prevailed, and they maneuvered the *Liberty* alongside the *Romney*.[11]

While the tug-of-war diverted attention, Harrison, his son, and Hallowell rushed up the wharf, seeking what they hoped would be the safety of their homes. Just as they reached the street, the crowd shifted its anger to the instigators of the affair. Harrison, immediately pummeled by clumps of dirt, stones, and projectiles of various types, was in the lead. His son, trying to shield him, followed close behind, but after about two hundred yards was knocked down and dragged off. Harrison received a blow in the chest, and as he anticipated the worst a bystander helped him escape. Other sympathetic souls rescued his son. Hallowell, in the meantime, had attempted to protect his colleague's son and was in turn attacked. After suffering "two bad Contusions on his Cheek and the Back of his Head," Hallowell was escorted away. Although Harrison believed they might have been killed, it seems unlikely that a multitude numbering between five hundred and a thousand could have been thwarted had murder been their intent.[12]

As the crowd continued to grow (Thomas Hutchinson estimated its size ultimately to be "2 or 3000 chiefly sturdy boys and negroes"), it resumed its search for the customs agents. Finding neither Harrison nor Hallowell at home, it settled for breaking the windows of their residences and those of the house of John Williams, an inspector general of customs. Its last target for the evening was Harrison's "fine sailing pleasure Boat," a craft known for its speed. Few events could have mortified the collector more than even the slightest damage to his prized possession, and probably that is why the crowd pulled the boat from the water and dragged it roughly a mile through the narrow streets to Liberty Tree, "where she was formally condemned, and from thence dragged up into the Common and there burned to Ashes." And finally people dispersed for the day.[13]

Rumors began circulating the next day that a crowd would reassemble that evening and attack the commissioners. Governor Bernard, alarmed by the riot and by the possibility of renewed violence, returned from his country house in Roxbury and tried to convince the Council that they jointly should request troops. The Council was unpersuaded and believed there would be no repetition of the previous evening. "Nor indeed did any such immediate Danger appear to me whilst I staid in Boston which was till Sunset," Bernard reluctantly admitted.[14]

The commissioners viewed their situation quite differently. For the past three and a half months, they regularly had received veiled threats and heard secondhand reports that a mob would march them to the Liberty Tree and attempt to force them to resign from their offices. The rumors and antics had been disturbing, though more annoyances than signs of real danger. Now, after the attacks on the customs officials and their property, the possibility that verbal abuse would expand to assaults on themselves and their families became increasingly likely. Having taken the precaution of seeking shelter in friends' homes on Friday, June 10, they took refuge aboard the *Romney* the next night. Days later, still apprehensive for their safety, they and their families settled into Castle

William. The commissioners' departure from Boston may also have been prompted by their desire for dramatic proof that the ministry must authorize the military to police the town.[15] Whatever their motives, they now were a diminished influence.

Although the commissioners experienced discomfort and the customs officers endured injuries and damaged property, the biggest loser by far was John Hancock, whose ship and cargo had been seized. Hoping to regain control of the *Liberty*, Hancock, through intermediaries, began negotiating with Harrison and Hallowell on Saturday afternoon. Should the sloop be returned to his wharf, he agreed to post bond and to relinquish the vessel should the admiralty court decide against him. The sweetener to the deal was the assurance that unruly mobs that otherwise might "pillage" customs officials and their friends would remain calm. Somehow the proposed settlement broke down Sunday evening, and the *Liberty* remained conspicuously anchored next to the *Romney*. Harrison and Hallowell attributed Hancock's reversal to "Firebrands" such as James Otis who wanted to keep the ferment alive. To their minds, the young merchant, "a generous benevolent Gentleman," was manipulated by the "Ringleaders of the Faction."[16] As usual, they didn't understand how widespread the opposition was becoming. Hancock certainly enjoyed the acclaim of the population, a welcome antidote to financial difficulties, but he, like many other Bostonians, was gradually being radicalized by the shortsightedness of British policy and the myopia of British officials.

With negotiations broken, Harrison and Hallowell feared further injuries and fled Boston for Castle William early Monday morning, "before the People were stirring." A few days later Hallowell sailed for London, where he presented messages from the commissioners and Harrison and gave the customs service's version of what had transpired.[17]

They were wise to leave, for on Monday "the People in Town were in great Agitation." To prevent a "tumult" that night, notices were posted throughout the town, requesting the Sons of Liberty to attend a meeting the following morning at Liberty Hall, the designation of the area immediately under and surrounding the Liberty Tree. As many as four thousand people assembled at the meeting time of 10 o'clock. Streamers flowed from Liberty Tree and rain fell from the sky. Wet and uncomfortable, the crowd traipsed to Faneuil Hall, whose capacity of one thousand people made it too small to hold everyone. With so many wanting to participate and hoping to stem violence, the selectmen called for an official town meeting that afternoon. Again the numbers were so large that the selectmen transferred the meeting to the Old South Church, a structure of sufficient size to contain the entire crowd.

Finally able to conduct business, the town meeting approved a petition to be delivered to the governor by twenty-one "gentlemen." The petition identified two prime grievances: taxes to which they had not given consent, and impressment. With the commissioners, the chief enforcers of trade taxes, removed from the town, they focused on their other grievance and requested Bernard to order the *Romney* out of the harbor. The twenty-one (including James Otis, John Hancock, John Rowe, Samuel Adams, and Daniel Malcom) traveled the four miles in their carriages to the governor's country house in Roxbury, where, as chairman, Otis presented the petition. Bernard received them "very cordially" and promised a response the next day.[18]

After his usual waffling on the legality of impressment and on his power to command a naval officer, Bernard assured the people of Boston that he would use his "utmost endeavors" to work out an arrangement with Captain Corner, and in this he was generally successful. Corner did not agree to end all impressment, but he consented not to impress any men "belonging to or married in the Province, nor any employed in the Trade along Shore, or to the Neighbouring Colonies."[19]

These conflicts produced generally favorable results. The commissioners had not renounced their offices as Andrew Oliver had in 1765, but they were no longer in town to supervise the despised laws. The captain of the *Romney* had not altogether forsworn impressing sailors, but he had promised to exempt those who mattered most to Bostonians. There still were fears of an expanded naval presence and an occupying army, but briefly—very briefly as it turned out—townspeople had some basis for optimism.

Two days before the *Liberty* incident, Wills Hill, Earl of Hillsborough, sent a letter to General Thomas Gage ordering a regiment "or such Force as you shall think necessary" to Boston. Hillsborough had become secretary of state for the colonies in January 1768. His was a new office, part of the reforms to control Britain's North American empire more efficiently. The obvious expectation was for him to have a firm hand in overseeing American affairs; unfortunately he soon had the opportunity to prove he was the right man for the job.[20]

In the spring, just as the ministry had sent troops to quell unrest in Ireland and Great Britain, Hillsborough had received a copy of the circular letter the Massachusetts legislature had sent to other colonies in February, as well as letters from the commissioners and Bernard detailing Boston crowd actions in March and their inability to enforce the law as fully as they would like. These missives projected images of a provisional government cowed by a popular faction, lawlessness, and imminent insurrection. Hillsborough had a number of options. He could accept the status quo: significant revenue coming from the tax on sugar and molasses (a tax unopposed by Bostonians, as we'll recall), coupled with public challenges in Boston to customs officials fulfilling their responsibilities. That choice, of course, would signify tacit acknowledgment of limited British authority. Alternatively, he could try to locate the source of Bostonians' discontent and strive to construct a solution that would produce revenue, resolve constitutional issues, and maintain British sovereignty. That choice would take time, patience, political skill, and a more accommodating personality than Hillsborough's. By this stage, with increasing parliamentary and colonial intransigence, it also might be impossible to achieve.

A third alternative was to send troops as a police force to support officials and to demonstrate Britain's power. That option might require a permanent occupying army and expenses greater than revenues, and likely would further alienate the colonists. Nevertheless Hillsborough chose the military alternative. Six weeks later, on July 30, after learning of the *Liberty* incident and of the commissioners fleeing the town, he ordered two additional regiments, the 64th and 65th, which had been stationed in Ireland, to Boston.[21]

Transatlantic communication of a message and its subsequent reply normally required at least three months, contributing to misunderstandings and distortion. Hillsborough's decision to send troops came before the *Liberty* episode, which preceded Bernard's learning of Hillsborough's reaction to the circular letter. On June 21 the governor conveyed to the legislature Hillsborough's demand that the assembly rescind its February circular letter and "declare their Disapprobation of, and Dissent to that rash and hasty Proceeding." The arrogance, clumsiness, and insensitivity of the British reaction grated on colonial ears. Not only was Hillsborough's order ill conceived, it was impossible to obey: the letter had been sent to the other colonial legislatures months before, and many of them already had replied.[22] The damage was done. Hillsborough clearly was only thumping his chest with the expectation that the Massachusetts legislature would cower.

Instead it emboldened the often divided and normally cautious House of Representatives. Its initial response was to gather as much information as possible, calling for a full copy of Hillsborough's letter as well as complete documentation of Bernard's letters to the secretary that apparently had triggered the outburst. Bernard was willing to comply partially. The remainder of Hillsborough's letter revealed that should the legislature not rescind its circular letter and condemn its intent the governor was required to dissolve the assembly. The dispatch also contained an implied threat of military intervention when it pledged, "Proper Care will be taken for the Support of the Dignity of Government." For his part, Bernard declined to divulge his communications to the ministry. "I shall never make public my Letters to his Majesty's Ministers, but upon my own Motion, and for my own Reasons," he announced loftily.[23]

Unwilling to acquiesce to Hillsborough's demand but hoping to avoid direct confrontation, the House stalled. When Bernard informed the legislature after a week that no answer would be interpreted as a negative, the legislature requested a recess to discuss the issue with constituents. The governor refused, insisting on an immediate reply to Hillsborough's order.[24]

The House countered with a lengthy analysis of what had led to the crisis. It attributed the situation to Bernard's having misrepresented its actions to the ministry. A petition for a redress of grievances was perfectly within the rights of British citizens, and the purpose of the circular letter was to inform the other North American colonies of the Massachusetts petition and to suggest that other assemblies send similar appeals. Acknowledging that a majority of the House had rejected the initial proposal to send a circular letter, it explained that the measure was reconsidered shortly thereafter and, contrary to Hillsborough's understanding, passed with a three-to-one majority, representing a broad cross-section, not a small, disloyal faction. And now, should the legislators refuse to rescind and repudiate their letter, the House would be dissolved. This was yet another attack on their rights. "If the Votes of the House are to be controuled by the Direction of a Minister," they reasoned, "we have left us but a vain Semblance of Liberty." They reminded Bernard that the source of their discontent was "the new

General Sir Thomas Gage, a portrait by an un-
known artist after an original by John Singleton
Copley. (Massachusetts State House Art Collection.
Courtesy of the Commonwealth of Massachusetts,
Art Commission)

Revenue Acts and Measures" and then informed him that in a vote of
ninety-two (including all four of Boston's representatives) to seventeen
they had rejected Hillsborough's demand. Acting quickly before being
dissolved, the House sent a letter to the secretary of state for the colonies
reviewing their actions and charging Bernard with misrepresentation.
Many legislators would have liked to send a letter to the king requesting
Bernard's dismissal but were unable to achieve majority support. At that
point, Bernard closed the House indefinitely.[25]

Unaware until late August of Hillsborough's decision to send troops,
Thomas Gage and Bernard each spent the greater part of the summer trying to find a way to station a military force in Boston without
having to take responsibility for its presence. Like Bernard, Hutchinson,
and Oliver, Gage believed that the source of Bostonian discontent was a
"Faction" that remained cautious until it was assured of broad support
from other colonies. Part of the problem was that royal officials in

Massachusetts were weak. Were they "less timid," Gage concluded, "the Faction would be less bold." In response to the commissioners' pleas from their Castle William refuge, he wrote that his inclination was to march troops into Boston immediately, but without the governor's specific application he lacked the necessary authority.[26]

Frustrated, Gage decided to provoke action, targeting those who could authorize the sending of regiments to Boston. As in September 1765, he dispatched two letters to Bernard. One reminded the governor of the general's sympathy and cooperation. The other was an order to the commanding officer at Halifax, empowering him to send troops for Boston. When he saw fit, Bernard could be saved the necessity of writing him and could simply transmit the requisition directly. Lacking confidence in Bernard's resolve, the general simultaneously urged the ministry to direct a military force to Boston. He believed the "Moderation and Forbearance hitherto shewn by Great Britain, has been Construed into Timidity, and served only to raise Sedition and Mutiny, to a higher Pitch." Boston and the entire province of Massachusetts were on the verge of rebellion. "Quash this Spirit at a Blow, without too much regard to the Expence," Gage advised, "and it will prove oeconomy in the End." The subjugation of Boston would stand as a warning to the other colonies and an encouragement to the government's friends.[27] Unbeknown to Gage, the ministry already had reached that conclusion.

Concerned about his own safety and seeming to forget Gage's earlier tactic for expediting a military presence, Bernard willfully misinterpreted the general's letters. He forwarded the order for troops to Halifax without any accompanying request of his own. Coyly suggesting in a letter to Hillsborough that he suspected at least one regiment was on its way, Bernard praised Gage for sparing him knowledge and therefore responsibility for the dispatch's contents. Even so, the more Bernard pondered Boston's likely reaction to the arrival of British troops, the more fearful he became that he would be blamed for them regardless of who had authored the application. He began to plan his escape to Castle William should it become necessary. His desperation grew when Gage disabused him of the fantasy that soldiers would come without the governor's explicit request.[28]

Bernard found himself in an impossible dilemma. He would "be made answerable to the Fury of the People for introducing Troops here" without the consent of the Council. Yet if he were unable to sustain the government and enforce the law, he would "be made answerable to the King for all the ill Consequences which shall follow the Want of Troops here." With little hope for success, Bernard decided to approach the Council one last time. Again he was disappointed, even chagrined. Not only did Council members unanimously disapprove of bringing a military force to Boston, they chastised the governor for the suggestion. After three years of sparring with the opposition, Bernard recognized his defeat. The House was long lost; now the Council had abandoned him. The stress of the constant battles had worn him down, and he began to consider leaving Massachusetts and its combative capital.[29]

At one level during the summer of 1768, it appeared that Boston had triumphed over its troubles. The commissioners had retreated to Castle William, impressment had halted, the House had refused to capitulate to Hillsborough's demands to rescind the circular letter, and the Bernard regime was greatly, perhaps fatally, weakened. There were reasons to rejoice.

But there still remained potential causes for apprehension. The Townshend Acts still were in place; customs officials, though diminished without the commissioners, continued to inspect cargoes and seize ships; Bernard had dissolved the legislature; two sixteen-gun sloops and two armed cutters, in addition to the *Romney,* were sitting in Boston Harbor by early July; and there was a persistent rumor of impending troops. Some observers perceived in these seemingly disparate problems a coherent plot. The taxes from the Townshend Acts and other duties were to pay the salaries of royal officials in the colonies. If those funds were sufficient for that purpose, the legislature—the people's representatives—was no longer necessary and could be dissolved. The ruling government then would consist of the governor and his cronies and enforcers whose responsibility was to collect the requisite revenue and to maintain public order. Comparing the present to the Stamp Act crisis, one writer concluded, "The design is more artfully laid, and more carefully disguised, than it was before; but is as certainly fatal to American liberty as it was then."[30]

For the first half of the summer Bostonians struggled to find an effective strategy of opposition. On July 2 a group of fifty to sixty men trooped to Commissioner John Robinson's house in Roxbury. They'd heard he had left Castle William and intended to surprise him. Much to their regret he was not there. They expressed their disappointment by pillaging his fruit trees and trampling his garden. On July 11 the selectmen hoped to strengthen the resolve of citizens—and to warn British officials—by ordering the "Magazine of Arms belonging to the Town to be brought out to be cleaned, when they were exposed for some Hours at the Town-House." Such a small-scale war game proved more pathetic than daunting. A few days later, town residents resorted to intimidation. Church bells rang as if for a fire, and a crowd assembled outside the house of John Williams, one of the customs inspectors. Voices from the crowd called for him to appear at the Liberty Tree the following day and there resign his commission. He refused to do either but agreed to answer questions at the Town House. Around noon, accompanied by "several gentlemen," Williams ventured out on the balcony of the council room and shouted to the fifteen hundred people assembled below that he was prepared to respond to any charges against him. None came. After fifteen minutes he "repeated his Proposal." Only a stray taunt floated up; otherwise there was silence. And then everyone departed, a few muttering displeasure at the fiasco. The embarrassed Sons of Liberty issued an explanation in the next *Boston Gazette*, claiming that it was an unauthorized event and reprimanding those who had taken their name without permission.[31]

As if that weren't enough, an errant sea captain, hoping to take advantage of the unsettled political climate, reclaimed his seized contraband cargo of molasses. About thirty men boarded his schooner one night and forced the two customs officers into a cabin, then hauled away thirty hogsheads of molasses. This put the lie to the townspeople's assertion that the *Liberty* didn't have to be removed from Hancock's wharf, for it was secure where it was docked. Trying to erase the contradiction, Boston selectmen pressured the ship's master to return the illegal goods, and the next day the molasses was back on the ship. "So we are not without a government," Bernard wryly commented, "only it is in the Hands of the People of the town, and not of those deputed by the King or under his Authority." These were all minor occurrences, none important enough to alter Gage's characterization of its being a summer without "tumults or riots."[32]

With the town adrift, a group of merchants decided to give nonimportation another chance. Apparently not prompted by the same public nudges of the previous March, a number of them negotiated an agreement on which they managed to get sixty signatures on August 1. By August 15 a substantial part of the mercantile community (according to the *Boston Gazette,* "with greater unanimity than in the Time of the Stamp Act") agreed not to send any further orders to Great Britain "for Goods to be ship'd this Fall" and from January 1, 1769, to January 1, 1770, not to order for themselves or other prospective purchasers any merchandise from Great Britain. They exempted coal, salt, and items needed for fishing, but specifically identified the Townshend Acts' taxable goods—tea, glass, paper, and painters' colors—as barred until "the act imposing duties on those articles shall be repealed." While they restricted trade with the British Isles, they allowed trade elsewhere, especially with the West Indies. That was important, for New England entrepreneurs made more money by shipping freight, regardless of its owner, than by selling any particular commodity. Bernard doubted that this nonimportation agreement would be any more successful than the one in March. He believed "the Non-subscribers, among which are some of the principal Importers of the Town, will effectually defeat this Scheme, if they are sufficiently secured from Mobs." For the moment this significant division among Boston's merchants (a split that largely determined future revolutionaries and future loyalists among their ranks) was benign.[33]

The annual celebration of August 14 helped disguise the schism. With grievances over British policy, poor economic conditions, and the possibility of military occupation mingling in their minds, the organizers and leading participants tried to achieve a balance between colonial rights and loyalty to Great Britain. As dawn broke and fourteen cannon discharged, spectators witnessed the British flag attached to Liberty Tree, a clear message of intent and aspirations. By late morning "principal Gentlemen and respectable Inhabitants of the Town" gathered under the stately elm, while people of lesser rank filled adjoining streets. The "fair Daughters of Liberty" smiled down from windows of nearby houses as they viewed the commemoration. Instrumental and vocal music commenced at noon, "concluding with the universally admired *American* Song of Liberty." The "Song of Liberty" consisted of amateurish but rousing lyrics grafted onto the traditional tune of "Hearts of Oak." It resembled a drinking song with its recurring chorus of "In Freedom we're born, & in Freedom we'll live, / Our Purses are ready, / Steady, Friends, Steady, / Not as Slaves, but as Freemen our Money we'll give." Fourteen toasts appropriately followed, beginning with "Our rightful Sovereign George the Third" and concluding with "The Glorious Ninety-Two, who defended the Rights of America, uninfluenced by the Mandates of a

Minister, and undaunted by the Threats of a Governor." And then, with a flourish of French horns and the thunder of cannon fire bringing the total volleys to ninety-two, about a hundred gentlemen retired to their carriages and ventured to the Greyhound Tavern in Roxbury, "where a *frugal* and *elegant* Entertainment was provided." They offered more toasts praising the monarch, sympathetic British politicians, and allies such as "the Farmer" and declaring their rights, then climbed into their carriages and paraded leisurely back to Boston.

Although Bostonians gradually were moving toward a more open and democratic society, the remnants of hierarchy were not shaken loose easily. Deference and rank still naturally coexisted with toasts to the "common Rights of Mankind."[34]

This was the last publicly supported celebration in Boston before the arrival of British soldiers. At the end of August, nearly three months after Hillsborough's authorization, Gage finally received orders to place a military force in the city. He quickly dispatched one of his aides, Captain William Shirreff, to determine what size force Bernard wanted and where they would be quartered. At their secret meeting, Bernard decided that two regiments were necessary. Although Gage preferred housing the troops in Castle William, the governor, wanting to avoid angering the town further by placing the military directly in the fort as well as desiring protection within Boston proper, chose to have one regiment quartered in town and the other in the barracks on the island beside Castle William. Gage took precautions to protect Bernard from the appearance of responsibility for ordering the occupying force and provided means to expedite troop movement. Shirreff brought orders from the general that allowed the governor to fill in the specifics and to forward them directly to Halifax under Gage's signature. When the aide returned to headquarters and informed the general of Bernard's decisions, Gage sent orders back to the governor as if he had originated them. Bernard was able to claim, as he soon did, that his hands were tied by others' judgments. Even with all these protections, Gage believed Bernard was still afraid. "Some People" who had wanted military support, the general delicately but pointedly wrote to Lord Barrington on September 10, "seem to be frightened, now they are comeing."[35]

Bernard indeed was worried that upon the troops' arrival there might be an insurrection. An article in the September 5 *Boston Gazette* particularly made him nervous. The writer "Clericus Americanus" for the most part avoided direct assertions but made his point through a series of rhetorical queries. Did all the recent parliamentary acts and ministerial actions violate their charter, which was the basis of their union with Great Britain? "If Governor Bernard can't issue writs for another assembly till further orders" and if the charter "is vacated and we reduced to a state of nature," shouldn't the towns select representatives for their own congress to govern in the vacuum while still remaining loyal under the auspices of the king? More forthrightly, Clericus recommended that if an army were sent, its soldiers should be viewed as fellow citizens. But if the troops were meant to subdue them, "we will put our lives in our hands" and pray.[36]

Some consoled Bernard that these were merely the "casual Raisings of an occasional Enthusiast," but he took them very seriously. The governor convinced himself that dribbling out word of the regiments' impending presence would allow the "Heads of the Faction" time to check their passions. On September 8 Bernard disingenuously told the moderate merchant John Rowe that he had "private advice that Troops were ordered hither" but no "public" confirmation yet. In the guise of friend of the people, he lamented that "he had Stav'd off the Introducing Troops as long as he could but could do it no longer." By nightfall all of Boston had the news. In the meantime Bernard hoped to minimize opposition by keeping the legislature closed indefinitely. He sought direct orders from Hillsborough to cancel the normal winter session so as to divert blame from himself and believed they had ample time to devise a strategy to bypass the May session as well.[37]

The news that British troops soon were coming to occupy their town alarmed Bostonians. On Friday, September 9, they called for a town meeting to convene on the following Monday to discuss what should be done. In the intervening Saturday night, individuals placed a turpentine barrel on the pole of the newly reconstructed beacon on the summit of Beacon Hill. Dating back to 1634–35, the beacon had fallen into disrepair and only recently been restored. The barrel hung roughly sixty-five feet from the ground, altogether more than two hundred feet above sea level. When lighted, it could be seen far inland. The lit beacon was a sign to the countryside of threatened invasion. Not wanting to risk an even more troubled or dangerous population, Bernard hurriedly instigated a meeting with the Council on Sunday afternoon, a highly unusual time for civic business. The Council, including the governor, wanted the barrel removed and requested the town's selectmen to take it down. But to no avail. Four days later Sheriff Stephen Greenleaf and some accomplices stealthily hoisted the provocative barrel off the pole without resistance or retaliation.[38]

On Monday the people of Boston assembled in Faneuil Hall. As various men made speeches (some incendiary, if Bernard's informants were accurate), they frequently referred to the town arms conspicuously lodged in the middle of the Hall since their cleaning months earlier. Less dramatically, the meeting voted for a committee to ascertain from the governor how sure was his information about a military force and to ask him to reactivate the legislature. The day's business concluded with the appointment of a committee to determine "the Measures they apprehend most salutary to be taken in the present Emergency."[39]

Bernard's response was terse. He based his understanding of impending troops on private sources. When he had official confirmation, he would inform the Council. As to the House of Representatives, he had no power to reinstate it until he received "his Majesty's commands."[40]

After the committee relayed its dismal report on Tuesday, the town meeting resolved to take more significant and innovative action. Faced with the constitutional grievances of taxation without representation and of a standing army about to be in their midst without their consent and having no means to seek redress without an assembly, the people of Boston voted for a convention of the province's towns to convene in their city on September 22.[41] Whether this was merely a vehicle for airing discontent, or supposed to serve as a temporary legislature, or intended as a reversion to Massachusetts Bay's original charter with no royally appointed officials was left unclear. The immediate question was whether other towns would send representatives.

Seeking a dramatic gesture, the town meeting then attempted to create the impression of potential armed resistance. Under the pretence of an approaching war with France, in full view of the town's weapons, and referring to the Massachusetts law that "every listed Soldier and other Housholder . . . shall be always provided with a well fix'd Firelock-Musket, Accoutrements and Ammunition," Bostonians in "a very great Majority" obliquely and yet pointedly voted "That those of the said Inhabitants, who may at present be unprovided, be and hereby are Requested duely to observe the said Law at this Time." In short, the town empowered those who lacked weapons at that critical moment to acquire them. Finally, those present at the meeting "expressed their high Satisfaction" that the merchants of New York City had supported the nonimportation agreement and voted to have a day of "Fasting and Prayer" on September 20, having now learned that four regiments would occupy Boston.[42]

The invitation for a convention that Boston's selectmen sent to other Massachusetts towns consisted of a familiar review of grievances and a solicitation for solidarity. Were British trade and tax policies, the ministry's demand that the House's circular letter be rescinded, the consequent dissolving of the legislature, the ineffectiveness of previous petitions for redress, and the imminent presence of a standing army not enough, the selectmen threw in the possibility of a war with France as an additional reason why towns should send representatives to the important gathering.[43]

Representatives from sixty-six towns and several districts were present on the first morning of the Massachusetts Convention on September 22. Within a week the number grew to ninety-six towns and eight districts. There were similarities to the House of Representatives. The delegation elected Speaker of the House Thomas Cushing as its chairman and Samuel Adams, House clerk, as its clerk. All four of Boston's members— Cushing, Adams, James Otis, and John Hancock—were also its legislative representatives. But there were important differences as well. Attendance alone was a filter for sympathy, if not kinship, with the opposition movement. Bernard could find few allies in the assemblage, and none of the notorious seventeen representatives who had voted to rescind and repudiate the circular letter made the trip to Boston. The delegates were a potentially defiant body, certainly a group prepared to challenge the governor.[44] As they met, ships from Halifax and Ireland were carrying two thousand British soldiers in their direction.

The Convention's first order of business was mild enough. It called on Bernard to reopen the House of Representatives. Implicit in the respectful request was the recognition of the legitimacy of the current provincial charter with its royally appointed governor and its elected legislature. There was no radical declaration of the Convention's authority as Massachusetts's sole governing body. Perhaps buoyed by the civility of its initial act, Bernard sent a note explaining his refusal to accept the Convention's message, for to do so would be an acknowledgment of its legal standing. The governor had not signed the communication, and the assembled delegates asked for an endorsed document. Continuing the game of cat and mouse, the reinvigorated Bernard addressed a message to the Convention's members as if they were private citizens. He admonished them that the Convention "to all Intents and Purposes" was a reconstituted legislature, a violation of the king's order. He excused their ignorance of the law and demanded they break up before doing any business. "But if you should pay no Regard to this Admonition, I must as Governor assert the Prerogative of the Crown in a more public Manner," he cautioned. "For assure yourselves (I speak from Instruction) the King is determined to maintain his entire Sovreignty over this Province; and whoever shall persist in usurping any of the Rights of it, will repent of his Rashness."[45] More shrewd than usual, Bernard deftly changed the subject from reauthorizing the legislature to the legality of the Convention and fired a warning shot to scare off the more timid delegates. He was partially successful.

By the end of the third day, the meetings had barely progressed beyond justifying their own existence and legality. In a lengthy reply to the governor, the body proclaimed its loyalty to "the Person and Government of our rightful Sovereign King" and its dual purpose of petitioning the Crown for a redress of grievances and of correcting misrepresentations of the colony's behavior. The people of Massachusetts were "disturbed" that previous petitions had been kept from the king and "greatly agitated" by the prospect of a standing army. The Convention intended to deliberate and advise about the best means to "preserve the Peace and good Order among his Majesty's Subjects." If Bernard believed the proceedings were "criminal," he should specify what was illegal. Maintaining his stance of not recognizing an illegal gathering, Bernard again refused to "receive the Message."[46]

The instigators of the assemblage must have been frustrated by these diversions but also heartened that each day brought more representatives. There was no evidence of delegates fleeing for fear of contamination by association.

The report that the Convention issued on September 27 was more moderate than the petitions and letters that had emanated from the House of Representatives. It reviewed grievances, including the approaching standing army and Bernard's refusal to recall the legislature. It reminded the population of repeated efforts for redress through the constitutional means of petitions and of the sad fact that those documents had been kept from the king and ignored by Parliament. Its most radical section was a sympathetic interpretation of street demonstrations. The "Tumults and Disorders that may have happened, have not arisen from the least disaffection to the Government as by Law established, or the Want of Loyalty to our King on the British Throne," it explained, "but merely from a pressing Anxiety of Mind on the Account of heavy and increasing Grievances." At this point of the report, it would have been logical to assert that extralegal activities were legitimate, given that the British government had rejected their appeals and dissolved their legislature. Instead the delegates pledged efforts to maintain public tranquility at this critical time and expressed hope for peaceful resolution.[47] That was it, the complete "result" of the Convention.

Those who expected a show of fierce opposition to Parliament, to the Bernard administration, and to a garrisoned Boston would have been disappointed, but such a stance would have verged on rebellion and few, if any, were so foolish as to imagine success. Though disheartened and frustrated, almost all citizens were genuinely loyal to Great Britain. Even if they fantasized about separation from the empire, they had to recognize that Boston couldn't do it alone. The Convention proved to be an early, small step toward independence.

On the very day of the issuance of the report, the 14th and 29th Regiments arrived on ships in Boston Harbor. Before the troops landed three days later, all but the Boston representatives of the now defunct Convention had rushed from town.

Chapter 7

Camping on the Common

Skyrockets exploded over Boston Harbor on the evening of September 29. Witnesses on passing boats "observed great rejoicings" and heard mocking strains of "Yankee Doodle" emanating from the British fleet anchored off Castle William. Flashes of light from the fireworks, which the British set off themselves, revealed the fourteen vessels with their cargo of twelve hundred soldiers and officers poised to invade the town.[1] The dreaded intrusion had become reality. Boston was to be occupied.

Based on letters and reports he had received, General Gage thought the town already in open revolt and expected violent resistance. Bostonians, not so foolhardy, had a different strategy for opposing the military presence and British policy and, for the time being, avoided direct confrontation. By four in the afternoon on October 1, the troops had landed with martial hoopla but met with no outward hostility from the townspeople, even when the 14th and 29th Regiments and part of the 59th Regiment were parading on Boston Common before marching to their as yet undesignated quarters.[2]

Redcoats were not an unfamiliar sight to many town residents. Just sixteen months earlier, Ensign William Dalrymple and twenty-seven Scottish recruits, on their way to join the 14th Regiment in Halifax, had briefly resided in the barracks at Castle William. Now Lieutenant Colonel Dalrymple had returned as the commanding officer of the occupying force. More vivid for Boston men who had served in the Seven Years' War were bitter memories of British regulars and their officers. Although they admired British discipline and courage, provincial veterans still resented having been treated as inferior to regular troops and officers. They had perceived the British as irreligious and been shocked

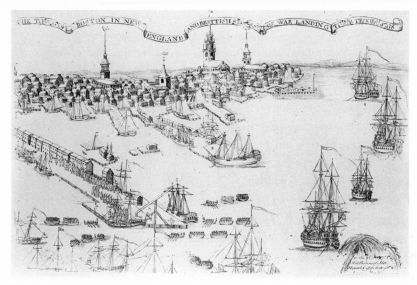

The Town of Boston in New England and British Ships of War Landing Their Troops! 1768, an engraving by Paul Revere. (Library of Congress)

by their profanity; by no means saints themselves, they nonetheless had been troubled by bawdy relations between redcoats and female camp followers. These cultural differences had often led to antagonisms, and Bostonians invariably recalled British soldiers as the aggressors, the instigators of altercations ranging from name-calling to riots.[3]

It seems unlikely that the soldiers were any happier being in Boston than Bostonians were in having them there. As has often been the case, the rank and file joined the military because the alternatives were even worse. Pay was low, discipline harsh, and conditions often grim, but even so army life was preferable to grinding poverty and possible starvation. At least the low cost of rum compensated for the unpleasant posting. To supplement their meager incomes, some soldiers took part-time work. Patrick Dines of the 29th, for example, found employment in a wig maker's shop. Others hustled jobs with rope makers and did a variety of tasks along the waterfront. But such competition depressed wages, reduced opportunities for locals, and deepened the resentment over the occupation. The hostile environment strengthened soldiers' bonds with each other, encouraging them to develop an identity separate from the townspeople.[4]

If a report on the composition of the 29th Regiment in 1773 reflects back to 1768, the men were experienced soldiers. Their ages ranged from eighteen to fifty, the average being approximately thirty-three. Most had enlisted at around the age of twenty, but it was not uncommon for them to have been much younger. James Bassett, the officer of the guard on the fatal night of March 5, 1770, had been only twelve when he began service in 1762. Some were married, and Boston selectmen worried about the potential expense of caring for their wives and children. (Unmarried redcoats produced their own problems, stemming from sexual frustration and demands for prostitutes.) The standard height set for men in the marching regiments was five feet, eight inches, and the regulars of the 29th just met the norm. They would have fallen slightly below average had it not been for their grenadier company. Like grenadiers in all British regiments, they were selected for their size. Their foot-high bearskin hats made them appear even taller and more imposing as they led charges on enemy forces.[5]

According to the same report, only a third of the men and noncommissioned officers in 1773 were English. More than 50 percent were Irish, slightly more than 5 percent were Scots, and seventeen individuals were listed as "Foreign." The foreign contingent probably came from the French West Indies. After the conquest of the island of Guadeloupe during the Seven Years' War, Admiral Edward Boscawen "procured eight or ten boys" whom he gave to his brother, at the time the commanding officer of the 29th Regiment. Boscawen thought the boys would be attractive and exotic ornaments and made them drummers, starting a tradition that continued until 1843. At the beginning of the Boston occupation, there was one drummer for each company; the number doubled in December 1769. Their dark skin distinguished them from their light-skinned comrades from the British Isles, and their yellow coats with red facing and lapels rendered them inescapably conspicuous.[6] The presence of British troops as a standing army was alarming enough for the residents of Boston, but having armed Irishmen and Afro-Caribbeans in their midst was a nightmare.

British officers in the rigid hierarchy of the military were supposed to stand out, from their uniforms to their bearing. Often sons of Britain's elite who had purchased their commissions, they had been raised to lead, to give orders, and to preserve class distinctions. They expected and demanded deference, but they also believed in honor, elegant manners, and noblesse oblige. Not even the radical *Boston Gazette* was immune to the appeal of senior officers. When Brigadier General Pomeroy left Boston in late June 1769 after commanding the troops for the previous half-year, the *Gazette* used the occasion to simultaneously condemn the occupation and praise Pomeroy, "this worthy good Officer" whose conduct "had in every Respect done Honor to the army, and as a Gentleman, his Departure is greatly regretted."[7] Bostonians typically did not extend the same high regard to junior officers, whose duties kept them closer to the men and their varied behaviors, whose social backgrounds sometimes were less distinguished than those of their superiors (and their commissions less costly), and whose experience in leadership and interaction with civilian populations were more limited.

With twelve hundred troops already in town and another thousand on the way, the most pressing issue was where to house them. Anticipating the need weeks before, Governor Bernard had called for a meeting with the Council on September 19. He informed them that General Gage had ordered two regiments from Halifax, one to be quartered at the barracks of Castle William and the other in Boston itself. He also notified them of Lord Hillsborough's July 30 letter, authorizing two additional regiments that would be brought over from Ireland, and requested the Council provide quarters. The Council replied by quoting the amendment of the Mutiny Act, often called the Quartering Act, whose first stage was "to billet and quarter the officers and soldiers . . . in the barracks provided by the colonies." Were barracks unavailable, civil officers of the town were to secure public houses, such as inns and taverns. Were public houses not sufficient, the governor and Council or their agent were to lease "so many uninhabited houses, outhouses, barns, or other buildings, as shall be necessary." The Council replied that as there were no barracks it wasn't their responsibility. Bernard retorted that dispersing troops in public houses throughout Boston and thereby mixing them with the general population would lead to bloodshed and that unheated barns and outbuildings were unacceptable for the cold winter. He reiterated his demand for barracks, patiently explaining that other buildings could be outfitted as barracks. The meeting concluded with the Council appointing a committee to confer with the selectmen about housing.[8]

Bernard suspected a plot to embarrass him and other British authorities. Should he and the military follow the letter of the law, there would be no shelter for the troops within the town. But should they seize buildings for the purpose, the opposition could resist the occupation with the law on its side. "So here is a System to make an Act impracticable,"

Bernard grumbled, "and then to oppose the King's Troops for not observing it!" And he sorrowfully acknowledged to Hillsborough, "The Act is impracticable enough without all this Contrivance." Bernard often exaggerated or misinterpreted the motives and actions of Bostonians, but this time he got them right. Recognizing the futility, let alone the possibility, of armed resistance, town leaders had developed a strategy for removing the troops from their midst: they would maintain the peace, thereby eliminating any justification for military presence, and they would invoke the Quartering Act to prevent soldiers and officers from residing within the town.[9]

When Bernard and the Council next met on September 22, there were no surprises but there was growing frustration. The committee reported that the selectmen concurred that the law required existing barracks to be exhausted before acquiring housing elsewhere. The barracks at Castle William, "which is part of the town of Boston," were capable of holding both regiments from Halifax, and there was plenty of time to determine where the regiments from Ireland might be quartered. An exasperated Bernard rejoined that although Castle William might be in the township it was not a part of the town and Gage had specified that one regiment be housed in Boston. Council members refused to budge. One of them, who must have read the Act very carefully, observed that "if there had been other Barracks in the Province, tho' at 50 Miles distant, they must be filled, before any Quarters could be demanded at Boston." Thwarted, Bernard fell back to threatening that the commanding officers would confiscate buildings for the troops if the town would not supply them.[10]

So matters would have ended for the day, had not the governor, desperate to find a solution, proposed that the Manufactory House be converted to a barracks. The Manufactory, a 140-foot, two-story brick building with an ample cellar, could easily contain an entire regiment. The province had constructed it to produce textiles that could reduce the demand for foreign goods and offer employment. After a few years, however, production had ceased, and at the time of Bernard's proposal squatters and a few weavers occupied the premises. He suspected that they had been "thrust" into the building when the people of Boston learned that troops were coming. That may be true, though the House of Representatives had been maneuvering to dislodge unlawful tenants since the previous February and most likely had not been successful.

Whatever the circumstances, the Council, wary about committing funds with the legislature dissolved and reluctant to cooperate, asked for time to consider. Two days later it informed Bernard that it would do nothing other than prepare the barracks at Castle William.[11]

As soon as the governor learned that the transport ships carrying the troops from Halifax had anchored in the harbor, he rushed to Castle William for a private conference with Lieutenant Colonel Dalrymple. After the two men reviewed prior negotiations with the Council, they decided to press their case again the following morning. Perhaps hoping to intimidate the Council, they convened the meeting in the military environment of Castle William rather than the familiar (and far more convenient) Town House, and invited the commanding officer of the fleet, Captain Henry Smith, to join them.

Dalrymple initially attempted to sway the Council with courtesy. He hoped that he was among friends and assured them that "his Men would on their Parts behave as such." Barracks where the officers could closely supervise the troops were important for "good Order," and he wanted to maintain good relations with the town. Hoping that such conciliatory remarks might persuade, he stated that his orders required that one of the barracks be in Boston. The Council members did not back down. They repeated to Dalrymple what they had told Bernard. The Quartering Act specified that barracks must be filled before other quarters were sought, and Castle William could hold both regiments. The Council bore no responsibility until troops fully occupied barracks and public houses. Shifting tactics and tone, Dalrymple angrily responded that he would not argue whether Castle William was or was not in Boston and that he was not accustomed to people disputing his orders. He "should most certainly march his Regiment in the Town"; if only public houses were available, he would take them, but he warned the Council of the potential consequences of townspeople encountering troops unsupervised by their officers.[12]

Before the meeting deteriorated further, Bernard leaped in and suggested reconsideration of the Manufactory House. The Council insisted that the room be cleared of visitors before conducting regular business. Dalrymple and Smith departed. Bernard then renewed his request, only to be met by the objection that the Council lacked the power to raise the necessary funds. The governor suggested that contingency funds he controlled could pay for renovating the Manufactory House for the troops, but still there was no assent. He then made his last offer for the day: he would be accountable for the Crown paying the costs, were the Council to authorize the use of the building. Bernard knew that to remain within the requirements of the Quartering Act he needed the Council's cooperation, but again it refused. With twelve hundred troops waiting to come ashore and with the ultimate responsibility for their housing on his sagging shoulders, he announced that he would assign the Manufactory House on his own.[13]

When Bernard returned to Castle William the next day to inform Dalrymple of his decision, he encountered Captain John Montresor, who had been sent by General Gage "to assist the Forces as Engineer, and to enable them to recover and maintain the Castle, & such other Posts as they could secure." Gage was under the impression that "Boston had revolted," and he had sent letters to Bernard and Dalrymple authorizing appropriate action. Dalrymple had already concluded that the situation was not so threatening, but he also had determined that both regiments should be stationed in Boston and was ready to land them without further preparation. All he needed was housing. Bernard empowered him to take the Manufactory House for one regiment; the other would camp temporarily on Boston Common.[14]

In 1768 the Common provided Boston's best location for a training ground. Unlike today, there were no swan boats, few trees except along the perimeter, no parklike terrain, no golden-domed Bulfinch capitol building nearby, and no urban hubbub. Situated on the relatively uninhabited southwest edge of town, it was a gently undulating open space—a good place for a stroll, an adequate spot to pitch a tent until winter approached.[15]

About 2 o'clock the next day, October 1, as troops began to congregate on the Common, Lieutenant David Cooper of the 14th Regiment inspected the Manufactory House to ascertain its condition and how many soldiers it would house. The resident overseer, John Brown, escorted him through the rooms, and Cooper left to report his assessment to Dalrymple. Almost immediately Cooper returned and notified Brown that Dalrymple had ordered the premises evacuated within two hours to make it available for the soldiers. Brown demanded to see Dalrymple, and at their meeting on the Common "complained to him of the hardship of being turned out of Doors from a House he had been placed in by the Province, and that without legal Warning." Dalrymple replied that

Governor Bernard had authorized the military's use of the Manufactory. Brown countered that the governor possessed no such power and that he would not comply. The conversation took place while the two men strolled to the nearby Manufactory, where the colonel lingered. Trying to avoid a confrontation on the troops' first day in Boston but needing shelter for the 14th Regiment, which had not brought tents, Dalrymple declared that "for the sake of the People" he would ask the selectmen for accommodations.[16]

The town officials agreed to open up Faneuil Hall to the troops after Dalrymple promised "upon his honor" to leave the Hall on Monday, two days later. When Faneuil Hall was found to be too small for the entire regiment, some of the soldiers took up residence in the Town House. On Monday the merchant John Rowe, serving as an intermediary and with an eye on the lucrative possibilities of supplying provisions and housing, informed the selectmen that Dalrymple had requested an extension until Wednesday. The colonel's frustration must have been stronger than his honor, for on Wednesday Rowe relayed the information that the 14th would remain in their temporary quarters until barracks were provided.[17]

So matters stood: the 29th Regiment littered the Common with their tents and equipment, the 14th filled Faneuil Hall and part of the Town House with guards posted at the doors, and the detachment from the 59th and the artillery train had somehow found housing in buildings on Griffin's wharf in the South End.[18] Boston had become a garrisoned town.

Unsuccessful in convincing the Council to quarter the soldiers in barracks, Bernard pressed them to supply provisions "for the usual Allowances." Here he was on firmer ground. The Quartering Act specified that the province in question must pay for candles, vinegar, salt, beer or cider, and a variety of other items. Food for the troops was the responsibility of the army. The Council hoped to negotiate and offered to comply if Dalrymple would do so as well. In short, were the colonel to withdraw both regiments to the barracks at Castle William, the Council would provide provisions. Bernard summoned Dalrymple to the meeting. Accompanied by Captain Smith, Dalrymple heatedly demanded quarters for his soldiers and warned the Council that if it did not fulfill its obligations under the Quartering Act it risked the king's displeasure. Afterward two members of the Council asked

A Prospective View of Part of the Common, 1902, an engraving by Sidney Smith after the 1768 watercolor by Christian Remick of the British troops on Boston Common. (I. N. Phelps Stokes Collection, Miriam and Ira D. Wallach Division of Art, Prints, and Photographs, The New York Public Library, Astor, Lenox and Tilden Foundations)

Bernard whether one of the regiments would be removed to the Castle if the Council furnished the "allowances." After hearing the inquiry, Dalrymple explained that he was ordered to station both regiments in the town, but that if peace continued he "made no Doubt but the General would allow one Regiment to go to the Castle; for which Purpose he had already wrote."[19]

Encouraged, the two Council members rejoined their colleagues, and by an eight-to-five vote agreed to supply the troops. But there was a catch. They attached a proviso that whoever they authorized "will take the risk of the Province's paying to him or them all such Sum or Sums of Money, so by them paid, laid out or expended for the Purpose aforesaid." The supplier, in other words, was taking a chance on whether Massachusetts would reimburse him. It was a clever move, for it reminded everyone that the legislature (which initiated revenue bills) was dissolved, effectively discouraged anyone from accepting the position of commissary, and still complied with the Quartering Act. Bernard tried to remove the clause, but meeting no success he nominated Joseph Goldthwait, who was approved to provide the supplies. On learning of the conditions and on the advice of Dalrymple, Goldthwait declined the appointment.[20]

Thomas Gage, discouraged to learn of the difficulties and wary that officials in Boston might give the citizens "just Cause of Complaint," arrived on Saturday, October 15. Governor Bernard called a meeting with the Council on Monday morning, and there Gage strongly made his case. He stated that as many as possible of the two regiments sailing from Ireland could stay in the barracks at Castle William but demanded that quarters be provided in town for the 14th and 29th Regiments and the spillover from the Irish regiments. After Gage left, the governor and the Council debated the matter until 8 o'clock that night, at which point six of the eleven councilors present voted to clear the Manufactory House to make room for soldiers of the 64th and 65th Regiments who could not be "conveniently accommodated" at Castle William.[21] Here at last was the opening Bernard had been seeking for a month.

During the afternoon of October 19, Sheriff Stephen Greenleaf, accompanied by Lieutenant Governor and Chief Justice Thomas Hutchinson, appeared at the Manufactory House. John Brown and other occupants were aware that Greenleaf's mission was to evict them, and Brown had already discussed the subject with several opposition leaders. As residents leaned out the open windows, Greenleaf addressed Brown, shouting out that he was authorized to claim possession of the Manufactory and that he required Brown "to clear it forthwith, for the reception of his Majesty's troops." Brown inquired who had issued the warrant. When he learned it had been the governor with the support of the Council, he proclaimed that they did not have sufficient power to evict him. He would vacate the premises only after the General Court had so ordered him. Hutchinson, who had maintained a low public profile since his breakdown ("a nervous disorder") a year and a half earlier, weighed in. He instructed Brown that the governor and Council were "the remaining authority of the province" and they had rightful legal power over the Manufactory. Brown should consider the "disagreeable" consequences of his refusal to cooperate. When Brown adamantly refused to yield, the sheriff read aloud the Council's decision and the governor's order and departed.[22]

Shortly after noon the following day, Greenleaf, perhaps with visions of the debacle between Daniel Malcom and customs officials in his mind, returned for another try. All of the doors and windows of the Manufactory were secured, but Greenleaf noticed that one of the cellar windows remained unlocked so that the weavers could enter and exit their workshop. After one of the weavers hoisted himself out, the sheriff rushed over to gain entrance. The weaver dashed back and attempted to restrain Greenleaf from opening the sash. The sheriff was the stronger of the two and managed to struggle his way in, feet first and with sword in hand. Only because of the obstacle of a loom, Brown, who was at the other end of the cellar, didn't attack immediately. "A small scuffle" soon ensued "in which neither party received much harm." Somehow Greenleaf found himself trapped in the cellar without an exit strategy, and it required a party of soldiers to rescue him. Once outside, Greenleaf deployed troops as sentinels at the doors and gate and stationed ten more in the cellar. When a crowd formed, he sent for a company of reinforcements.[23]

The Manufactory was under siege. Soldiers isolated the inhabitants of the building. The *Boston Gazette* reported, "Friday morning bread and water were denied, and no person allowed to speak to them for several hours. The sick were denied the visits of their physicians, and Dr. Church's apprentice in the afternoon had several pushes with a bayonet as he was attempting to convey them medicines." Several town leaders mingled with the growing and resentful crowd outside and attempted to maintain peace. Others informed Council members of the situation. Hurriedly the Council, worried by the volatile confrontation and its own role in instigating it, decided to explain to the governor that they meant only to empty the Manufactory "by law," not force, a disingenuous distinction (and a clear sign that the Council was abandoning responsibility for the state of affairs). The possibility of violence convinced Bernard to withdraw the troops. By early evening the siege had ended.[24]

Yet the problem of finding quarters for the troops within the restrictions of the Quartering Act remained. Citing the Council's approval of the 64th and 65th Regiments eventually using the barracks at Castle William as evidence that all barracks were filled, Bernard called together the town's justices of the peace, seeking an order to authorize public houses for quartering the 14th and 29th Regiments. After several days of negotiation, the justices declined. According to Bernard, two of the twelve justices supported billeting the troops and the law required no more than a single town official's assent, but in the highly charged political climate of Boston they were unwilling to act so conspicuously. The governor ("at the End of my Tether") on October 26, thirty-eight days after initiating discussions with the Council and still under the obligations of his office to obtain housing for the troops, gave up hope for cooperation and appointed another to procure quarters at the Crown's expense.[25]

Gage had expected such an outcome and already had assigned officers to locate and rent houses for themselves and buildings for their men. Almost four weeks after Dalrymple had pledged that the 14th Regiment would be in Faneuil Hall for only two nights, the soldiers left for converted warehouses and other structures. A remnant of the 14th stayed in the Town House for an additional three weeks before moving out. The 29th decamped from the Common and moved into former sugarhouses and commercial buildings.[26]

As Gage, Bernard, and Lord Barrington knew, they had violated the terms of the Quartering Act to house the troops within Boston.[27] The barracks at Castle William were empty when they quartered regiments in the warehouses and dwellings, a breach of the letter of the law. Officers had lodged soldiers illegally and consequently were subject to being cashiered. But their options had been limited. They could billet soldiers outside of Boston proper, obeying the Act and countermanding the intent of military occupation, or they could house soldiers in Boston without the authorization of provincial and local officials, breaking the law but fulfilling their orders to police the town.

The list of abridgments of British law and constitutional principles was growing, as were measures and behaviors that reduced opportunities for institutional redress. British authorities were taxing colonists without their consent, dissolving legislatures, ignoring petitions, establishing a standing army in peacetime, sending troops as a police force without the explicit request of the governor and Council, and now violating the Quartering Act. Colonists were beginning to perceive this series of grievances as a conspiracy to deprive them of their rights. In this case, they were wrong. It was not a conspiracy. The sad fact is that British officials viewed colonists as less than full citizens of the British empire. They were not equals; they were subordinates. It was preferable to follow the law and the constitution, but the demands of the state superseded the rights of colonists. The citizens of Boston had without question manipulated the law's purpose in order to thwart the presence of soldiers. As Gage put it in reference to the section of the Quartering Act forbidding military officers unilaterally to house troops, "The Clause in Question is by no Means calculated for the Circumstances of this Country, where every Man studies Law, and interprets the Laws as suits his Purposes, and where the Measures of Government are opposed by every Evasion and Chicane that can be devised."[28] Gage's claim applied to him as well, and yet he had gone even further to suit his own purposes because he had the power to do so. He prevailed this time but in doing so left Bostonians with fewer options within the bounds of the law.

Promoting desertion was another way to undermine the standing army, as colonists recognized almost immediately, and unhappy soldiers were plentiful among the regiments. Despite the sullen greeting they received as they garrisoned Boston, the troops realized that a new life in the countryside might be an improvement over their current condition; at least forty of the regulars deserted within the first two weeks of the occupation. Bostonians and others apparently encouraged and assisted soldiers to flee. Certainly the senior officers held that view. On October 3 the regiments formed on King Street, and they heard a proclamation offering a reward of ten guineas, the rough equivalent of two thousand dollars at today's purchasing power, to any soldier who identified "any one who should attempt to seduce him from the service." Dalrymple assured the men that "he would take care that it should be the last offer he [the offender] should make."[29]

That was just the beginning. To prevent easy access to the countryside, the military had a guardhouse constructed at the Neck. Although unknown assailants had destroyed the initial building before it was completed, the structure soon was resurrected. Guards inspected any suspicious cart or person entering or leaving the town. Soldiers in civilian garb scoured outlying areas for escaped comrades. Sentries were posted outside the houses of officers and the barracks of troops and challenged passersby. Residents were accustomed to responding to the town watch at night on Boston's darkened streets, but they resented the redcoats who confronted them. The most shocking preventive measure occurred on the morning of October 31. In front of the regiments assembled on the Common, Private Richard Ames of the 14th Regiment solemnly was marched out, placed before a firing squad, and executed for desertion.[30] This was not the Boston its residents had known before occupation.

As shocking and more immediately threatening, British soldiers challenged Boston sensibilities on slavery and race. On October 28 Captain John Wilson of the 59th Regiment, accompanied by two other officers, and perhaps all drunk, encouraged some African American slaves to attack their masters. He assured "them that the soldiers were come to procure their freedoms, and that with their help and assistance they should be able to drive all the Liberty Boys to the devil." Although it is unlikely that any slaves perceived Wilson's remarks as anything more than inebriated mischief, several Bostonians lodged complaints about "a dangerous conspiracy" with the selectmen, who immediately instructed the town's watch to scrutinize "Negros & to take up those of them that may be in gangs at unseasonable hours." On two occasions earlier in the month, Boston residents had witnessed the "very disagreeable spectacle" of Afro-Caribbean drummers of the 29th Regiment, already controversial figures in their eyes, administering punishment to white soldiers. Right on Boston Common, the drummers whipped nine or ten offenders of "sundry misdeameanors" on one day and two or three others, including "one Rogers, a New-England man," on another.[31] Public whippings and other punishments were traditional and familiar to all Bostonians, but this role reversal stirred racist fears.

African slavery in Boston was nearly as old as the town itself. In 1638 the Salem sea captain William Pierce brought a cargo of slaves from the West Indies, apparently the result of an exchange for Indians captured in the Pequot War. It was an unusual event. Though in 1645 Emmanuel Downing, brother-in-law of John Winthrop, argued strenuously the economic necessity of a slave labor force, New Englanders found widespread adoption of the institution impractical. Unlike the Chesapeake colonies to the south, New England had a glacier-scraped, thin soil, a short growing season, and a population explosion. Labor exchanges with neighbors and the work of sons and daughters generally were sufficient for the demands posed by family farms. The external circumstances of soil, climate, and labor supply, rather than higher morality or stronger virtue, explain why slavery didn't become an integral component of the New England colonies. Late in the seventeenth century, royal agent Edmund Randolph estimated that there weren't more than two hundred slaves in northeastern British America, and they were broadly dispersed. New England slave owners typically held only one or two forced laborers and they were in constant contact with their bondsmen.

Rarely absentee owners, they worked, ate, and slept in near proximity to their slaves.[32]

Those were the conditions that shaped the peculiar institution and attitudes toward Africans in New England's first century. Massachusetts gave slavery legal status in 1641 by sanctioning the enslavement of "lawfull captives taken in just warres, and such strangers as willingly selle themselves or are sold to us." Theoretically any individual or ethnic group could fit this definition, but practically it applied to Indians and more typically to people of African descent. Slaves were property who could be purchased and sold, but they also were recognized as persons. Both free and enslaved Africans possessed significant legal rights: they could own and sell property; they were entitled to trial by jury; they could act as witnesses for and against white people; they received the same legal protections in criminal cases as anyone else; and they could sue, even for their freedom if there were questions about the legitimacy of their enslavement. Bonded and free African Americans could legally marry a spouse of their choosing regardless of ethnicity, and churches accepted them into membership. New England offered the least harsh slavery in the British colonies. But it still was bondage, and there were limits. African Americans could not participate in church governance or vote or hold office in civil society. They could join militias during war but not during peace. There occasionally were work restrictions to protect the employment of white craftsmen, such as when Boston enjoined carpenter Thomas Deane not to hire a "Negro" as a cooper.[33]

During the seventeenth century, New Englanders were guilty of ethnocentrism—particularly vicious when directed at Indians—and perhaps mild racism. With the growth of the African American population in the eighteenth century, racism became more prevalent. As a result of the slave trade and reproduction, the black population grew much more rapidly (one historian places the increase at nearly 50 percent per decade for the first half of the century) than did the white population. The greatest growth came in Rhode Island, where by midcentury more than 10 percent of the total population was African American, southeastern Connecticut, and Boston. Boston's black population in 1710, mostly slave, numbered between three hundred and four hundred. By 1742 it had grown to 1,374 and approached 8.5 percent of all Boston residents. The census for Boston in 1765 reported a decline of both whites and blacks but still a substantial number of people on the tightly clustered peninsula. Of the town's 15,520 inhabitants 811 were "Negroes and Molattoes," 5.2 percent of the whole.[34]

The "Numerousness of Slaves" certainly was on the mind of Samuel Sewall, perhaps the wealthiest man in Boston in the early eighteenth century and the judge in the witchcraft trials of 1692, who recanted his role and wrote the antislavery tract "The Selling of Joseph" in 1700. The Calvinist Sewall believed "that all Men, as they are the Sons of Adam, are coheirs: and have equal Right unto Liberty, and all other outward Comforts of Life." Slavery violated God's order and was wrong. Rather than calling for an outright abolition of bondage, however, he advocated halting the importation of slaves. People should not be dragged from their native land, their spouse, and their children. Moreover white servants with limited terms of indenture would be more productive than African slaves who would be "Unwilling Servants" as they yearned for "their forbidden Liberty." Sewall recognized that few of his fellow citizens could "endure to hear of a Negro's being made free" and doubted that assimilation and integration were possible. "And there is such a disparity in their Conditions, Colour & Hair," he warned, "that they can never embody with us, and grow up into orderly Families, to the Peopling of the Land."[35] Even the enlightened Sewall, who opposed slavery on the basis of common humanity, also held the racist view that the cultural and physical differences between whites and blacks would keep them forever apart. His solution, like that of moderate antislavery proponents of the nineteenth century, was containment. During the period leading up to the American Revolution, a growing number of Bostonians agreed that slavery should be stopped, and nearly all white residents of the town believed Africans to be persons, but also of a lower and potentially more dangerous order that, whether free or enslaved, must be controlled.

From Sewall's humane tract against slavery in 1700 to Captain John Wilson's frivolous and taunting call in 1768 for a slave rebellion, there were sporadic attempts to end the peculiar institution in Massachusetts. More often there were efforts to restrict the African Americans in their midst. In 1701 Boston's selectmen took Sewall's proposal seriously and advised the town's representatives to promote "the bringing of white servants and to put a Period to Negros being Slaves," but in 1705 Massachusetts enacted a law prohibiting "Negroes" or Indians from marrying whites, becoming the only New England colony to forbid mixed marriages.[36]

The most disturbing evidence of Boston's racism during the colonial period came in 1723, when the town sent fifteen proposed laws for the "Better Regulating Indians Negros and Molattos" to the General Court—a comprehensive Black Code. Six laws applied to slaves or servants, but over half were directed exclusively at free people. Among the proposals were restrictions on firearms and other weapons, on gathering in groups, and on alcohol. More unusual and heartless was the requirement that "every free Indian Negro or Molatto Shal bind out, all their Children at or before they arrive to the age of four years to Some English master, and upon neglect thereof the Select men or Overseers of the Poor Shal be Empowered to bind out all Such Children till the age of Twenty one years." Boston and other New England towns frequently forced poor residents to indenture some of their children to reduce the costs of poor relief, but this proposed law, which removed children regardless of the family's financial circumstances, was unprecedented. It appears to have been designed to prepare children for subservience—and offer cheap labor—rather than to trim the town's financial obligations. The Massachusetts legislature was unable to craft a bill that satisfied both the House and the Council, and the colony's first flirtation with Jim Crow died.[37]

Boston nonetheless continued to pass laws restricting the rights of African Americans. Most pertained only to slaves and servants, but some affected all black Bostonians. Concerned about large groups forming, particularly after dark, the town ordered in 1723 that "all Indians Negros and Molattoes shall be Buryed halfe an hour before Sun Set at the Least." Five years later, in 1728, it prohibited all African Americans from carrying sticks or canes. A special watch patrolled the streets to apprehend "all Negro and Molatto Servants" who were out after 10 o'clock at night. Penalties were imposed for loitering on the "Lord's day," and innkeepers and sellers of alcoholic beverages lost their license if they sold liquor to "Negroes or Mollatto Servants."[38] And so it went.

While Bostonians in the 1760s railed against the Stamp Act, the Townshend Acts, and other impositions on their liberty, many of them owned slaves. Samuel Adams, John Hancock, James Otis, John Rowe, and Thomas Hutchinson were among the town's slaveholders. It was a rare week when at least one Boston newspaper didn't publish an advertisement for a slave to be sold or to reclaim a runaway. The same issue of the *Boston Gazette* that reported Andrew Oliver's being driven from office as the province's stamp collector ran the following ad: "A likely Negro Girl, about 16 Years of Age, capable of doing all sorts of Houshold Work, to be sold only for want of Employment." Such irony and hypocrisy were not lost on some of the *Gazette*'s readers. Shortly after the assembly was dissolved in July 1768, "Æquus" lambasted the contradictions of slavery. "I Observed in your last Paper the following Advertisement, viz. *To be Sold a Negro Boy, 16 Years Old, for no Fault*. The poor Boy is acknowledg'd to be guilty of no fault: Is it not then a glaring Absurdity," he pointedly questioned, "that he should be *Sold!*"[39]

Æquus was not alone. Opposition to slavery grew hand in hand with resistance to British policies that deprived colonists of their constitutional rights, and even some slaveholders, including James Otis, raised their voices against the institution. Members of the Massachusetts House regularly sought to abolish slavery and to stop the importation of slaves into the province. The Boston town meeting fully supported the bill in 1767, but once again the assembly couldn't concur with the Council and the measure failed. Part of the opposition may have come from slave traders and their allies. Since the late seventeenth century New England had been more heavily engaged in the slave trade than any other region of the British colonies. The northeastern section may not have been as suitable for large-scale slavery as other colonies, but its vigorous maritime enterprises meshed easily with the transportation and selling of human cargoes. By 1767, however, the slave trade was in decline, and the antislavery bill prohibited the importation of slaves only into Massachusetts, not elsewhere.[40]

A greater obstacle than slave traders to ending slavery was the lingering fear of free African Americans. Like other British colonists, few Bostonians could shake their racist assumptions about the inferiority of people of African descent and their potential danger to whites. As fair-minded a person as John Adams under the guise of "Humphrey Ploughjogger" resorted to a racist opposition to the Stamp Act in 1765 when he wrote, "Providence never designed us for negroes, I know, for if it had it wou'd have given us black hides, and thick lips, and flat noses, and short woolly hair, which it han't done, and therefore never intended us for slaves."[41] The white citizens of Boston recognized the injustice of slavery and the rough parallels to their own situation; they understood that Africans were persons, but they had greater difficulty accepting black equality than did British ministries tolerating the full rights of colonists. Captain Wilson's drunken remarks and Afro-Caribbean drummers whipping white soldiers rubbed a festering scab and intensified the resentment of British occupation.

Chapter 8

Occupation

The presence of an occupying force altered both Boston's political dynamic and the focus of the opposition movement. Eliminating the restrictions of the Townshend Acts and the violations of their constitutional rights remained the ultimate goals of most Bostonians, but removing the troops became their immediate objective. Daily encounters with redcoats reminded townspeople of their subordinate status, but rather than organize public demonstrations to voice their resentment they chose to return to the tactic of "no mobs" to prove how ill advised the sending of the military had been.

With General Thomas Gage still in Boston, the Council attempted to convince him to withdraw the troops. It argued that the events of the preceding March 18, the original cause of the order to garrison the town, were "trivial" and that those connected with the *Liberty* episode of June 10, though "criminal," had been provoked by the commissioners and their minions to justify naval ships in Boston Harbor and soldiers in the town. No one had threatened the commissioners. They had been perfectly safe but fled the town for the *Romney* and Castle William as a charade to prove that their lives were in peril and Boston a lawless place. Gage could see for himself that "the Town and Province, are in a peaceful state." In this context the Council concluded that "his Majesty's service does not require those regiments to continue in the Town" and requested that they be placed at Castle William or nearby Point Shirley. The approaching regiments from Ireland should be diverted to their original destination, "a different part of North America."[1]

Gage was not yet prepared to change course or publicly agree that the troops were unnecessary, but he offered hope that the occupation would be short-lived. He responded that the soldiers would follow "discipline and order" and not distress the citizens. Should the town's behavior support the Council's "construction of their past actions," he would recommend "withdrawing the most part of the Troops." It was a cautious and diplomatic reply, a carrot and a stick. Days later, in a letter to the Earl of Hillsborough, the general was more candid and a bit skeptical of reports that British officials had sent from Boston. Based on the "best Information I have been able to procure," he wrote, he agreed with the Council that the "Disturbance in March was trifling." He believed that the *Liberty* "riot" provided the commissioners with "Sufficient Reason" to be alarmed for their own safety, but he acknowledged that they had not been attacked and he was uncertain whether they would have been had they stayed in Boston. In his mind, the best reason for the troops' presence was the resolves from the town meeting calling for the Massachusetts Convention, for he thought its intentions "suspicious."[2] After observing Boston firsthand, Gage had doubts whether the crowd actions of March and June justified military occupation. Nonetheless he distrusted the town's political leadership.

By late October the commissioners were weary of their self-imposed exile at Castle William and, gaining confidence from the presence of British regiments, inquired whether they might safely return. Governor Bernard presented the question to the Council for its opinion. One of the Council members stated that the commissioners would be safe as long as they "behave themselves as they ought to do, which must be very differently from what they had done before." Another asserted that they never had been in danger in the first place but had retreated to Castle William for political purposes. Increasingly impatient with the Council, Bernard pressed for a more definitive response. He was then assured that the commissioners might safely return. The governor relayed the Council's assessment to the commissioners, but he intentionally neglected to answer their question as to whether any civil magistrate would order troops to quell a disturbance, a legal requirement for the use of military force among a civilian population. Still, that was response enough for the commissioners, and after five months' absence they came back to Boston on November 9.[3]

When the various commissioners attended church services the following Sunday, there were no incidents and no celebrations. No public demonstrations confronted the customs board, but neither were

Castle William, 1773, an ink and watercolor drawing. (Library of Congress)

its members welcomed. Commissioner Henry Hulton discovered that no one would rent him a house; he settled for leasing lodgings within the town and purchasing a property five miles away in the countryside. Even after some individuals broke the windows of his new residence, he envisioned a more tranquil existence in which he would engage in the Crown's business four days a week in Boston and enjoy "quiet with [his] family" the other three at his country estate.[4]

His social life also kept him relatively isolated from detractors. Every other Wednesday, Hulton and others employed by the British government, including military and naval officers as well as "a few families in town"—all told about sixty couples—held an assembly for dancing and mutual entertainment. A writer in the *Boston Evening-Post* warned the "Young Ladies of Boston" not to attend, for they would damage their reputation by associating with people, "some of whom are profest enemies to the country which gave you birth, and who are even now endeavoring to rob you, your friends, relations and country, of the invaluable blessings of the best constituted government upon earth." Denial of social pleasures alone was not a sufficient inducement, and soon a competing assembly, the Liberty Assembly, danced the night away on intervening Wednesdays.[5]

Before leaving Castle William, the commissioners, emboldened by the regiments' arrival in Boston, instigated the prosecution of John Hancock and five of his confederates. They already had seized the *Liberty* and its cargo, and in August the vice admiralty court had condemned the ship, though not the goods. But the customs board previously had not dared to go further. On October 29 Advocate General Jonathan Sewall filed suit against Hancock, Daniel Malcom, Nathaniel Barnard, John Matchet, William Bowes, and Lewis Gray for landing wine without paying duties. Hancock, as the principal, faced a particularly heavy penalty of triple the value of the wine, nine thousand pounds. Defending him in perhaps the most important case of his early career was John Adams.

The trial commenced on November 7, but there followed delay after delay. Finally, on January 2, the prosecution called its first witnesses, who included some of Hancock's "nearest relations" as well as tradesmen with whom he did business. Thomas Kirk, the tidesman and earwitness who belatedly recalled overhearing casks of wine being hauled off the *Liberty*, was only as reliable as whatever corroborative evidence could be found. The prosecution must have hoped that Hancock's kinsmen and business associates would substantiate Kirk's claims. Adams presented the defense witnesses in mid-February, and it appeared that closing arguments and the conclusion of the trial were imminent. That was not to be. Much to the "astonishment of the publick, and as it is said, even to the judge himself," the commissioners brought forward additional witnesses. Apparently they now realized that their case, as it stood late in the trial, was too weak for a guilty verdict. A month later Sewall, most likely fearing an acquittal, withdrew the charges.[6] Rather than demonstrating their augmented power, the commissioners failed to convict Hancock and made themselves even more detested in the process.

A new publication, the *Journal of the Times*, covered the entire trial, the only news source to do so. From September 28, 1768, to August 1, 1769, it maintained a daily account of life under military occupation. Originating in Boston and written in secret, copy was sent to the *New York Journal* and then reprinted in the *Pennsylvania Chronicle* and other colonial newspapers. Not until December 12 did the initial entries of the *Journal* appear in the *Boston Evening-Post*, its first appearance in the town, and from then until the *Journal*'s demise the following August the *Evening-Post* published succeeding items. As a result, Boston readers of the *Journal* were always more than a month behind actual events. That may have lessened the impact of its articles. Less charitably, Thomas Hutchinson thought the time lapse fuzzed memories "so as to make the aggravations more easily received."[7]

Hutchinson was absolutely right that the *Journal* had a point of view hostile to the troops and British officials and sympathetic to the opposition movement, but those drawbacks shouldn't discredit it as a valuable eye-witness to the times. Although its specific authors remain unknown and despite its obvious spin on the events of the day, the *Journal* is one of the best sources, occasionally the only source, on life during the first ten months of the occupation of Boston.

Article after article commented on the occupation's impact. Not only were soldiers stationed at the guardhouse at the Neck to deter would-be deserters, but sentries were posted throughout the town, as the *Journal* made abundantly clear. They were placed in front of residences of senior officers and primary government officials as well as before each barrack; they guarded the customs house on King Street; and they manned the main guardhouse next to two cannon aimed at the doorway of the Town House, home of the General Court, across the street—an intentionally provocative and taunting reminder of their presence. Soldiers stopped carriages and carts as they entered and left the city, supposedly to search for deserters. If Boston citizens protested the impositions and the military's proper authority, however, sentries overzealously responded. When "gentlemen and ladies" returned from the countryside in their carriages and ignored the checkpoint, guards threatened them, in one instance warning that they would "have their brains blown out unless they stopped."[8]

As daunting were the challenges that sentries made to people on foot, particularly at night. Bostonians willingly accepted the inquiries of the town's watches, but they resented the British soldiers' demands of "Who comes there?" As much as they now grasped that they were living in a garrisoned town, they acknowledged only civil authority and resisted the military as much as possible. Harrison Gray, a prominent merchant and a member of the Council, told soldiers who challenged him one evening that he was not obliged to respond. They retaliated by thrusting their bayonets toward his chest and detained him for half an hour. Gray brought charges against the soldiers, but the province's attorney general wouldn't indict them.[9]

In large part, these frequent incidents grew from the clash between civilian and military traditions. Soldiers expected military rules to apply and orders to be obeyed. The residents of Boston believed they were British citizens not subject to a standing army in peacetime. Wanting

GRENADIER 29TH REGIMENT, 1769.

Grenadier of the 29th Regiment, 1769. In H. Everard, *History of Thomas Farrington's Regiment subsequently designated the 29th (Worcestershire) Foot, 1694 to 1891* (Worcester, England, 1891), 61. (Reproduced by permission of The Huntington Library, San Marino, California)

to avoid a violent escalation, Colonel Joseph Pomeroy, who replaced Dalrymple as the overall commander of the regiments, ordered in mid-December that the challenges be suspended, and for the most part they ceased during the remainder of the occupation.[10]

Just the reverse were confrontations between the town watch and soldiers. In an almost parallel universe to sentry postings, watch houses were scattered throughout Boston and town watches walked night streets; the responsibility of these appointed citizens was to prevent crime and keep order. They, too, challenged people, though only after dark. Military officers especially took exception to the perceived audacity of ordinary residents demanding to know their identity. As the *Journal of the Times* reported, one November night two officers retorted to the

Town House watch that they had no right to stop officers on the street, for they were the "King's soldiers and gentlemen, who had orders from his Majesty, and they were above the Selectmen who gave them their orders." Four regiments and strong liquor, a potentially violent if not deadly combination, fortified them.[11]

Similar altercations—threats, brandished swords, and fights—occurred at all of the watch houses, but the close proximity of the main guardhouse and the Town House made that central area a frequent (and occasionally farcical) battleground. On January 19, 1769, after beating a pedestrian, several officers with swords in hand attacked the Town House watch. In the course of the brawl, one of the watch snagged an officer with his billhook (a hand weapon with a hook on the end of the blade) and hauled him into the watch house. Fellow officers soon rescued him but were unable to retrieve his sword. The next day the watchmen brought the captured weapon to Judge John Ruddock, "who by the help of the sword, gained knowledge of the owner" and thereby convicted him.[12]

There were other tensions between Bostonians and the military occupiers. Despite its Puritan reputation, Boston was an international seaport with all the vices of a substantial eighteenth-century city. From its inception, the town had known drunkenness, profanity, prostitution, irreligion, and disturbances on the Sabbath. And, well aware of human foibles, it had attempted to moderate bad behavior but had not expected to eliminate it. For the most part, the soldiers and officers shared the culture and values of the residents of Boston, and the officers administered discipline, often at the end of a whip, to check the very abuses of power that disturbed and humiliated Bostonians. But the soldiers were not welcomed by the citizenry; they were poor, and many were unmarried, alienated, and lonely. Cheap rum often was their comfort, and inebriation became a prime source of social disorder. The military didn't introduce vice to Boston, but raised it to new levels. The *Journal of the Times* expressed Bostonians' growing fear that by placing troops in the town "our enemies are waging war with the *morals* as well as the *rights* and *privileges* of the poor inhabitants."[13]

Even ordinary military routines irritated some residents' sensibilities, particularly on Sundays. The fifes and drums that accompanied the changing of the guards disrupted the solemnity of religious services and attracted "boys and Negroes." In late December 1768 the selectmen asked Colonel Pomeroy to halt the practice, and there were fewer public complaints afterward. Years later, in his *Autobiography*, John Adams remembered how annoying it had been to have soldiers drill below his windows overlooking Brattle Square each morning. The daily reminders convinced him that Britain would not alter its course. "My daily Reflections for two Years, at the Sight of those Soldiers before my door were serious enough," he wrote. "Their very Appearance in Boston was a strong proof to me, that the determination in Great Britain to subjugate Us, was too deep and inveterate ever to be altered by Us."[14]

The most egregious form of subjugation consisted of assaults on townspeople. The extant evidence makes it difficult to ascertain who instigated some of the attacks, but Bostonians were naturally inclined to blame the troops. It appears that some of the time, perhaps often, a beating was retaliation for an insult or taunting gesture from a resident. On one occasion, an apprentice was watching a dancing assembly when the sentry who had been guarding the door came up behind him and struck him on the head, knocking him to the ground. The soldier maintained that someone had spat on him. Attracting greater attention was an altercation in front of Judge John Ruddock's house. A group of sailors accompanied by a woman were strolling and encountered a contingent of soldiers, one of whom asserted that the woman was his wife. In the ensuing melee, at least one bystander suffered "a considerable wound on his head." On hearing "a great cry of murder," Ruddock, a Boston selectman, and his son rushed from their house, and the judge grabbed two of the "assailants" and called on those present to assist him. The aid that arrived, unfortunately for Ruddock, was thirty to forty soldiers who, with fists and bayonets, sought to free their comrades. After receiving several blows, Ruddock and his son retreated to the safety of their house, having been chased as far as the entryway. A corporal in the fray, John Norfolk, a year and a half later offered a slightly different account, claiming that the younger Ruddock had been an aggressor who roughed him up and took his bayonet. Although several soldiers were identified and charged, none was brought to trial.[15]

Lieutenant Daniel Mattier escaped prosecution altogether, while the soldiers who helped him attack Joshua Hemmingway and ransack his house pled guilty but were freed by order of the attorney general. Mattier and his men believed Hemmingway had shot the lieutenant's dog and decided to administer retribution. Armed, they forced their way into his house, terrorized his family, and damaged possessions. At first, Mattier's confederates pled not guilty, but, promised leniency, they reversed themselves. The soldiers were pleased with the legal process, Hemmingway and his family must have been angered, and the *Journal of the Times* fretted that it was a bad precedent.[16]

The attorney general may have acted properly when on several occasions he refused to prosecute accused and indicted offenders— some charges were doubtless trumped up—but he would have been hard-pressed to justify the escape of John Riley, a grenadier in the 14th Regiment. Jonathan Winship, a butcher from Cambridge, had angrily rebuked Riley at the Boston market for striking him the previous day. Forgoing a verbal response and apparently with Colonel Dalrymple's approval, Riley simply repeated his earlier action and knocked Winship to the ground. Winship hastened to Edmund Quincy, a justice of the peace, and pressed charges. Within the day, Riley appeared, pled guilty, and was fined thirteen shillings for the offence and court costs. When he stated that he was unable to pay, Quincy released him under the security of John Phillips, a sergeant in the 14th, until the next day. Riley returned as promised, and when asked whether he was ready to pay his fine, he retorted that "he would not pay it." As Quincy prepared the paperwork to incarcerate Riley, Lieutenant Alexander Ross of the regiment, an acquaintance of the judge, walked in and unsuccessfully attempted to convince Quincy to remit the fine. A large number of soldiers (Quincy estimated twenty) who planned to stage a rescue if needed already were gathered in the street. As Ross prepared to leave, Quincy ordered him to control his men to avoid a riot. Ross claimed he was unable, and at that moment Riley made for the door (whether encouraged by Ross is unclear). The constable Peter Barbour, with the assistance of a few Boston residents, attempted to restrain Riley but were forced back by soldiers with drawn swords. The defendant made his escape and was not seen again. Four soldiers and Ross later were fined for their roles in the episode.[17]

Few offenses could be more disturbing to the populace and more damaging to the reputation of the regiments than attacks on women, and the *Journal of the Times* was full of such accounts. For the most part, these were cases of sexual harassment. Soldiers insulted and made lewd comments to passing women. When they stopped or followed women or if a man escorted a woman, the possibility of violence increased. One evening a householder, "hearing the cries of two women in the night, who were rudely treated by some soldiers, ventured to expostulate with them" and for his troubles received a blow from a musket. On another evening soldiers knocked down a sea captain who had objected to rude comments directed at two "married women" he was accompanying. On several occasions women who were being harassed took refuge in neighboring houses, only to have the offending soldier enter the premises and wound the "master of the house" who had come to their defense. Women also were the victims of beatings (by cutlasses, bayonets, fists, and muskets) and would-be abductions. Soldiers attempted to drag women into barracks and sailors to pull them onto ships, but there is no record of a successful kidnapping.[18]

In some instances, the *Journal* may have exaggerated or fabricated stories, but it is equally likely that women who were attacked or raped kept quiet. The near absence of rape charges is striking. There is only a single account of an attempted rape. One April evening, a soldier spied an "aged woman" sitting by a table on the ground floor of her home. He entered and seeing a Bible beside her commended her piety. After a short discussion of religious topics, he "acquainted her that he had a bad swelling on his hip, and should be glad of her advice." While she was replying, he grabbed her shoulders, flung her to the floor, and attempted to rape her. Her "resistance and screams" prompted him to flee before neighbors arrived. As he left he managed to steal some clothes she was washing and ironing, the source of her livelihood. She filed a complaint with Judge Ruddock. The only reported rape in all the pages of the *Journal* offered scant evidence of a soldier's involvement. On the morning of June 27, Sarah Johnson collapsed and died on her way to the market. The jury of inquest upon the testimony of physicians concluded that she had been raped and beaten, allegedly by "soldiers unknown," three days before, "which probably was the cause of her death." That was the entire account. Both the *Boston Evening-Post* and *Boston Gazette* offered the same narrative, nearly word for word, but the administrative-leaning *Boston Chronicle*, *Massachusetts Gazette*, and *Boston Post Boy,* despite publishing other tales of unnatural deaths, left this one out.[19]

Better substantiated were the robberies, burglaries, and thefts that resulted from the onslaught of the four regiments on the town. Three soldiers hailed a citizen on the street and robbed him of his money after he refused to acknowledge their command. Another soldier mugged the journeyman of a silversmith and took what coins he had. Troops burgled a shop and stole leather. A soldier and two "Negroes" broke into Michael Malcom's house and removed a variety of silver objects. In midwinter local newspapers warned Bostonians not to purchase wood or ashes from soldiers, because of the likelihood that the wood had been stolen. In a rare laudatory account, the military received compliments for helping to extinguish a fire in the new county jail. "The officers & Army behaved extremely clever on this Occasion & ought to have the Publick thanks of this town," John Rowe confided to his diary and probably expressed in person to the officers. Even the *Boston Gazette* grudgingly acknowledged that the soldiers and sailors had been "very serviceable in assisting and relieving the inhabitants." The bad news for the military was that one of the three culprits who had set the fire to escape their second-floor cell was a soldier and a convicted thief.[20]

The townspeople of Boston were not merely passive bystanders during the occupation. Often the victims of abuse, they were sometimes also the instigators. Despite the popular movement's tactic of "no mobs," individuals and groups (ranging from a few people to perhaps as large a gathering as thirty residents) attempted to intimidate and even torment the troops in their midst.

Conspicuous targets were sentries posted at various guard stations, barracks, officers' dwellings, and imperial buildings throughout the town. Sometimes in response to an inquiry of a passerby's identity or an order for companions to disperse, sometimes from the sheer pleasure of taunting authority, sometimes out of inebriation, and sometimes out of malice, Boston citizens heckled the intruders. "Bloody backed Scoundrel," "Lobster," "Thieving Dog," "Red Herring," and various combinations, they jeered. Often the epithets carried a political message. "Damn the King, Damn the Governor, Officers and Soldiers," sentries and other redcoats were told. "They had no business" in Boston and no right to command its citizens. Snowballs, chunks of ice, stones, and brickbats frequently accompanied the angry words.[21]

Sergeant of the guard Thomas Smilie of the 29th Regiment witnessed at least four of these incidents. One evening at about 9:30, Cornelius Murphy, a private attached to Smilie's guard, paced before the residence of Lieutenant Colonel Maurice Carr. A number of men approached, and two of them headed toward the colonel's door. Murphy interceded and demanded their purpose. They answered that they "wanted to get

Revenge on some more of the bloody back Rascals." The sentry pushed them back with the butt of his musket and told them to move on or face more severe consequences. When a large stone narrowly missed him, he raised his gun to frighten the culprit. The man cowered, but others taunted Murphy to fire. At this impasse, Carr and his adjutant appeared and quelled the disturbance.[22]

Private William Godson had a similar experience. As he was standing sentry before one of the barracks of the 29th one dark night, several townspeople crept into the yard of an adjacent residence and began throwing stones, breaking some barracks' windows. Godson ordered them to desist. Without a response they left the yard and assembled before Godson, shaking sticks in his direction and prompting him to call for the sergeant of the guard. Confronted by cries that they "had no Right to Keep Sentry's there" and abusive language, Sergeant Smilie tried to cool their temper. Despite their retorts that they had "a better Right there than him or his Bloody Back Rascals," they eventually left without further damage.[23]

Smilie repeated his performance in April 1769, coming to the rescue of a sentry who had left his post before a barracks gate to avoid stones and other airborne objects. Leaving the guardhouse the sergeant positioned himself before the crowd and asked their intent. "You Bloody Back Rascals," was shouted in response, "our Town is free, We will have no Soldiers in it but our Selves, which we think better Soldiers than You." Smilie called out the guard to disperse them, only to have the townspeople return a short while later.[24]

In June, roughly three months after a bloody altercation with soldiers in front of his father's home, John Ruddock Jr. led a group of stone-throwing provocateurs. When Smilie entreated them to stop, he was met with the angry rejoinder that they would "Either Kill or be Killed" before they would go away. Grabbing the young Ruddock and hoping his father would calm the situation, Smilie held him until Judge Ruddock arrived in his chaise. Contrary to Smilie's expectation, the magistrate was furious and swore there would be retribution. He made clear that the sergeant should watch his back when away from the barracks.[25]

Smilie's encounters with Bostonians were threatening but stopped short of violence. Private John Timmons wasn't so fortunate. Between 9:00 and 10:00 in the evening of June 14, 1769, Timmons was at his sentry post before the main guard when a stone or brickbat struck him, causing him to fall. Upon recovering he heard a woman shout "Murder" and that the "rogues" had departed toward the Old South Church, a few blocks south. Other unknown voices called the woman a "whore" and instructed her to remain silent. Not recognizing that it was a set-up, Timmons left his post and rushed after the men. Rounding the corner of the church, he was immediately battered by clubs, dragged along the street, and kicked. Only the sounds of the approaching main guard drove off the assailants, wigmakers John Reed, Josiah Davis, and John Paymount. A Mr. Winslow, who resided nearby, brought the bleeding Timmons into his home until the regimental doctor attended to him.[26]

The assault on Timmons was unusual. Sentries might expect occasional verbal abuse and errant objects, but rarely concerted physical attacks. Away from the relative safety of guard houses and barracks, however, individual soldiers and even a group of three or four had to be wary, particularly after dark. Harassment was common enough, but, according to soldiers' depositions taken the summer after they left Boston, bodily attacks occurred at least once during most months of the occupation. In November 1768 as Corporal William Lake was walking in the North End at about 7 p.m., a townsman clubbed him to the ground. In April 1769 several residents struck Private William Banks and told him that "he nor any of his Cloth had any business in Boston." On July 14, 1769, a number of Bostonians knocked Corporal Robert Balfour to the ground and, while he was lying there, told him they would have done the same to his colonel.[27] And so it went.

On Christmas Day Corporal John Shelton and Privates James Botham and William Mabbot were walking along a street in the North End when Shelton was knocked down. The three of them quickly realized they were outnumbered and in danger. Ducking into a shop they were fortunate that the owner directed them along a back way to their barracks.[28]

Not even the Common in broad daylight was secure for Corporal William Halam. Recuperating from an illness he had stepped outside the hospital next to the Common only to be struck by sticks and called "a bloodyback'd rascal." May 29, 1769, proved to be a bad day not only for Halam but for any British troops on Boston Common. Five other soldiers in three separate incidents also were driven from the area. On June 4 Halam, still recovering at the hospital, went for a walk on the Common and was again beaten up. Perhaps Halam was a troublemaker or simply unlucky, for five months later a number of townspeople attacked him as he was striding to his barracks and stole his hat and bayonet.[29]

Sergeants William Jones and Richard Pearsall had hoped for a pleasant summer's day away from Boston. They had been issued passes for a trip across the Charles River to Charlestown. Jones brought his wife and child. Aboard a ferry for their return they observed a horseman trying to force his way on the craft. Jones volunteered that the ferry was so crowded the boatman already had turned away would-be passengers. The horseman, in frustration and probably at the sight of Jones's military garb, damned the sergeant as a "Rascal" and a "Scoundrel," whipped him with a riding crop, and also whipped his wife. Other "Inhabitants" grabbed Pearsall's collar, tore his shirt, and hit him several times. The situation might have turned more grave had not "some Gentlemen" intervened.[30]

Jones and Pearsall sought legal action. They first contacted Colonel Carr, who ordered them to lodge their complaint with Major General Alexander Mackay. Mackay asked for witnesses, and the "gentlemen" who had interceded on the ferry substantiated Jones and Pearsall's account. The general rewarded the sergeants with half a pound each for their good behavior but advised them "to drop all prosecution as no redress would be obtained for A Soldier in Boston." That was the conclusion of several soldiers who tried to bring townspeople to trial for assault. Even John Timmons—armed with the names of the three wigmakers who had lured him away from his post and beaten him— couldn't find a magistrate who would issue a warrant.[31]

Bostonians often couldn't convince British officials to prosecute soldiers, and the troops were unable to persuade local magistrates to bring residents to trial. Few altercations between members of the occupying regiments and citizens of Boston, regardless of who was responsible, resulted in justice. Soldiers' anger grew, townspeople felt increasingly alienated from the representatives of British power and from the empire itself, and the threat of violence lingered as close as an inadvertent bump in the street.

When the Massachusetts House of Representatives last had met the previous July, there had been no concerns over soldier or citizen misconduct and retaliation. Although there were a few naval ships in Boston Harbor, most conspicuously the *Romney*, there were no troops in town. British trade and tax policies had undermined the Bostonians' shaky economy and fragile rights, the commissioners and their subordinates remained prickly irritations, and Governor Francis Bernard and his Crown colleagues proved more devoted to the advancement of their careers and fortunes than to the well-being of colonists. But there were no troops. Now redcoats crowded the streets of Boston, and two cannon were aimed at the Town House entrance.

Before the legislature resumed sessions on May 31, 1769, nearly a year after it had been dissolved, Bernard had lobbied for structural change in the Massachusetts government. He believed that certain Bostonians should be punished for instigating the Convention and that the government should be transformed so as to be more responsive to British dictates. Specifically he argued that the Crown should appoint the Council rather than its being an elective body in order to bolster the governor and British policy and that Parliament should remove seated judges and appoint new justices on the grounds that the local magistrates had not enforced the Mutiny Act in accordance with Parliament's wishes. Bernard also identified nine Bostonians as deserving of special punishment. For their participation in calling the Massachusetts Convention, the moderator of the town meeting (James Otis), the town's selectmen (Joseph Jackson, John Ruddock, John Hancock, John Rowe, and Samuel Pemberton), the town clerk (William Cooper), and the speaker and clerk of the Convention (Thomas Cushing and Samuel Adams) should be barred from "setting in the Assembly or holding any Place of Office during his Majesty's Pleasure." The House of Lords encouraged the king to investigate whether treason had been committed, but otherwise Bernard's suggestions went unheeded.[32]

The Massachusetts legislature was unaware of Bernard's proposals, but nonetheless opened the session already angry with the governor and outraged by the presence of troops. Bernard's heavy-handed dealings strengthened the alliance between the Council and the House. For the time being, the assembly focused on the troops. Immediately the House declared that warships in the harbor, troops in the town, and cannon pointed at the door of the very building in which they deliberated were an affront to their dignity and an obstacle to free, legislative proceedings. They requested that Bernard accordingly remove the military outside of the port and town during the duration of the session. Governor Bernard, in response, claimed he had no authority to do so and soon thereafter rejected eleven of the candidates for Council seats, selected by the House and the past year's Council.[33]

With few options available to alter Bernard's position, the House chose to do nothing. Literally. It would not act on ordinary business, such as authorizing the payment for the provincial debt and the salaries of government officials. One of the few exceptions to its inactivity was the resolution to organize a celebration of the king's birthday. Previously the governor had invited the Council and House to the festivities, but this time the legislature seized the initiative. Joined by "a great Number of Merchants and Gentlemen of the first Distinction," representatives made toasts to "The King, Queen and Royal Family," "The Restoration of Harmony between Great-Britain and the Colonies," and a series of British allies and republican heroes.[34] Fueled by alcohol, they loudly demonstrated their loyalty to the king and their disdain for Francis Bernard.

Two weeks into the session, hoping to break the impasse or at least to strengthen public support, the House replied to the governor's disclaimer of authority to remove troops and ships. It was a peculiar situation: the people's representatives advocated greater power for the Crown's appointee while he dodged the responsibility. Attacking on several fronts, the House reasoned that the justification for the occupation was invalid, for the town had been misrepresented as rebellious. Boston, like other "populous Cities," experienced disturbances from time to time, but its citizens remained dutiful and loyal subjects. The governor, moreover, as the "King's Lieutenant, Captain-General and Commander in Chief," had command over "all Officers, civil and military, within this Colony." If the highest civil official in the province had no control over the military, concluded the House, they truly lived in a despotic state. The armed forces in their midst had no checks; their power was absolute.[35]

The increasingly impatient Bernard, who knew he was soon returning to England, had no desire to engage in a debate and merely repeated that he had "no Authority to give Orders for the Removal of the King's Ships out of the Harbour, or his Troops out of the Town." Two weeks of legislative inactivity had been a waste of time and money ("upwards of five Hundred Pounds lawful"). If the troops prohibited the assembly from the freedom of open deliberation, he had a remedy. He would move the General Court across the Charles River from Boston to Cambridge, where there was no military presence. And that is what he did. As soon as the legislative session transferred out of Boston, the two cannon opposite the Town House—provocative symbols of might and oppression—were removed and shipped to Halifax.[36]

The change of venue did little to alter the discourse. The House continued to provide arguments against troops being stationed in Boston; Bernard continued to call for the legislature to address public business. When the House resolved that should it resume regular responsibility it was doing so through necessity and not establishing precedent, the governor briefly may have imagined the logjam had been broken. But more days passed, and the assembly still took no action. With nothing better to do and aware of Bernard's impending departure, four weeks into the session the House once again petitioned the king for his dismissal. The next day Bernard pointedly reminded the legislature that at the king's request he would soon leave for the mother country "to lay before him the State of this Province" and needled it with the possibility that his absence would be temporary. That presented too large and irresistible a target for the House to ignore, and it mockingly approved his assignment. "We are bound in Duty at all times," it wrote the governor, "and we do more especially at this Time chearfully acquiesce in the lawful Command of our Sovereign." The House was heartened that the king, once he learned the true state of the province and the grievances it held, "will in his great Clemency and Justice frown upon and for ever remove from his Trust all those who by wickedly misinforming his Ministers, have attempted to deceive even his Majesty himself." The legislators had no expectation that Bernard ever would be governor again.[37]

Nearly six weeks into the legislature's inactive session, Bernard belatedly, and perhaps reluctantly, laid before the body the expenses for quartering and provisioning the troops. He offered an account of past expenditures and a requisition for future charges. Six days later there was no word from the House. More politely than before, Bernard notified the assembly that he needed an answer. He distinguished between expenses that belonged to the Crown and those that were the responsibility of the province according to parliamentary law.[38]

Members of the House were well aware that they must make a decision and inform the governor. First, however, they decided to have some fun. Castle William, where the commissioners and their families had resided for four and a half months, was provincial property. The House resolved that the commissioners owed Massachusetts fifty-four pounds, four shillings in rent. Fully aware of how Parliament had treated New York when its legislature balked at paying military expenses, representatives then debated how they should respond to Bernard's request and to the

Mutiny Act. The usual quibbles with process and the letter of the law prefaced their determination, a resounding negative. The Mutiny Act was "the most excessively unreasonable" of all the recent "Regulations." Since assemblies had no control over expenditures, there was a potentially bottomless pit. "For in Effect," the House declared, "the yet *free* Representatives of the *free* Assemblies of North-America are called upon, to repay of their own and their Constituents Money, such Sum or Sums as *Persons* over whom they can have no *Check* or *Controul* may be pleas'd to *expend!*" If they were free representatives, they had the right to judge what was a reasonable expense. Complying with the Mutiny Act would forfeit their freedom. Foiled for the last time, Bernard prorogued the General Court.[39]

Contrary to his assertions, Bernard—unexpectedly—had been given the power to remove all the troops from Boston. In early June General Gage sent him orders for dispatching the 64th and 65th Regiments to Halifax. Hillsborough, allowing for the possibility of total withdrawal, had earlier suggested to Gage that two regiments depart from Boston but had left it to the general's discretion to determine how many troops should go altogether. Since his fall visit to Boston, Gage had suspected that the military was unnecessary for protecting British officials. He had viewed the call for the extralegal Massachusetts Convention as a potential act of rebellion and had wanted the army to display Britain's might to would-be rebels. That objective now accomplished, Gage preferred to remove all four regiments from the hostile environment of Boston.[40]

The general could have ordered the departure of the entire military force, but he was a cautious man who avoided making controversial or risky decisions on his own. When he wrote to Bernard with the orders for the 64th and 65th, he asked whether all of the troops should leave. The governor, on the advice of the commissioners and others, urged that the 14th and 29th be retained for the sake of British officials and their allies. "And yet if the Troops are removed," he wrote, justifying his decision to Lord Barrington, "the principal Officers of the Crown, the friends of Government, & the importers of goods from England in defiance of the Combination, who are considerable & numerous must remove also."[41] As he offered the same explanation to Gage, Bernard was well aware that he would soon be sailing for England. His and his family's safety was not at stake, and he had the opportunity to depart with unusual goodwill. Perhaps he genuinely believed that the commissioners and others were in danger without military protection. Or perhaps he relished one last chance to thwart his detractors.

By late June the two regiments prepared to depart in piecemeal fashion. On June 21, the 65th Regiment embarked from Castle William and three days later set sail for Halifax. Along with General Alexander Mackay and Commodore Samuel Hood, Bernard overreacted to some routine resolutions of the assembly that aired its grievances and held back the departure of the 64th. Eventually their alarm subsided. Four companies left on July 11, with the remainder of the 64th Regiment leaving aboard the *Romney* on July 25.[42]

And finally the eagerly anticipated exit of Governor Francis Bernard arrived. He bid farewell to his residence on July 31 and spent the night at Castle William. In the morning he took a small craft to the *Rippon*, and it weighed anchor around 10 o'clock. Fifteen cannon fired salute as the ship's sails filled with wind. Bernard must have sighed with relief that his ordeal was over and that he had conducted himself with the dignity befitting his office. But after a mile or so, the wind died. The *Rippon* was in the Boston doldrums. It took three days before the breezes pushed her into the Atlantic at last, during which Bernard became a captive spectator to the joyous celebrations ashore. St. George's flags suddenly appeared on the Liberty Tree and on Hancock's wharf, streamers "flung out" from merchant ships in the harbor and from rooftops, bells rang throughout the town, and small cannon fired jubilantly until sunset. As darkness set in, bonfires were lit on Fort Hill "in plain sight of the ship, whence Sir Francis had the satisfaction to witness the festivity of the people at his departure," and on a hill at Charlestown. Soon the countryside was filled with light, as other towns joined the celebration.[43]

Executive authority transferred to Thomas Hutchinson, who was sworn in as acting governor. The honor fulfilled Hutchinson's life-long ambition, but he was sufficiently astute to recognize the difficulties that lay ahead, even for a native son. Nearly a year earlier, Andrew Eliot had anticipated the shift of power and questioned whether Hutchinson was wise to accept. "He is, I believe," Eliot wrote, "a sincere friend to his country; but in the present situation of things, it will not always be easy to determine what is right and best. A Governor must obey orders from home, however disagreeable to the people, or even to himself; and it will be quite impossible to give satisfaction on both sides the water."[44] Here was the opportunity for Hutchinson to prove his mettle, to avoid the landmines laid by all sides, and to restore harmony with the mother country. He had baggage, he had made mistakes, and the situation may have been impossible for anyone to resolve, but Hutchinson welcomed a new beginning, even with a thousand soldiers still patrolling the streets of Boston.

With the troop level cut in half and the detested Bernard gone, the annual commemoration of the uprising against the Stamp Act on August 14 was particularly festive and well attended. The ranks of the Sons of Liberty had swelled to the point that nearly any well-to-do man who opposed the occupation, trade regulations, and Parliament-instigated taxes was a member. About 11 o'clock in the morning a crowd of Sons of Liberty gathered around the Liberty Tree and proposed fourteen toasts. As usual, the first toast to the king demonstrated the participants' loyalty to the empire. The remainder honored heroes and abused the "Traducers of America." Because of its novelty, the most noteworthy toast called for "An honest Successor to the late abandoned Fugitive [Bernard]." But the day demanded more, and 355 of the assembled Sons of Liberty climbed into 139 carriages and rode to the Liberty-Tree Tavern in nearby Dorchester. Sheltered by a tent, they dined amid flapping streamers, lively music, and occasional cannon fire. Then more toasts, forty-five in all, were in order. Desiring to return home in some stage of consciousness, they restrained themselves to a bumper (a full glass) for the first toast and "as moderately as each Gentleman inclined" for the succeeding forty-four. By 5 o'clock in the early evening, they formed a wobbly procession that "extended near a Mile and a half" for the return trip. On reentering Boston, they circled the Town House and "retired each to his own House." Both the *Boston Gazette* and the *Boston Evening-Post*, whose editors had attended, ambiguously concluded, "The Amusements of the Day were conducted with that Propriety and exact Decorum, which Gentlemen ever observe."[45]

This group was quite different from the Sons of Liberty who had opposed the Stamp Act. The association had evolved into a social club of wealthy and middling citizens. Among those who traveled to Dorchester were forty-nine graduates of Harvard College. Of the 148 whose occupations are known, seventy were merchants and thirty-one others, such as sea captains and shopkeepers, were connected to trade. Twenty-four were engaged in the professions of law, medicine, and education. Only twenty-two were artisans, and with few exceptions they were skilled craftsmen, including printers, braziers, and the silversmith Paul Revere. Their most common attribute was experience in town government. By the August 14 celebration 123 had held some town office, and 34 others would enter public service in the years soon after. Every current selectman was present, as were several Suffolk County justices and all four Boston representatives to the General Court. This was a well-networked group with thirteen clubs, often with overlapping membership, represented. The North End Caucus, the Merchants' Club, and the Masons (if the two lodges are combined) had at least twenty members each participate. Most were forty-five or younger, but their ages ranged from seventeen-year-old Andrew Henshaw to sixty-nine-year-old Richard Dana.[46] Conspicuously missing were lesser skilled artisans, such as Ebenezer Mackintosh, and laborers. Perhaps the "lower sort" took part in the morning's festivities, but they were almost entirely excluded from the afternoon's posh event. Those in attendance represented a broad cross-section of Boston's substantial citizens.

The significance of the event is how many mainstream Bostonians now identified themselves as Sons of Liberty. Bernard and the military occupation inadvertently brought together economic rivals and began to radicalize the population. Such a union was not permanent in all cases. Seventeen of the August 14 celebrators later became loyalists. But for the most part, Bostonians were changing. The occupation was taking its toll, and it would continue to do so. In the summer of 1769 the moderate minister Andrew Eliot reexamined his previous position. "I have sometimes given offence by opposing some measures among us which I thought rash," he wrote a British correspondent, "but I begin to think I have been mistaken. Every step the ministry takes, serves to justify our warmest measures—and it is now plain that if they had not had their hands full at home, they would have crushed the Colonies, and that, if we had not been vigorous in our opposition, we had lost all."[47] Eliot was not alone in holding these emerging and increasingly militant views.

Chapter 9

The Merchants and John Mein

With soldiers all around them, Bostonians had fewer options for over-turning Britain's trade and revenue policies than they had had during the Stamp Act crisis. Petitions to the king, the ministry, and Parliament clearly were ineffective, even when they were actually read. Intimidation of British officials had halted implementation of the Stamp Act, and nonimportation had pressured British manufactures to lobby for its repeal. But intimidation of customs agents no longer was an option, for it would justify the continuing presence of troops. Nonimportation, fortified by consumers' willingness not to purchase prohibited goods and by the enlargement of domestic manufacturing, therefore appeared to be the only recourse open to loyal subjects. Reluctantly merchants and traders agreed to stop importing British goods, though not indefinitely or without exceptions. Rather than insist on a boycott until Parliament terminated all duties, they limited the Nonimportation Agreement to the period from January 1769 to the end of December 1769, and they exempted a few commodities, primarily items needed for fishing.

Major merchants prepared in advance. They had the means, and at least some of them the ruthlessness, to stockpile during late 1768 and to gouge consumers as products became scarce. Many also welcomed the opportunity to retrench from mounting debts resulting from the trade imbalance with Great Britain. In 1768 the total value of exports from New England to Great Britain had been 89,000 pounds, whereas imports had been 441,000 pounds. By contrast, trade with the West Indies neatly balanced imports and exports, and profits made by commerce with southern Europe and Africa and particularly from shipping throughout the world provided the cash necessary to maintain the complex economy.

Merchants who were engaged in trade outside of Great Britain, and thus unaffected by the Nonimportation Agreement, and wealthy shipowners who transported other people's commodities, barred or not—a significant omission of the Agreement—stood to flourish. Domestic manufactures of proscribed British goods, such as paper, glass, and textiles, even thrived from their enterprises when demand increased.[1]

As is frequently the case in times of crisis, the burden of sacrifice was not equally distributed. While 1769 progressed and the shelves of less affluent traders grew bare, smaller merchants and shopkeepers faced financial ruin. Artisans, such as coopers, and laborers, such as dockworkers, became unemployed or underemployed; sailors scrambled for berths on merchant ships. In February one writer condemned what must have been a growing public grievance. He complained that some merchants were undermining the intent of the Nonimportation Agreement by ordering in advance "3 or 4 times as much goods as they would otherwise have done" or by continuing to import. The citizens of Boston shouldn't rely on the public spirit of all merchants; they must encourage local manufacturers and stop purchasing proscribed items. He shrewdly advised, "If we don't buy, our merchants will not import," and if they don't import, British policy must change.[2]

Advertisements in Boston newspapers supported his argument. In March 1769 there were nearly as many advertisements from retailers as there had been the previous October, and they featured such items for sale as tea, British textiles, housewares, and the all-encompassing "English and India goods." Several ads, though fewer than before, assured the consumer that the products had been "just imported."[3] The time frame of "just imported" was ambiguous. (Did the phrase mean "immediately" or "recently"? 1768 or 1769?) It could have meant the previous day; for although 211 merchants and traders signed the Nonimportation Agreement, there were no penalties for violations, whether committed by a signer or a nonsigner. That was but one of several loopholes that weakened the measure's objectives. An importer, truthfully or not, might claim that weather or some other unforeseen circumstance had delayed a shipment that should have arrived before the Agreement went into effect. Without knowing when a prohibited item had reached Boston, a consumer might unwarily purchase it under the assumption that it had arrived in a timely fashion. Merchants and shopkeepers did not post dated manifests on their store windows, and consumers who keenly wanted specific articles might throw suspicion aside. And there was the lingering question of how much was too much. Was a small chest of barred goods a violation? Was a single piece of British linen a violation? Were twenty pieces? Should small amounts be ignored? What was the upper limit of "small"? Until there was enforcement of the Nonimportation Agreement with penalties, answers to those questions had little consequence.

Finally, on April 21 the merchants (almost certainly assisted by nonmerchants from the opposition movement) formed a committee of seven to investigate the level of compliance with the Nonimportation Agreement. Six days later the committee reported that five or six persons had acknowledged infringements and agreed to place the proscribed goods in warehouses supervised by the merchants' association. The merchants appointed another committee to confer with nonsigners who had imported barred commodities.[4]

On May 2, after a report by the second committee, the body of merchants concluded that only six of the 211 signers of the Agreement had broken their word "through Inattention," by neglecting to countermand their orders placed in the fall, and that they now had rectified their dereliction. On the whole, nonsigners had complied, "except six or Seven Persons, whose Importations appeared to be as usual." The association then voted to publish the Agreement in Boston newspapers, to renew their pledge, and not to purchase goods from persons who continued to import from Great Britain. The Sons of Liberty reinforced the merchants with an article in the *Boston Gazette* advocating that people cease all transactions with violators of the Agreement. They may also have been the authors of the handbills posted throughout the town that named those who persisted in engaging in the prohibited trade.[5] Now that the culprits were identified, consumers no longer had the excuse of ignorance, and they might be accused of unpatriotic behavior were they observed doing business with the "enemy."

Although not one of the named himself, the editor of the *Boston Chronicle*, John Mein, leaped to their defense by challenging the integrity of the signers. According to Mein (who had acquired from the commissioners or their subordinates manifests of ships from Great Britain that had docked in Boston since January 1), 190 people had imported large numbers of trunks, bales, cases, hogsheads, casks, and other containers of goods on twenty-seven different ships. He knew the identity of the importers, "many of whose names appear in the subscription for non importation," but because "it is a most inhuman and insidious measure to publish the names of persons with design to injure them" he would refrain from doing so. Should fellow citizens doubt the authenticity of his claims, they could view the "list of importers" at his office.[6] The implication was that signers were every bit as guilty of violating the Nonimportation Agreement as were those listed in the handbills and that the merchants' association was discriminating in favor of its friends—or at least those who played the game properly—to the disadvantage of longtime foes, such as the sons of Thomas Hutchinson.

It was a clever piece of counterpropaganda. There was no way to determine whether the imported goods were proscribed, or whether signers had behaved hypocritically, or whether there was any information not already taken into account by the merchants' committees. But the discerning reader who had fulfilled his civic obligations to his financial detriment or who refrained from purchasing coveted articles for the well-being of the community must have become skeptical, perhaps angry.

Why Mein entered the fray at this point is unclear. He had lived in Boston for less than five years, and the *Boston Chronicle*, which he published with John Fleeming, had existed for only a year and a half. For the most part, his newspaper, more than any other Boston publication, focused on foreign affairs; and although it sympathized with the Bernard administration and British policy more than did the *Boston Evening-Post* or the more radical *Boston Gazette*, it was more centrist than the mouthpiece of the administration, the *Massachusetts Gazette*. Mein was thirty-two years old when he migrated to Boston from his native Edinburgh. He came with sufficient funds or credit to establish a bookstore, a circulating library, and a printing firm. The bookstore was well stocked, and it remained politically neutral enough for John Adams to frequent the premises comfortably.[7] It is possible that enlarging his enterprise with a newspaper may have stretched him financially and made him vulnerable to suggestions from the commissioners and their friends, but few disputed that he had a hot temper and strong convictions.

The first clear indication of Mein's volatile temperament came in January 1768, soon after he had launched the *Boston Chronicle*. Its first issue contained a piece criticizing William Pitt, a politician with plenty of warts but a favorite of Boston's opposition movement. In a fairly innocuous article, "Americus" in the *Boston Gazette* countered that Pitt was a defender of American freedom and should not be disparaged, and he questioned whether the *Chronicle* was maintaining the neutrality it proclaimed in its prospectus. Almost as an aside, he suggested that Mein and Fleeming's newspaper had a "Jacobite" cast (basically meaning it favored the ministry).[8]

The ink for "Americus'" piece was barely dry when John Mein stormed into the *Gazette*'s office, demanding to know the author's name. Benjamin Edes admonished him that as a printer he should know better than to ask "such an unpertinent, improper question." Too angry to care about journalistic ethics, Mein retorted that if Edes didn't divulge the author he would assume Edes was responsible "and the affair shall be decided in three minutes." Edes told him he was too busy and that Mein should return the following morning. The *Gazette*'s editor may have been stalling, or he may have sought the author's permission to reveal his identity, but in either case when Mein returned, Edes repeated that he would not give him the name. Mein challenged him to a fight and, after Edes declined, left the building. Unfortunately for John Gill, the *Gazette*'s coeditor, Mein encountered him on the street that evening and struck him with his cane. Gill retaliated with a lawsuit in which the jury found in his favor. After appeals Mein eventually paid seventy-five pounds (a substantial sum, roughly equivalent to twelve thousand dollars today) plus court costs for the pleasure of venting his temper.[9]

The attack on the merchants' association was more threatening to the popular movement than the caning of an editor. The Nonimportation Agreement hinged on the trust of merchants and consumers throughout the colonies, and suspicions could tear the thin fabric of opposition to British trade and tax policies. Hurriedly Boston merchants published a request for people "to suspend their Judgment," for "the Matter will shortly be set in a *true* light."[10]

One week after Mein's article appeared, the merchants answered the charges. They essentially responded that there was no news; they already had taken action against signers who had broken the Agreement, a small number of persons, by placing the proscribed goods "under the direction of the Committee." By combining all ships (including some that would have arrived before the end of 1768 but had been blown off course), all types of cargo (both items allowed, which constituted the bulk of the shipments, and barred articles), signers and nonsigners, Boston residents and inhabitants of other places, and traders and other people such as clergymen "who only had a single Article for their Family Use," Mein had distorted the record and created an impression not supported by the facts. The merchants defied Mein (or the people they suspected of being behind him) "to publish the Names of the Importers, the Quality of the goods imported, and to point out the particular Signers, if they can produce any, that have imported any other goods than what is above expressed."[11]

So matters stood during the next month and a half, while half the soldiers left Boston and Bernard prepared to depart. Fewer merchants and shopkeepers had merchandise to sell, and now their advertisements emphasized that they had complied with the Agreement. John Gore Jr. emphasized his "North American Manufactures"; Henry Lloyd sold "American cordage"; Thomas Walley proudly offered the "much admired New-England Flour Mustard" and paper "made in Milton"; and the sea captain Samuel Dashwood made clear that his products had been imported "last Fall."[12]

With rumors circulating that the ministry was about to repeal duties on glass, paper, and painters' colors so as to pacify British manufactures and to discourage those commodities being produced in America, the merchants chose to strengthen the Nonimportation Agreement. The boycott of prohibited goods would continue until all revenue acts were repealed, extending beyond 1769 if necessary. Shipowners no longer were free to transport banned articles owned by third parties. Those who breached the accord would have their names published in Boston newspapers, and there would be an additional subscription of consumers pledging not to purchase goods from violators. The merchants' committee pressured colleagues to sign the new agreement and convinced most of those traders who previously had been recalcitrant to place barred shipments under the care of the association. Not even John Rowe escaped censure for importing porter. Only a few importers refused to bend, and on August 14 their names were revealed to the public: Elisha and Thomas Hutchinson Jr., sons of Thomas Hutchinson; John Bernard, son of Francis Bernard; "Richard Clarke and Son"; Nathaniel Rogers; Theophilus Lillie; "James McMasters and Comp."; and John Mein.[13]

The furious roar that Bostonians soon heard (and must have anticipated) emanated from the sheets of Mein's *Boston Chronicle*. Believing that he had been unfairly designated as an importer, Mein fought back. He defended his own actions, attacked the perceived hypocrisy of his detractors, and in issue after issue throughout the remainder of the year published the cargo manifests of ships that had arrived from Great Britain after the Nonimportation Agreement went into effect on January 1. On August 17, in the first wave of his relentless editorial tsunami, he explained that in his multiple roles as printer, bookbinder, and bookseller he employed seventeen people, "fourteen of whom live under my own roof." Whenever possible he purchased paper from manufactures in Milton, but they were unable to supply him fully. As a consequence, some of the paper he acquired came from Great Britain. No more than twenty pounds' worth of materials he and his employees used for bookbinding, however, was manufactured outside of Massachusetts. His business as a bookseller required importing books—a necessity for a civilized people—and he should be praised rather than persecuted. Mein's bottom line was this: if he should sign the Agreement and curtail his purchases from Great Britain, he would have to lay off most of his workers, and they would become destitute or a burden to the town.[14]

Struggling merchants and shopkeepers, artisans, laborers, and consumers must have felt some stirring of sympathy for this argument, and they must have resented being caught between the strictures of British revenue and tax policy and the pressures of Boston's nonimportation. But the daily presence of an occupying army as well as the detested commissioners and the customs service reminded most Bostonians who they were and whose side they were on. Mein, a recent immigrant from Scotland, hadn't developed such an attachment; he and his fellow Scots in Boston remained unswervingly loyal subjects to the Crown.

The manifests Mein published proved a greater threat to nonimportation and the popular movement than did his analyses. Mein detailed the cargoes of ships by importer, types of import, and quantity of goods. Readers could discover that the *Snow Pitt* carried twenty-four casks of shot, three hogsheads of line, and twelve bales of blankets and other supplies for John Rowe. As it turned out, the shot and line were exempted from the Agreement and the blankets and other goods were for the army, but there was the name John Rowe, a leading figure in the merchants' association. Just as before, Mein printed everything and didn't differentiate. In his net he caught John Hancock, a signer, and Thomas Hutchinson Jr., a nonsigner. Prohibited glass and linen appeared next to coal and salt, both allowed. People of Boston mingled with other residents of New England and beyond. Three of the six members of

Vol. II.
No. 134.

The Boston Chronicle

[285]

No. 120.

From THURSDAY August 17, to MONDAY August 21. 1769.

Copy of the Articles of Agreement concerning Non Importation, entered into and
signed August 1768.

First, That we will not send for or import from
Great Britain, either upon our own account, or upon commission; this fall, any other goods than what
are already ordered for the fall supply.

Secondly, That we will not send for or import
any kind of goods or merchandize from Great Britain, either on our own account, or on commission,
or any otherwise, from the 1st of January 1769,
to the 1st of January 1770. EXCEPT

Salt,
Coals,
Fish-Hooks,
Lines,
Hemp,
Duck,
Bar-Lead,
Shot,
Wool-Cards,
and Card-Wire.

Thirdly, That we will not purchase of any fac-
tor, or others, any kinds of goods imported from
Great Britain, from Jan. 1769, to Jan. 1770.

Fourthly, That we will not import, on our own
account, or on commission, or purchase of any who
shall import from any other Colony in America, from
January 1769, to Jan. 1770, any Tea, Glass, Paper,
or other goods commonly imported from Gr. Britain.

Fifthly, That we will not, from and after the
1st of January 1769, import into this province any
Tea, Paper, Glass, or Painters colours until the act
imposing duties on those articles shall be repealed.

To the PUBLIC. August 21th, 1769

HAVING learnt, the day after my last Publication, for the first time, that the
Chairman of the Merchants, really imported
goods from England, preceeding the year 1761,
I, with the utmost readiness, admit, during
the period of, his Importations, he ought to
be considered as a Merchant; but being now
occupied in a business so very different and
having created Importation entirely for many
years——however honourable he may be by
station, or however respectable in his business, as a Distiller, he can, at present, have
no title, even to the name of Merchant.

THE PUBLIC, will no doubt perceive, that
the cargoes of the vessels, are given without
regard to what was excluded from or included
in the Non-Importation agreements; a regard to
justice inducing me to lay the whole before
them——and as the penetration of the can
did readers must, often naturally, lead them
to secure to the articles, agreed upon August
1768, they are, for that purpose, inserted anew
in this paper.

That the "Well Disposed Merchants" who
took the Lead at the different Meetings, have
displayed ill grounded and pointed antipathy,
in my case, must appear evident, as well as
great partialities to others, when they allowed
so many respectable and so many large Importers, as were mentioned in our list and in this
Paper, to pass unnoticed.——A charge, which tho'
sufficiently obvious already, shall be more fully demonstrated in the course of this laborious,
yet necessary Undertaking.

Indeed these Few "Well Disposed" Leaders,
not only, acted unjustly, with regard to me,
who never was no considered myself in the
light of a Merchant; but they have also
imposed, upon the really well disposed part
of the Gentlemen present at these Meetings,
(who implicitly trusted to their information
and report), by exhibiting a partial list of the
Importers, and have since, by their Advertisement, attempted to impose on the Public
in general.

The Manifests of the three following Vessels will contribute greatly to place this in
a proper point of view.

Summary of the Cargo of the Snow Pitt, William Tapscott, Master, from Bristol, taken from the
Cockets and Manifest, sworn to by the Master, June 15, 1769.
List of Articles allowed to be imported by the Agreement, August, 1768.

By J. Rowe, D. and W. Hubbard, T. Russell,   270 Bars of Lead
to Order, Clark and Nightingale, J. Rotch   38 Casks of Shot
and Son, P. Frye, Wm. Tapscott.   5 Casks of Lines

List of Articles not allowed to be imported by the Agreement August, 1768.

27t Casks of Nails	6 Boxes Pipes	60 Sheets, 4 Cases, 2 Bot-
96 Casks Cheese	2 Boxes Pans	toms nine wrought Copper
70 Baskets Cheese	1 Box Buttons	1 Box Glass Ware
30 Casks Wrought Iron	289 Boxes, Half and Quarter	1 Package Brass Manufactory
14 Bales Woolens	Boxes Glass	5 Casks Pewter
24 Bundles Pans	16 Sides Glass	2 Casks Shoes
12 Packages Linen	61 Boxes, Bundles and 1	5 Bundles Spades
2 Hogsheads refined Sugar	Cask Tin Plates	3 Bundles Scythes
2 Packages Hats	52 Bundles Steel	1 Box Ribbons

IMPORTERS NAMES.

Timothy Newell,	N Sparhawk,	Mifflin and Company
John Rowe,	William Scott,	A. Usher,
George Erving,	Constant Freeman,	J. Royal,	Wm. Wilson
James Warden,	Ralph Inman,	Clark and Nightingale,	S. Sanford,
Rufus Green,	Andrew Brimmer,	J Rotch and Son,	Bennet and Company
Wm. Coffin junr.	John Cutler,	Thos. Robie,	Willing and Company
D. and W Hubbard	To Order	Peter Frye,	Wm. Perry,
D. Sylvester Gardiner,	All the above in Bos-	Folsom, & Co.	W. Tapscott.
Nathaniel Rogers,	ton.	E. Doane,	
	Eldridge Gerry,		

Of the above Articles those in Italic pay the new Duties here; the Names of the Importers of which
are also in Italick: For a distinct State of the whole, [See last Chronicle, Thursday August
17th 1769.

Manifest of the Cargo of the Brigantine Last Attempt, Nathaniel By-
field Lyde Master, from London, taken from the Cockets and Manifest, sworn to by the Master, April 10, 1769, which Day the Vessel was
entered at the Custom-House, Boston:—Owner, JOHN HANCOCK,
Esq;—The Coals were shipped, January 12, 1769, and the Rest of the
Cargo between the 26th January and the 3d February, 1769.

Marks.	Numbers.	Packages	Contents.	To whom Consigned.
T. P.		34 Casks	Cheese	
N B.		10 Boxes	Lemons	
R. M.		5 Chests	LEAD SHOT	Robert Moodie, Boston
		6 Barrels	Gunpowder	
R F.		3 Boxes.		Ralph Fisher	ditto
N. S.		1 Case		John Leverett	ditto
WP.		smatted Parcels		
O in a		Sheets 100lb LEAD		Edward Lyde	ditto
diamond		2 Barrels	Gunpowder	
		10 ditto	ditto	
N L.		2 Boxes		Nath. Byfield Lyde	ditto
		2 Casks		
B. L.		80 Casks	Gunpowder	Byfield Lyde Esq;	ditto
		63 Chaldrons	COALS	John Hancock Esq;	ditto
N. B. L.		15 Barrels	Gunpowder	
R. R.		5 ditto	Ditto	
W B.		15 ditto	Ditto	
		3 ditto	ditto	
J. S.		10 ditto	Ditto	Where the Contents of the
W. 00		5 ditto	Ditto	Packages in any of the Ma-
S		5 ditto	Ditto	nifests are not, mentioned the
		5 ditto	Ditto	Cockets were wanting.
N 4 C				
4 in a		10 ditto	Ditto	
diamond				

Manifest of the Cargo of the Brigantine Lydia, Joseph Hood, Master,
from London, taken from the Cockets and Manifest, sworn to by the
Master, April 18th, 1769, which Day the Vessel was entered at the
Custom-House, Boston:—Owner, JOHN HANCOCK, Esq;—The
Goods were shipped between the 5th January and 12th February, 1769.

Mark.	No.	Packages.	Contents.	To whom consigned.
		50 Chaldron	COALS	
J. H.	1 to 5	5 Bales	100 pieces British Li-	John Hancock Boston
			nen	
W. B.		1 Cask	500 weight wrought	Wm. Bowes ditto
			iron	
T. G.	1, 2.	2 Bales	218t ells German and	Thomas Gray ditto
			570 ells Russia Linen	
		50 Matts	100 pieces Russia Duck	
			4 pieces British and Irish	
			Linen	
			57ells Russia Linen	
D. M.		1 Trunk	7 pieces Callicoe	Daniel M'Carty
			2 pieces long Cloth	
			4 pieces Taffities	
			7 pieces British Linen	
		1 Trunk	3 pieces Stuff and Ha-	
			berdashery	
		2 Trunk	48 pieces Stuff	

Boston Chronicle, front page of August 21, 1769 issue. Ships' manifests, much
to the chagrin of many prominent merchants, dominated the newspaper and
continued to do so throughout the late summer and fall.

the merchants' steering committee and five of twenty-four members of other merchant committees were listed in the first two and a half weeks of published manifests alone. Before he was through, Mein printed hundreds of names, including those of forty-six men who attended the Sons of Liberty celebration that August.[15]

The merchants' association clearly could not leave those insinuations unanswered, but its initial response was weak at best. Rather than analyze the manifest of the *Snow Pitt* that Mein printed on August 17 and offer a benign interpretation, the organization examined the cargo of a Captain Scott's ship that had recently docked. The account may have been more current and more appropriate to conditions as of August, but by not countering Mein directly it was unconvincing.[16]

Still, there were signs that pressure from the supporters of nonimportation was working. Richard Clark and Son capitulated. In exchange for having his firm's name removed from the public register of nonimportation violators whom consumers should shun (a group that the *Boston Gazette* featured in the upper left corner of its first page in every issue beginning August 28), Clark agreed to abide by the association's restrictions and to store prohibited goods under its supervision. Another breakthrough was the agreement of auctioneers not to sell any goods or merchandize that may have been imported in defiance of the Agreement.[17] But these indications of success were not sufficient to neutralize the potential harm of Mein's published manifests, particularly when they presented Boston's most prominent merchant, John Hancock, in an unflattering light.

In the August 21 issue of the *Boston Chronicle* all three published manifests were from ships owned by Hancock, and Mein identified him as the importer of "100 pieces British Linen" (constituting five bales), a substantial amount of a proscribed commodity. Not willing to wait a week for the next issue of the friendly *Boston Gazette*, Hancock's chief subordinate, William Palfrey, rushed a rejoinder into the *Massachusetts Gazette* three days later. Because Hancock was "out of the Province," Palfrey took the responsibility of defending his reputation. "The Man who seeks the Welfare of his Country," Palfrey reasoned, "cannot fail to render himself obnoxious to those who are using every Artifice in their Power to enslave it." It was all a misunderstanding perpetuated by Mein, who intended to mislead people "who are ignorant of the Nature of British Manufactures." The one hundred pieces of British linen were in fact one hundred pieces of Russian duck, an exempted textile, and customs officials in Britain frequently labeled "duck" as "linen" in the cockets they signed. Taking no chances that readers might note that Thomas Gray's imports in the same manifest were described as "Russia Duck" (a confusing inconsistency, if that, of a customs agent), Palfrey had several "gentlemen" inspect the invoice and three of the bales, and he declared under oath before a justice of the peace that all five bales were Russian duck.[18]

Mein retaliated by printing the entries of British linen attested to by George Hayley, Hancock's business associate in England, and customs officials in England and Boston, slyly inquiring whom one should believe. "This affair then at present rests between Mr. Hayley, a Merchant in London of great character and extensive business, and Mr. William Palfrey, clerk to Mr. Hancock," Mein rhetorically concluded. Hancock wanted no more scrutiny. More than a month after he and other merchants agreed not to ship proscribed goods for third parties and shortly after the exchange between Palfrey and Mein, he finally instructed his British associates to prevent all goods "except Coals, Hemp, Duck & Grindstones being put on board any of my vessels."[19] With that, Hancock was in full compliance. Mein had hoped to discredit his opponents, but inadvertently his public exposures in fact strengthened the Nonimportation Agreement.

Recognizing the need for a thorough and timely explanation of the printed manifests, representatives of the merchants' association made a full, many-pronged assault on August 28 in both the *Boston Evening-Post* and the *Boston Gazette*. In essence, they argued that the manifests were old news that did not reflect the present. The ships had arrived in the spring, before the merchants' association had bolstered enforcement of the Agreement, and even then there were few violators. By August the importers who refused to cooperate had been publicly identified, and they constituted a small fraction of Boston's merchants and traders. The manifest of the *Snow Pitt* that had arrived on June 1, for example, showed thirty-one importers, only fifteen of whom were Boston residents. Four of those fifteen had signed the Nonimportation Agreement. Timothy Newell imported tin and iron plates, which at the time of the order were understood to satisfy the Agreement and later were specifically excluded from proscription. John Rowe imported shot and lines, exempted items, and consigned supplies for the army. George Erving imported linen and

A LIST of the Names of those who have AUDACIOUSLY counteracted the UNITED SENTIMENTS of the Body of Merchants throughout NORTH-AMERICA; by importing British Goods contrary to the Agreement.

John Bernard,
Nathaniel Rogers,
Theophilus Lillie,
James McMasters & Comp'y.
John Mein,
Thomas Hutchinson, Junr. and
Elisha Hutchinson.

Boston Gazette, upper left corner of front page of September 4, 1769, issue, displaying the names of nonimportation violators.

beer, a violation, but they arrived despite his countermanding the order and he had placed the merchandise under the association's care. The goods listed for Daniel and William Hubbard "were only directed to their care for Stephen Ayrault, a merchant at Newport."[20]

And so it went through the various manifests: mistakes, misunderstandings, and inaccuracies. The vast majority of the importers were nonsigners or residents of towns other than Boston. Many were not engaged in trade but had acquired a single item for their families, or were clergymen who had purchased books for themselves, Harvard College, or Indians. One thousand three hundred pieces of glass were in fact bottles of beer, which had been used as provisions on the ship or consigned to a Portsmouth merchant. "British linen" was English and Russian duck, "German linen" was small duck, and "turnery" was wool cards. Theirs was not a perfect response, but it went a long way toward their claim that signers of the Nonimportation Agreement were keeping their word and that opponents of the Agreement and of the popular movement once again were misrepresenting Boston citizens. In reply Mein merely demanded that the authors reveal their names; he made no attempt to rebut their analysis. The merchants' association, anticipating more publications and suspecting doctored information, applied to customs officials to see the official manifests but were denied.[21]

While Mein was skirmishing with Boston merchants, copies of letters the commissioners had sent to England during the *Liberty* episode in June 1768 surfaced. Justifying their part in seizing Hancock's ship and their retreat to the *Romney* and then Castle William, the commissioners had depicted Boston as riotous and insurrectionary. The letters reinforced impressions that misrepresentation had prompted the sending of troops and fueled rumors that popular leaders might be tried as rebels.[22]

The increasingly unstable James Otis became particularly agitated. On the morning of Friday, September 1, accompanied by Samuel Adams, he ventured to the meeting place of the board of commissioners and spoke with Henry Hulton and John Robinson. Refusing to step inside, he insisted that they meet elsewhere for undisclosed business. He may have had a fight in mind or he may have wanted only to clear his name by words, perhaps an apology. The following morning, at a coffee house, Otis had a brief conversation with Commissioner William Burch and a more extended—and unpleasant—exchange with Robinson. Over dishes of coffee, Otis sought to learn what the commissioners had written about him. Robinson didn't believe that Otis's name had appeared in the board's communications to the Treasury, but he thought it improper to divulge the contents of private letters. Otis complained that his character had been falsified and demanded justice, and Robinson, who could be as irascible as Otis was erratic, haughtily replied, "[I am] ready to give you the satisfaction you have a right to expect from a Gentleman."[23] And then they parted, for the day.

During the next few days Otis exhibited more signs of restlessness and a seething resentment. As he, Edes, Gill, the two Adamses, and others prepared the September 4 issue of the *Boston Gazette*, he talked endlessly. "Otis talks all," John Adams confided in his diary. "But he grows narrative, like an old Man. Abounds with Stories." The more Otis pondered the commissioners' letters, the angrier he became. He took to heart the insinuations that American colonists were "Traitors and Rebels" and lashed out in the *Gazette*, calling the commissioners "superlative blockheads" and focusing his wrath on John Robinson by asserting, "I have a natural right if I can get no other satisfaction to break his head." But words on the page provided him no catharsis. That evening at the Club, one of his social groups, his fury raged on, and he attacked all in sight and in mind. "There is no Politeness nor Delicacy, no Learning nor Ingenuity, no Taste or Sense in this Kind of Conversation," Adams wrote to himself. With his own strong sense of honor and outrage, Robinson, when he read Otis's threat, determined to achieve his own satisfaction.[24]

The confrontation came quickly the next evening. Otis and Robinson met at the British Coffee House, hardly a neutral site, for it was the favorite haunt of army and naval officers, customs officials, and their friends and allies (including John Mein). When Robinson entered the establishment between 7 and 8 o'clock, he noticed that Otis had no sword and so first went to another room, where he left his own. Both men had new walking sticks, Otis having purchased one identical to Robinson's, and both demanded satisfaction. Otis suggested they go outside to fight, but Robinson grabbed him by the nose, an indignity that demanded retaliation or the loss of honor, before he could go further. Immediately they struck each other with their sticks and continued to do so until bystanders grabbed the two men's weapons and encouraged them to fight with their fists.

Denizens of the Coffee House encircled the two combatants. John Gridley, a young friend of Otis, observed the struggle from outside. When Robinson's associates began to push and pull Otis, opening him to Robinson's blows, Gridley rushed in to prevent a pummeling. Someone grabbed Gridley's right shoulder, but he freed himself and took hold of the collar of Robinson's coat, which ripped to the pocket. Bystanders immediately struck Gridley on the head with their sticks, and one person hit him above the wrist, breaking his arm. In the general mayhem, people other than Robinson may have struck Otis as well, and someone purportedly shouted, "Kill him!" Robinson's allies tossed Gridley out of the Coffee House. He returned only to be thrown out again. Bleeding and with a disabled arm, Gridley entered a side door and found a stunned Otis. He accompanied Otis to the front room and had him sit for a few minutes, and then the two men, assisted by friends who arrived after the fight was finished, left for medical care. Robinson, fearing prosecution or worse, went into hiding. Despite a gash in Otis's forehead and Gridley's fractured arm, neither man sustained severe injuries, but that didn't stop rumors forming that Otis had survived an assassination attempt.[25]

William Browne, who reputedly struck Gridley and Otis, was the only one of Robinson's associates identified as having taken part in the brawl and thus became a scapegoat. He was detained the day after the fray and brought before two magistrates and two thousand angry Bostonians at Faneuil Hall that evening. James Murray, a Scottish merchant, friend of the court faction, owner of one of the warehouses where troops were barracked, and a recently minted justice of the peace, boldly marched into the assembly. As soon as he was recognized, some of the multitude wished to force him out, but Selectman Jonathan Mason, a prominent member of the popular party, proclaimed, "For shame, gentlemen, do not behave so rudely," and escorted Murray to the selectmen's section. Hisses greeted Murray, and he bowed in sarcastic reply. The ritual repeated itself, and then Murray took his seat. The justices invited Murray to join them, but he declined.

In short order, evidence was presented and Browne was bound over for trial. When the defendant was unable to post bail and no one else offered to help, Murray, while indicating to the judges that the gesture was not meant to imply that he exonerated Browne, paid the bail himself. As Murray attempted to leave the Hall, someone yanked off his wig, revealing his bald head. Members of the popular party quickly surrounded him to prevent further abuse. One of the group, Lewis Gray, made clear its concern: "No violence, or you'll hurt the cause." As they made their way out of Faneuil Hall, Murray's wig disdainfully danced on a stick close behind.[26]

Boston newspapers published eyewitness accounts for the next several weeks and Otis sued Robinson (a case that was settled years later, long after Robinson had departed from Boston), but the Otis-Robinson episode was only a brief diversion from the greater struggle to remove British troops and repeal British revenue measures. Robinson soon reemerged to marry Nancy Boutineau, the daughter of an affluent Boston lawyer, and there were no demonstrations against him. Townspeople again elected Otis the moderator of their meeting, as his service to the community neared its end and as he sank deeper into mental illness. But redcoats still patrolled the streets, maintained their guard posts, and harassed citizens, and customs agents still seized ships, confiscated cargoes, and enforced hated laws.[27]

John Mein continued being a prime adversary. Manifest after manifest, accompanied by editorial essays, flogged the Nonimportation Agreement in successive issues of the *Boston Chronicle*. Mein repeated his assertions that he was not a merchant and should not be lumped with people who made their living through importation, and that he and a few others had been unfairly singled out while others escaped public censure.

Whatever Mein's motives, he threatened the popular movement's efforts to reverse British policy. As individual merchants explained why their names appeared in the manifests, Mein, a self-appointed arbiter, praised those he believed and condemned those whose accounts didn't coincide with his assessment, or who ridiculed or attacked him in their own defense. He lauded Thomas Gray for "having acted with the candour and good manners becoming a gentleman of his fair character," Francis Johonnot for his clarity, and Benjamin Andrews for placing his name by his newspaper statement; he excoriated William Palfrey (John Hancock's surrogate) for his disingenuousness and Francis Green for "throwing out the most illiberal abuse, without the least shadow of argument." He was most effective when he raised potentially divisive questions: What goods were stored under the supervision of the merchants' committee? Where were they stored? What access did owners have to them? Who were the owners of those articles? Who were the signers of the Agreement? Everyone knew that repentant merchants who, intentionally or not, had violated the Agreement and had placed their goods under the care of the merchants' association held an advantage, once the duties were repealed and trade resumed. They would not have to wait at least three months for orders to reach Britain and shipments to return. There also were suspicions, which Mein tried to cultivate, that some merchants had access to their impounded wares and were surreptitiously selling them.[28]

The merchants' association focused on holding subscribers to their word, intensifying the pressure on those who defied them, and fortifying their reputation outside of Boston, while individual merchants, rather than the steering committee, responded to the manifests and to Mein's charges. Thomas Handasyd Peck, a merchant identified in a *Chronicle* listing, not only contradicted under oath the manifest that indicated he had imported forty dozen hats in a case, but also offered a public demonstration of its impossibility. The day after the manifest was printed, Peck attached a box with the mark "THP No. 5" to his shop window. Next to it he placed the inscription, "This is the Case that John Mein in his Paper of Yesterday says contain'd FORTY DOZEN of Hatts, imported in the Thomas, William Davis Master, by Thomas Handasyd Peck. Measurement of the Box: 23 Inches long, 14 1/2 Inches wide, 16 Inches deep, N.B There was not one Hatt in the box. Query, Does he Lie or not?" That noon Peck, "attended by his Servant with the Box on his Head, and the Town Bellman," paraded down King Street, stopping at the Exchange, the Town House, and John Mein's bookstore, among other places, "to the very great Diversion of a large Number of Spectators." Mein protested that the official documents at both ends of the voyage showed forty dozen hats and that he had "proved in the clearest manner" what he had asserted, but it is unlikely that his retort quelled the derisive laughter.[29]

The merchants' association attempted to shift the argument. It reported that Thomas Hutchinson had joined his sons in the importation of tea and coyly queried whether he also had been a partner in their purchase of "near 3000 Packs of Playing Cards." Tea was notorious for being one of the Townshend taxable commodities, but playing cards had the added liability of being "the best Means of Dissipation, which is the surest Step to Slavery." Less than two weeks later, the sons found the sign board for their store "besmeared" by "some Boys." The besmearing agent wasn't described, but its smell was apparently pungent. More important, the Hutchinsons had received the message that the merchants' association was growing weary of their recalcitrance. William Palfrey, clearly writing for the association, published an article in the *New-York Gazette* on September 18 criticizing Mein, defending Hancock, and reassuring New York readers that Bostonians were respecting and enforcing the Nonimportation Agreement and were trustworthy allies.[30]

As if to verify Palfrey's contentions, the association denied the request of five Scottish shipbuilders for exemption from the Agreement and forced the recent immigrant Patrick Smith to reship his merchandise to London. And the Boston town meeting voted to enter the names of Agreement violators into the record so that posterity would know who had "preferred their little private advantage" over the common good. The association, which had become nearly synonymous with the popular movement by this point, also gave hope that there were alternatives to the declining stock of imported textiles. In Boston and throughout the province, young women met in spinning matches and produced substantial quantities of yarn. How well-placed was that hope was open to debate. The wealthy and politically astute James Bowdoin believed that American manufactures hadn't progressed "so rapid as the warm Sons of Liberty has represented on the one hand, nor so small & diminutive as ministerial sycophants have represented on the other."[31]

After nearly a year of efforts to curtail trade with Great Britain, however, there were clear signs of success. Advertisements in October issues of Boston newspapers for merchandise from Britain had diminished significantly from the spring, and almost everyone who offered British goods for sale attached a statement similar to Hammatt & Brown's "last year's Importation." Gilbert Deblois clarified that his winter goods had been "imported last Fall," and he offered his customers up to three years to pay. Others promoted colonial commodities. John Gore Jr. offered "North America Manufactures for Men's Winter Wear," and Joseph Dawson claimed that his fruit trees produced "as good Fruit as any that comes from England." [32]

By themselves such advertisements were not irrefutable proof that there had been change, for the market could have gone underground, obscured from the light of public exposure. But there was more substantial evidence. On October 4 Thomas Hutchinson Jr., Elisha Hutchinson, and Theophilus Lillie agreed to the merchant association's terms. They promised not to sell items prohibited by the Nonimportation Agreement and to store chests of tea and other goods under the supervision of the merchants' committee. Public odium and declining sales must have combined to persuade them to capitulate. In the Hutchinsons' case, their process for laundering their inventory had been revealed the previous month: they sold their ware to middlemen, who in turn disguised the importers' identity from purchasing shopkeepers, thus circumventing the censure of vending proscribed articles. Exposure now eliminated, or at least reduced, that source of income, and in that context they chose to gain public approval rather than wallow in unprofitable abuse. The October 9 issue of the *Boston Gazette* proclaimed only the names of John Bernard, Nathaniel Rogers, James McMasters & Company, and John Mein as "noncompliers." Bernard, Rogers, and McMasters had reluctantly appeared before the merchants' association (apparently Mein did not receive the courtesy of an invitation) and insolently refused to subscribe. Within a week Rogers changed his mind, and then there were three.[33]

Who could hold out longer, the vast majority of Boston merchants and shopkeepers or the noncompliers, was an open question. The answer depended on how long it took Parliament to repeal the revenue measures. Nonimportation was having an impact in Britain. For 1769, exports from Great Britain to New England totaled 228,000 pounds, a decline of 213,000 pounds from the previous year. Considering that merchants from Newport and Providence, Rhode Island, and Portsmouth, New Hampshire had not joined their counterparts in Boston, New York, and Philadelphia; that some articles were exempt from the Agreement; and that enforcement had been lax for the first four months of the year, the level of compliance in Boston by the last three months of the year was remarkable.[34] But the citizens of Massachusetts's premier port city could maintain the boycott for only so long without courting financial devastation. Conditions already were dire for many.

With tensions high, almost any incident could have set off large-scale violence. In late October three episodes took Boston to the edge. In one, Robert Pierpoint, coroner for Suffolk County, charged Ensign John Ness of the 14th Regiment with stealing wood and assaulting him. After a constable delivered a warrant to Ness at the guard house at the Neck, Pierpoint showed up to ensure that the officer, when relieved, would appear before Justice Richard Dana. As a crowd formed, the two antagonists exchanged angry words, and Ness, sensing potential danger, called out the guard to form with fixed bayonets. After another unit arrived to relieve them, Ness and the soldiers marched back to their barracks. On the way they encountered insults, attempts to break into their ranks, and thrown objects. Bostonians had experienced a year of occupation and, despite entreaties from popular leaders to maintain the peace, were finding it increasingly difficult to contain their rage. Whether intentionally or not, one frightened soldier fired his musket in warning and others thrust their bayonets to force the crowd back. Both Ness and Captain Ponsonby Molesworth were indicted for ordering the troops to fire on civilians, but neither was convicted.[35] The town narrowly escaped a bloody riot between soldiers and its citizens.

As might be expected, John Mein was a protagonist in a skirmish that took place a few days after the Pierpoint-Ness event. Tired of his status as a scapegoat for merchant abuse, being a prickly person who relished a fight, and perhaps anticipating an escape from his economic plight in Boston to greater financial reward in London, he escalated his attacks in the *Chronicle*. In the October 26 issue, almost as a prank he placed in the upper left corner of the first page the names of six men he believed to be the merchants' steering committee (mimicking the *Boston Gazette*'s list of noncompliers). More provocatively, in response to Daniel Bailey's complaint of not receiving payment for Mein's debts, he printed brief caricatures of key popular leaders with the threat that he would expand them in subsequent issues if the "well disposed" published more "abusive letters, &c." Although he disguised their names, Mein made it obvious whom he was lampooning. Among the dozen of the first round were Johnny Dupe, "alias the Milch-Cow" of the "Well Disposed" (John Hancock); Counsellor Muddlehead, "alias Jemmy with the Maiden Nose" (James Otis); and Samuel the Publican, "alias The Psalm Singer, with the gifted face" (Samuel Adams).[36]

In the afternoon of October 28, when the *Chronicle* appeared (apparently it had been delayed), Mein and John Fleming left their store and ventured onto King Street. Each carried a loaded pistol, as had become their habit. Blocking their path were several men, including Thomas Handasyd Peck and Samuel Dashwood, who "thought themselves ill treated in a late Publication" of Mein's. After being "catechised" by the growing crowd and exchanging angry words with them, Mein pulled his pistol and "threatened to fire if they did not stand off." Closely followed as they hastened up King Street, Mein and Fleming fled into the guard house across from the Town Hall, and one of the two (the crowd believed it was Mein, but evidence points to Fleming) wildly discharged his pistol as they "retreated" into the building. Upon application, Justice Dana issued a warrant for Mein's arrest, but friends spirited him away. He remained in hiding for a few days, before seeking refuge on a ship in Boston Harbor. Unapprehended he sailed for England in the second week of November, never to return.[37]

George Gailer was less fortunate. Arriving in Boston as a sailor aboard the sloop *Success*, he immediately informed authorities of the presence of one or two unreported casks of wine, and customs officials seized the ship. Although he was spotted and pursued on the very afternoon of the Mein episode, he scurried into a house, where he stayed until evening, hoping to escape under the cover of dark. When he tried to slip out quietly, he was detected, and then his ordeal began. Stripped to the waist, he was painted with tar, covered with feathers, and placed on a cart. People "oblig'd him to hold a large Glass Lanthorn in his Hand that People might see the doleful Condition he was in, and to deter others from such infamous Practices." For the next three hours the cart with its terrified passenger was pulled through the main streets of Boston, stopping briefly at the Liberty Tree, where Gailer swore never to inform again. As the cart, rider, and joyful crowd passed Mein and Fleeming's printing office, three shots were fired from inside the building. Some of the procession ran into the office to capture the culprits, but only the guns remained. The interruption did not deter the parade that eventually concluded about 9 o'clock, after Gailer repeated his oath and begged forgiveness.[38]

In less than a week three incidents had produced crowds and gunfire. Yet no crowds had been confronted by troops; no gunmen had been arrested or convicted. These were lessons that everyone immediately learned. As acting governor, Hutchinson had hoped to convey a different message. While a terrified Gailer was touring the town, Hutchinson met with Colonel Dalrymple, who prepared his regiment for action and provided each soldier with thirteen rounds of ammunition. Unable to gather a majority of the Council and gain the authority to use force, and with the crowd dispersing voluntarily, Hutchinson lost the opportunity to tame the population. He therefore resorted to a proclamation calling for apprehension of the participants in the tar and feathering and a warning against similar demonstrations in the future. He took no official notice of those who fired weapons.[39]

In late July, when the merchants' association strengthened the Nonimportation Agreement, the merchants agreed that they would not import goods "unless the Revenue Acts are repealed." That potentially extended the Agreement beyond December 31, 1769, the end date of the original accord. At the time there was reasonable expectation that Parliament would terminate the duties before the end of the year, and so the amended language was somewhat ambiguous. Merchants could interpret it to mean that importation of British merchandise could recommence earlier rather than later. By mid-October it was evident that the Townshend Acts would extend into the new year, and the association began a new subscription in support of a boycott of indefinite duration.

After nearly a year of financial sacrifice, Boston merchants and shopkeepers were wary of signing, but they also didn't want to provoke the animosity of the community. John Hancock, for one, had to get his own house in order. His English business associates, Haley and Hopkins, had been shipping proscribed articles to several Boston merchants, and they recently had used one of Hancock's ships for the transactions. The merchants' association intervened and compelled the violators to send their goods back to England. Hancock, wanting to salvage Haley and Hopkins's reputation and his own honor, offered use of his ship "freight free." He warned his partners to desist for the time being and suggested they share the expense.[40]

As the end of the year grew near and as "a number" of signers of the original Nonimportation Agreement refused to subscribe to the amended version, the merchants' association intensified its pressure and added new names to its published list of noncompliers. The December 11 issue of the *Boston Gazette* advised its readers not to purchase from John Bernard, James McMasters, and John Mein (the three holdovers), as well as Patrick McMasters, Henry Barnes (an out-of-town importer), and Ame and Elizabeth Cumings or risk being considered "Enemies to their Country." The Cumings sisters were the first women to be listed. Between 1761 and 1770 no fewer than forty Boston women in thirty-seven separate shops (these were not street vendors) advertised their wares in Boston newspapers. A few, such as Mary Jackson, sold brass and iron goods or glass, stoneware, and china, but most offered garden seed or clothing and fabric. Four of the fourteen known to be engaged in business while the Nonimportation Agreement was in effect signed the document. Jane Eustis, a subscriber to the original Agreement, was one of the few who advertised in 1769 after May, and she was closing her shop after at least eight years to sail for England.[41]

Why the merchants' association chose to make examples of Ame and Elizabeth Cumings is unclear. Part of the explanation may be their social network. When their mother's death orphaned them, Elizabeth Murray, the sister of the Scottish merchant and future loyalist James Murray, provided them with the financial support and advice needed to establish their own store, and for at least six years the Cumings sisters had been successful shopkeepers. Had they stopped importing millinery, jewelry, and fabrics, they would have jeopardized both their livelihood and the expectations of their friends. When in November the merchants' committee requested that they place their imported goods under its care, they, never having subscribed to the Agreement, defied its wishes and landed on the list. Their friends in the tight community of court faction, customs officials, military officers, and Scottish merchants and all of their families came to their aid, and they experienced "more custom than before."[42]

So it was as 1769 came to a close. There were only half the number of soldiers as when the year began, but animosity between townspeople and the military continued to grow. The crowds had returned, and John Mein had departed. Nonimportation remained strong, but the effects of diminished commerce cut across economic strata and threatened the well-being of merchant, shopkeeper, artisan, laborer, sailor, and consumer alike. Self-interest, even survival, competed with loyalty to Boston and colonial rights. Clergyman Andrew Eliot pondered how many merchants would demand the return of their goods, temporarily stored under the supervision of the merchants' association, on the first of January. He expected a crisis.[43] As was often the case, he was right.

Chapter 10

Prelude to a Tragedy

When it met on December 28, 1769, the merchants' association clearly had evolved into a far more complex organization. No longer was it composed only of merchants and traders, numbering no more than a few hundred (and often well under a hundred) in attendance, whose prime motivation was advancing their specific interests. Now over a thousand people filled Faneuil Hall, and this larger group, transformed by a broad cross-section of Boston residents and designated "the Body," sought to terminate the Townshend Acts, remove the troops, protect their rights, and promote their well-being. They participated as citizens of a commonwealth who, through collective action, could stand up as equal members of the British empire. They viewed the Nonimportation Agreement as the sole "pacifick" and effective method for attaining a redress of their grievances, and just as well-stocked merchants benefited from the Agreement, so did manufacturers and artisans who produced articles banned from importation. Prolonging the boycott beyond December 31 did not simply denote good citizenship; it also could be the pursuit of self-interest.[1]

Rumors floated through town that some persons who had agreed to store their proscribed goods until the Nonimportation Agreement had ended and until imported merchandise had begun arriving in Boston (a means to even the playing field for those who had been faithful to the compact) already were selling prohibited items or intended to resume selling them on January 1. A committee of inspection had surveyed stored goods and reported to the Body that they had identified three violators, John Taylor, Theophilus Lillie, and "Benjamin Green and Son." The meeting voted to ostracize the culprits and anyone else who

View of Faneuil-Hall in Boston, Massachusetts, 1789, an etching by Samuel Hill that appeared in *Massachusetts Magazine*. This simplified version is in Samuel Adams Drake, *Old Landmarks and Historic Personages of Boston*, revised ed. (Boston, 1906), 134.

did business with them in the future. It also warned others who were considering the resumption of trade in proscribed merchandise that they would be treated similarly and would "not only be unworthy of the future confidence and favor of the publick, but must expect to incur their just resentment, by being thoroughly despised and neglected." To enforce compliance, the Body directed the committee of inspection to examine all stored goods "at least once a week."[2]

Benjamin Green and his son chose to begin negotiating a deal with the Body, but John Taylor and Theophilus Lillie decided to defend themselves in public print and to challenge the conclusions, the legitimacy, and the justice of the meeting. Taylor provided a history of his predicament. When the merchants' committee approached him on August 4, 1769, he had not previously subscribed to the Nonimportation Agreement. The committee asked him to sign a document pledging that he would not import forbidden goods from Great Britain before January 1, 1770, that he would "deliver up" to the merchants' supervision all such merchandise still to arrive, and that he would not conduct business with people who refused to make a similar agreement. Taylor assented to the first two stipulations but would not consent to halt bartering and selling with noncompliers. According to Taylor, the committee thought his position reasonable and had him sign "an Agreement, leaving out that Clause."[3]

The merchants' association was not so charitable and declared Taylor's partial settlement "unsatisfactory." Summoned to the meeting by the association, Taylor was intimidated into full conformity. He rationalized his behavior with the expectation that his stored goods soon would be returned to him. He was under the impression that "storing the Goods was made use of only as a blind, and that all those, who had delivered their Goods to the Committee, had them return'd in a very short Time, and some [he] knew had been permitted to sell them." He also asserted that one of the merchants from the committee declared to him that their aim was the "Repeal of the Revenue Laws" and that articles already imported "could have no tendency to effect the End proposed, as the Manufacturer must receive his Pay and the Merchant his Profit, but would be only hurting ourselves," thus implying that discreet sales were condoned.

When Taylor's goods arrived in October, the merchants' committee, unaware of his interpretation, allowed him to store the items in a room over his shop. Disingenuously, he maintained that there was no time limit for when the goods could be sold. He fulfilled his end simply by going through the motions of placing the goods in storage. The "few Woolen Goods" he sold were not a violation, for no one had told him "it was expected [he] should keep them stored for any Time whatever." The blame was with the committee for not being sufficiently clear; the Body should not have impugned his character.

Theophilus Lillie provided the public with a similar account, but with some important differences that later would have reverberations. On August 4, 1769, a committee of William Whitwell, Thomas Boylston, and Benjamin Austin visited Lillie and asked him to sign an agreement identical to Taylor's original document. Finding the group polite and cordial, he consented and believed that would put an end to the matter. When the merchants' association rejected the abridged compact, Lillie, unlike Taylor, refused to capitulate. The consequence was his name appearing in Boston newspapers and on handbills as an "enemy to our

country." He charged that there had been attempts to discourage customers from entering his establishment: "My sign-board was defaced, and
my name brushed out, and I suffered many other indignities." Warned
by friends that worse was ahead, in early October, on the condition that
his goods could remain in his store, he acquiesced to the Agreement. For
a short while fellow merchants and shopkeepers welcomed Lillie back
to their society. Even so, the committee of inspection regularly reviewed
his holdings. Still bristling with resentment, Lillie could contain himself
only so long, and eventually he told the inspectors, "[I] had not promised
to keep them any certain time; and what I did promise was forced out of
me, and could not be considered as obligatory."[4]

On December 10 the committee once again sought to view Lillie's
stored goods, and this time he told them he did not want to be interrupted
and "would not submit to such slavery any longer." Samuel Dashwood,
a member of the committee and a sea captain accustomed to people
obeying his orders, flew into a rage, as Lillie told it, and challenged
him to step outside: "[He threatened to] break my neck, my bones, and
the like." Other committee members were more conciliatory, and they
persuaded Lillie to allow the inspection. Convinced that others did
not have to endure such treatment and even were selling freely, Lillie
declared he would sell his goods, too. Once again he became an "enemy
to our country."[5]

Where Lillie departed from Taylor was in expanding his defense
beyond personal experience and raising issues of natural rights. He
insisted that "people who contend so much for civil and religious
Liberty" were depriving him of his "natural Liberty." Neither he nor
a representative consented to the establishment of the Nonimportation
Agreement, and he was being punished after the fact. When he had
ordered the proscribed goods, there had been no compulsion or law to
subscribe to the Agreement. "My storing my goods," he complained,
"must be considered therefore as punishment for an offence before the
Law for punishing it was made." Given the choice of bad alternatives, he
sided with the British government. "I own I had rather be a slave under
one Master," Lillie reasoned, "for if I know who he is, I may, perhaps, be
able to please him, than a slave to an hundred or more, who I don't know
where to find, nor what they will expect from me."[6]

Lillie's exasperation with his detractors and his concerns about his
financial plight were valid, certainly understandable, but his demand

that he must give his consent, or have a representative who did, for a law to be valid pushed the individual rights argument to the extreme. He questioned whether a society had the right to pass legislation that was compulsory for individuals to obey if they had not supported the measure. This was more than the protection of minority rights (although his concern about ex post facto punishment touched on the issue); this was a case for individual vetoes. In this world, legality required unanimity.

Such opinions must have held some currency in Boston, for at nearly the same moment Lillie was composing his defense "Determinatus," writing in the opposition movement's *Boston Gazette*, offered a much different construction of the appropriate relationship between society and the individual. He suspected that a "Cabal" was attempting to undermine resistance to the Townshend duties by forwarding the proposition that "[we have the] right to carry on our own trade and sell our own goods if we please." He countered that there was a social good that superseded individual liberty. Rhetorically he queried, "Have you not a right if you please, to set fire to your own houses, because they are your own, tho' in all probability it will destroy a whole neighbourhood, perhaps a whole city! Where did you learn that in a state or society you had a right to do as you please?" "Determinatus" insisted that these were not ordinary times and that the "fate of unborn millions" was at stake. Avarice, pride, and self-interest must be put aside for the greater good.[7]

Under different circumstances Lillie and "Determinatus" might have switched arguments. That doesn't mean that these views were held lightly. It indicates, rather, that there was no firm agreement on the responsibilities of the individual and of the state or on the appropriate balance of the two. A political and social philosophy was evolving, and ideas could be weapons as well as beliefs.

Had John Taylor and Theophilus Lillie been the only apostates, the popular movement might have been annoyed but not especially troubled that the Nonimportation Agreement was being jeopardized. Faced with potential widespread defection at the start of the year, however, it quickly mounted a campaign to plug the trickle before it became a flood. On January 17, 1770, the Body met again at Faneuil Hall to hear a report from the committee of inspection that identified Thomas and Elisha Hutchinson, William Jackson, Nathaniel Cary, Benjamin Green and Son (negotiations temporarily had broken down), Theophilus Lillie, John Taylor, and Nathaniel Rogers as persons who had violated their word not to sell stored goods "till a general importation might take place." The meeting selected the wealthy merchant William Phillips to be its moderator and then appointed committees to call on the accused and invite them to appear before the assembled multitude. For reasons ranging from being away from home to outright refusal to attend, none of the men materialized. Upon learning that the Hutchinson brothers had assured "two Gentlemen" that they would return the tea they had removed from storage, the assembly instructed the "two Gentlemen" to get the assurance in writing. William Jackson, who indicated that he "was ready to treat with any Committees," received a harsher response. The entire assemblage of roughly a thousand persons and a small committee marched to Jackson's house. Although only the committee was empowered to treat with Jackson and the "whole body" was to post vigil "orderly and peaceably," Jackson would not allow the committee into his house. Everyone returned to Faneuil Hall, where they decided to adjourn until the following day.[8]

The next morning began inauspiciously. In the presence of "upwards of a thousand" Bostonians, the committee of inspection reported that the Hutchinsons had changed their minds again. They would not relinquish their tea. Here was the critical test. Should the recalcitrants, particularly the Hutchinsons, stand firm, others would be encouraged to join their ranks. The Body condemned that group for "sacrificing the right of their country to their own avarice and private Interest" and voted for all assembled to accompany William Molineux to each violator's home, where he would read a proclamation demanding that they return their proscribed merchandise to storage. Should any of the charged persons wish to negotiate, four other men were appointed to join Molineux in the deliberations.[9]

The first stop was the residence of Thomas Hutchinson, where his adult sons still lived. Rather than allow the committee to meet his sons inside, Hutchinson himself threw open a window and began a heated conversation with Molineux. He took offense that the king's representative was being treated in such a manner. Molineux, with the crowd silently behind him, explained that they had come to discuss the violation with the principals, not with the acting governor. Undeterred, Hutchinson went on the attack again, claiming that his sons' agreement was not a binding contract. Molineux retorted they were bound by honor to keep their word. Neither man budged, and the two sons "gave no satisfaction." The Body then ventured to the other houses and enjoyed no greater success. They maintained order among themselves, not even huzzahing as they left Nathaniel Roger's house (the last of their tour), but apparently failed to intimidate or convince any of the holdouts.[10]

When the Body met for the third successive day, this time with twelve hundred people present, they finally received good news. Nathaniel Cary, who had been away during the deliberations, sent written confirmation that he would abide by the revised Nonimportation Agreement, but he was the only one who did so. Just as the crowd was prepared to vote on censuring the others, the moderator William Phillips informed them that the Hutchinsons had relented and would place their tea and the money they had gained through sales under the moderator's care. As reported to the assemblage and in the newspapers, the acting governor had met with Phillips and transmitted the agreement. Privately Hutchinson believed that leaders of the Body and, to a certain extent, his own sons had sandbagged him. As he wrote to Bernard (now safely in London), his sons had arranged the deal with Phillips on their own, and the moderator merely had asked to show the minutes of their pact to their father. In short, Hutchinson had been out-maneuvered. The public impression was that he was a party to undermining the resistors of the Nonimportation Agreement, and he could counter only by placing his sons in a worse light. Despite his hunger to be appointed governor and to appear a strong advocate of British policy, he kept publicly silent but suffered the displeasure of his regular allies.[11]

Hutchinson may have hoped to redeem himself when he sent to the Body at its next constituted meeting the order "to separate and disperse." He declared it an illegal assembly and cautioned, "Such of you as are Persons of Character, Reputation and Property" should disassociate from those who might commit "irregular Actions." He would have preferred being joined by the Council, but he was unable to convince a majority of its members to coauthor the statement. In return, the people at Faneuil Hall wrote Hutchinson that they had read his address "with all that Deference and Solemnity which the Message and the Times demand" but disputed his assertion that their meeting was unlawful.[12]

Once Sheriff Stephen Greenleaf departed with the response, after assuring the assembled multitude that he desired "to be considered in the Light only of the Bearer of his Honor's Letter," the Body took up the day's serious business. Boston citizens voted that they would henceforth have no transactions of any kind with William Jackson, Theophilus Lillie, John Taylor, and Nathaniel Rogers, who had "severed themselves from the Commonwealth." They voted to ostracize anyone who would dare to violate the Nonimportation Agreement for two years from the infraction. They renewed their condemnation of John Bernard, James and Patrick McMaster, Ame and Elizabeth Cumings, and John Mein. And they agreed to abstain from drinking tea and to encourage their families to do the same.[13]

One other vote attempted to cover an embarrassment of their own. In the interval between meetings, some person or persons had attempted to set fire to William Jackson's house. Although members of the Body were quite willing to intimidate their opponents and had little sympathy for Jackson, they drew the line at arson, and they offered a reward of one hundred dollars to anyone who could identify those responsible. They suggested that the perpetrators were enemies who sought to disgrace "the Friends of Liberty and this Country," but it was far more likely that the arsonist came from their own ranks.[14] Once again the popular movement had to walk the thin line between the threat of violence and actual violence. It was one thing to terrorize royal appointees through the vague threat of destruction of property and personal attacks, but something altogether different to provide examples that would justify the despised military occupation.

Despite John Mein's being in London and its mounting debts, the *Boston Chronicle* under John Fleeming continued to be the voice of resistance to nonimportation. Sometimes using ridicule, sometimes raising issues of equity and rights, the *Chronicle* and its writers hoped to divide Boston and undermine the opposition movement. One author, recognizing that humor can be more devastating than logic or facts, proposed that "there be no more marrying nor giving in marriage till the Revenue acts are totally repealed." That would prevent the creation of another generation, thus sparing it from the "most abject slavery." All women must be stored, and he volunteered himself to chair the committee that kept the keys. "If any man should refuse to deliver up his wife or daughter upon such an interesting occasion," he slyly observed, "he must be deemed An Enemy To His Country." He promised that he and his "'Well Disposed' Brethren, would engage, with the kind assistance of the Ladies, to carry on the Horn Manufacture to great advantage" (a reference to cuckolding husbands). Being public spirited, he would demand no fee for his service to the community.[15]

Even leaders of the Body may have chuckled at the parody, but they were not amused when "A New-England Man" called for the names of people who had paid duties during 1769 and the *Chronicle* obliged. As with the manifests, the new lists were a mixed bag that included nonsubscribers, nonresidents, and only a few prominent defenders of the Nonimportation Agreement (including John Rowe and Samuel Dashwood), but they had the potential to spread discontent as the economic malaise dragged on.[16]

The *Boston Evening-Post* and *Boston Gazette* rushed out articles to counter the *Chronicle*'s influence. Several who were listed offered explanations as to why their names appeared. John Greenleaf was an apothecary, and the so-called green glass he had imported were containers for medicine; Eleazer Johnson explained that the contents ascribed to him belonged to others and that he had paid duties so that the ship could unload its cargo; and Joseph Jackson claimed that the proscribed goods were for people outside the province and had been ordered before the Agreement. Samuel Dashwood, the sea captain with a short fuse, made the mistake of attacking his accuser in print and of disguising the fact that the "gentleman in Portsmouth" who in fact purchased the glass under Dashwood's imprimatur was his brother-in-law; for the next several weeks he was immersed in a series of charges and rebuttals.[17]

More effective were articles such as the one written by "Miles Standish," who reminded readers what the struggle was about: the grievance was with Parliament, which had been encroaching on colonial rights. He rekindled memories of the hardships of their ancestors and what they had accomplished and urged Bostonians, "Do whatever is in your power to maintain your invaluable rights," in particular to boycott British goods. In a similar spirit, three hundred "Ladies in this Town" signed an agreement "totally to abstain from the Use of Tea," and they were joined by 126 "young Ladies of this Town" who pledged to deny themselves "the drinking of Foreign Tea, in hopes to frustrate a Plan that tends to deprive the whole Community of their all that is valuable in Life."[18]

By mid-February 1770 public sentiment against "the importers" became more heated. Nearly simultaneous to their names being published in handbills and newspapers, their store windows were broken and their signs vandalized. Pressure kept building not to frequent the shops of nonimportation violators.[19]

In the midst of these disputes came conflicting reports of a battle between soldiers and citizens in New York City. Boston residents were aware that there had been a controversy over the New York Assembly passing legislation in December to supply troops, and in late January there were tales of skirmishes involving the city's Liberty Pole. There was a brief paragraph in the February 1 edition of the *Massachusetts Gazette* describing a bloody fight that included one death, but the February 5 issue of the *Boston Chronicle* claimed the account was "not authentic." Finally, on February 19, both the *Boston Evening-Post* and the *Boston Gazette* printed an extensive report, covering two full pages of supplement, that must have shocked Bostonians as they learned what could happen in their own city.[20]

Around 8 o'clock at night on Saturday, January 13, 1770, a group of about forty soldiers from the 16th Regiment, probably full of rum, decided to cut down New York's Liberty Pole in the Common across from the upper barracks (now the financial district, close to Wall Street and Broad Street). The Pole was substantial, not something to be felled in a single blow, and the soldiers positioned some of their number as lookouts to prevent detection. Before long, of course, some residents discovered the shenanigan in progress and hastened to a nearby tavern run by a Mr. Montanye. A few disbelievers ventured out and spied a hole being bored in the Pole for the placement of powder. Returning to the tavern they realized there were too few of them to thwart the soldiers and instead hollered "Fire, in order to alarm the inhabitants." Soon they saw a flame traversing a fuse connected to the Pole, but much to their delight it was extinguished before an explosion occurred. They rewarded the soldiers' demolition skills with hisses, and the soldiers responded by storming the tavern, where they beat a waiter, insulted the patrons, and broke panes of glass, lamps, and bowls before quickly retreating to their barracks for cover.[21]

New Yorkers who had not heard of the episode from their neighbors learned of the assault on their Liberty Pole in an article by "Brutus" that appeared on Tuesday, January 16. "Brutus" called for a meeting the following noon at the Liberty Pole to discuss what had occurred and also the town's broader relationship to the troops. He protested that the army was "not kept here to protect, but to enslave" the residents, and yet the assembly was providing funds to supply them and their fellow citizens were employing them to the detriment of the town's poor. The latter was a particularly resonant point, in New York as much as in Boston. Soldiers moonlighted to supplement their meager wages and provisions, typically working much cheaper than the going rate. The city's laboring poor, already reeling from the consequences of the Nonimportation Agreement, were deprived of employment or forced to accept compensation even lower than normal. "I hope my fellow citizens will take this matter into consideration," "Brutus" pleaded, "and not countenance a set of men who are enemies to Liberty, and at the beck of tyrants to enslave, especially when it will bring on you the just reproaches of the poor."

Before the town met the next day, soldiers returned Tuesday evening to complete their task. Again they filled a bored hole with powder, and this time they produced an explosion, splitting the Liberty Pole. Townspeople searched the area for the culprits, but the soldiers hid in a nearby house that had been "a temporary barrack." Sneaking back at about one in the morning, the saboteurs cut down the damaged Pole and sawed it into pieces, which they threw down at Montanye's door, and slipped back to their barracks.

When incensed townspeople congregated for their meeting on Wednesday, January 17, they formed a committee to apply to the owners to demolish the house that had concealed the soldiers. That was a mild response, but soldiers nearby "drew their cutlasses and bayonets" and taunted the people to pull it down. The timely arrival of magistrates and officers separated the would-be combatants and averted a melee. Merchant sailors had their own grievances with the soldiers, who were their competitors for dockside jobs, and they "turn'd ashore all the soldiers they found at work on board the vessels and obliged such of them as were at work in stores to quit it."

The soldiers, many of whom were not strangers to poverty and misfortune, resented their treatment. For nearly four years they had been the recipients of scowls, insults, and reluctant support from an ungrateful population they believed they were protecting. The attack on the Liberty Pole was the result of long-festering wounded feelings and was directed at the Sons of Liberty, whom they called the "real enemies to society." Members of the 16th Regiment created a handbill expressing their side of the story and began posting it throughout the town on

January 19. Four lines of a poem prefaced their tract and summarized their aggrieved views:

God and a Soldier all Men doth adore
In Time of War, and not before:
When the War is over, and all Things righted,
God is forgotten, and the Soldier slighted.

Isaac Sears and Walter Quackenbush, both Sons of Liberty, were not sympathetic to the regiment's perceived plight. Witnessing a group of soldiers about to display the broadsides, Sears collared the one who "was fixing the paper" and demanded to know what right he had "to put up libels against the inhabitants." Quackenbush grabbed the vulnerable soldier who was holding the papers. When one of the other members of the party "drew his bayonet," Sears hit him in the head with a ram's horn, thus driving off all but the two restrained soldiers, whom they promptly marched to the mayor's residence. As a crowd of angry New Yorkers gathered, twenty soldiers from the 16th, displaying cutlasses and bayonets, strode down to rescue their comrades. Townspeople pulled rungs from nearby sleighs to use as weapons and prepared to do battle. The two captured soldiers called to their fellows to desist and "to leave them to the determination of the Mayor," and the mayor and an alderman came out of the building and ordered the soldiers to depart. A violent conflict was averted, or at least postponed, as the soldiers, after a pause, trekked back to their barracks. Townspeople accompanied them, but the soldiers, their weapons still unsheathed, restrained themselves. As they reached the summit of Golden Hill (now the general area of John Street, east of William Street, in lower Manhattan), they were reinforced and, according to the account in Boston newspapers, turned on the locals with the cry, "Where are your Sons of Liberty now?" And the fracas was on. Both soldiers and residents were injured in the ensuing fight, later to be named the Battle of Golden Hill, but no one was killed.

The following day scattered skirmishes erupted again, the most notable being tussles between soldiers and sailors. There were contradictory reports on how the fight began, but antagonisms between the groups were of long standing, and most likely soldiers wanted to retaliate for being driven from their part-time jobs just days before. The conflict occurred near the New Presbyterian Meeting House. When the mayor and alderman saw soldiers headed toward that destination, they rushed to intervene. The mayor commanded the troops to return to their barracks. Even in the presence of a swelling crowd of New York residents, however, the soldiers held their ground. Recognizing the futility of his attempts, the mayor prepared to seek the help of officers but was detained by citizens who feared a bloodbath in his absence. Rumors quickly spread through the city that soldiers were slaughtering the inhabitants. More people hastened to the scene. Twenty men from the lower barracks augmented the rioting troops, and it appeared that injuries would become more grievous than bruises and gashes. Instead, and fortunately, the soldiers thrusting their way with swords and bayonets returned to their quarters. The "battle" was over. New Yorkers salvaged their dignity by constructing a new Liberty Pole in a more secure location.

Bostonians—resident, soldier, and sailor alike—must have pondered what might ensue in their own town. Just as in New York, there were antagonisms between inhabitants believing they were occupied by a foreign force and soldiers perceiving mistreatment from an ungrateful citizenry. Just as in New York, there was competition for low-paying work between moonlighting soldiers and desperate residents. Just as in New York, there were conflicts between merchant sailors and the men of the regiments.[22] But in Boston, still with two regiments totaling one thousand troops, there was the potential for a more deadly confrontation.

Three days after Bostonians learned the details of Golden Hill, boys and young men, with older residents watching and encouraging them, set out to torment Theophilus Lillie and to discourage would-be purchasers from buying his wares. That morning they planted a "large Wooden head carved and painted" and a board covered with paper depicting four of the Nonimportation Agreement violators outside of Lillie's shop and in the middle of the prime thoroughfare leading into the North End of town. No one who lived in the vicinity could miss the display or its implications. One of Lillie's neighbors was "the informer" Ebenezer Richardson, who had been implicated in reporting alleged smuggled goods to the customs service at least as far back as the Daniel Malcom episode in September 1766. Richardson determined that it was his responsibility to clear the street of the provocative objects. First he attempted to persuade a passing "countryman" to ram the totems with his wagon. The man refused, as did a "Charcoal-man," even after Richardson told him he was a magistrate. Undaunted, Richardson decided to dismantle the "pageantry" himself, but the horse and cart he drove "passed without disturbing it."[23]

Discouraged, Richardson accepted his defeat and began walking the "50 or 60 paces" to his home. In that short space he encountered Edward Proctor, Thomas Knox, and Captains Riordon and Skillings and engaged them in a shouting match. Most likely at least one of them called him an informer, and he "cry'd out, perjury! perjury! often repeating it as he passed them." As he reached the doorway of his house, he parted with the menacing words, "By the eternal G-d, I will make it too hot for some of you before night!"[24]

Had the incident ended there, it would have merely been a matter of insults and hard feelings; but of course there was more. The exchange had attracted the attention of youths, who began yelling "Informer" outside his house. Too agitated to ignore the taunts, Richardson and his wife stepped outside, returned the abuse, and demanded that the youthful crowd disperse. The boys retreated and advanced like waves on a beach, releasing "light rubbish," lemon peels, eggs, and the like. When someone from within threw a brick at the people outside the house, one of the older observers entered the fray and heaved it back, breaking the first of many windows. The objects then escalated from small stones to large stones, whizzing in both directions. To stop the tumult, Richardson opened his door and cocked his gun. But the projectiles and heckling continued to fly, and minutes later Richardson pointed his gun out a window, pulled the trigger, and blasted birdshot into the congregated boys.

Samuel Gore and Christopher Seider fell to the ground. Both were spectators at the wrong place and at the wrong time. Gore, the nineteen- or twenty-year-old son of Captain John Gore, suffered shot in both thighs and two fingers. Dr. Joseph Warren, who removed the slugs and who later was killed at Breed's Hill, thought that Gore might lose the use of his right forefinger but was not in danger of dying. Seider, the eleven-year-old son of a poor family who had been placed with a Madam Apthorp, was more severely wounded. Hearing noises as he left school with other boys, he hurried to see the spectacle and was almost immediately struck by birdshot. One of the eleven pea-size shots that punctured his chest and abdomen pierced a lung. He died that evening.[25]

Witnesses to the shooting rushed to the nearby New Brick Meeting House and rang its bell to summon town residents. Shortly the expanding crowd surrounded Richardson's house, while some of their number

Life and Humble Confessions of Richardson, a depiction of the fracas that killed Christopher Seider. (The Historical Society of Pennsylvania)

entered and seized Richardson and George Wilmot, who was found in the compromising position of holding a gun loaded with "179 goose and buck shot." As the sheriff escorted the two men to Judge John Ruddock, one person tried to throw a noose over Richardson's neck but failed. Ruddock ordered that they be sent under guard to Faneuil Hall to be examined by himself and three other justices: Richard Dana, Edmund Quincy, and Samuel Pemberton. In front of a crowd estimated at a thousand people, the magistrates committed Richardson and Wilmot to prison to await trial. Their trek to the jail was perilous. Angry townspeople were ready to take immediate vengeance, and only the intervention of some "Gentlemen of influence" prevented mortal retribution.[26] For all they knew, Richardson and Wilmot would go unpunished, as had been the case in previous months, when on three occasions people who had fired guns into crowds had escaped prosecution or conviction. And the two accused men already were among the most unpopular in Boston. The incident made the town all the more turbulent, but further violence was averted temporarily.

Seider's funeral offered some comfort to his family, catharsis to the community, and political ammunition for the opposition movement. The procession began at the Liberty Tree, where the Sons of Liberty had attached a sign, in part reading, "Thou shall take no Satisfaction for the Life of a Murderer;—He shall surely be put to Death." Led by "about Five Hundred School Boys," the coffin was carried through Boston streets trailed by "at least two thousand" mourners "amidst a Crowd of Spectators." Hutchinson estimated the funeral to be "the largest perhaps ever known in America." Seider was buried on the grounds of his parents' house, located conveniently close to the Liberty Tree. There were efforts to elevate him to martyrdom. An article in the *Boston Gazette* noted that although Seider's family was poor it consisted of "Persons of Sobriety, Industry and good Morals," and "A Mourner" observed that "this little hero and first martyr to the noble cause" displayed a "manly spirit" and a firm mind, and by the evidence of "several heroick pieces found in his pocket" there was "reason to think he had a martial Genius, and would have made a clever man." Christopher Seider may have occupied a larger segment of Boston and American memory were it not for events that transpired two weeks after his death.[27]

Chapter 11

The Massacre on King Street

By early March 1770, many Bostonians were openly expressing their frustration, anger, and resentment at the representatives of British might. They had lived through seventeen months of military occupation, more than two years of the presence of the commissioners and the enforcement of the Townshend Acts, and a decade of economic hardships. They increasingly realized that British authorities viewed them as subordinates rather than as equal members of the empire. Acting Governor Thomas Hutchinson, meanwhile, still yearned to remove the "acting" from his title, and he and his associates fretted that power had shifted to the popular movement. In their splendid isolation the commissioners continued to fear violence against their persons and their property but nonetheless remained eager to prosecute infractions of trade laws, no matter how small the offense. And the troops, like those in New York City, resented being stationed among a people who showed them too little respect and too much animosity. Political rivalries, strife over maintaining nonimportation, and competition for jobs compounded the general discontent. It wouldn't take much to ignite a lethal explosion.

The final steps toward tragedy began midmorning on Friday, March 2. A few hundred yards apart in the South End of Boston were Green's barracks, which housed part of the 29th Regiment, and the substantial enterprise of John Gray, which consisted of rope walks measuring 744 feet long, a warehouse, a residence, and several outbuildings. Gray employed a regular crew of journeymen and apprentices but often hired temporary workers as well. That morning, a soldier from the 29th (possibly Private Patrick Walker) ambled by the rope walks, and William Green, a journeyman, shouted to him, inquiring whether he wanted work. It was a setup, aimed at producing laughter and humiliation. When the soldier, who like other members of the occupying force needed to augment his meager income, eagerly answered yes, Green gleefully responded, "Then go and clean my s—t house." The soldier furiously retorted that he would seek satisfaction and was not afraid of any rope worker. While the soldier attempted to restore his dignity, Nicholas Ferriter, a rival for employment who had been hired only for the day, stealthily climbed out a window and pulled the soldier's feet out from under him. As the soldier fell, his coat flew open, revealing an unsheathed cutlass. John Wilson, another rope worker, grabbed the sword and took it inside. Without his weapon and badly outnumbered, the soldier stormed off.[1]

Twenty minutes later he returned with eight or nine comrades armed with clubs. The group entered Gray's warehouse and challenged the three or four men there to explain the treatment of their fellow soldier. Recognizing that soothing words would not resolve their predicament, the besieged warehousemen called for help. Soon thirteen or fourteen rope workers arrived, and the assembled force drove off the soldiers. Undaunted, the members of the 29th rallied thirty or forty soldiers. Led by a tall, Afro-Caribbean drummer and armed with clubs and cutlasses, they set off to get revenge.[2]

In a house between Green's barracks and the rope walks, sixty-nine-year-old justice of the peace John Hill observed the growing body of soldiers racing back and forth and hollered at the drummer, "You black rascal, what have you to do with white people's quarrels?" Well experienced with racism, the drummer shrugged off the insult, replying, "I suppose I may look on," and continued his march toward the anticipated fray. Hill trailed after and attempted to use his authority to halt the altercation. No one paid attention to him; but when soldiers knocked down a rope worker and began to beat him with their clubs, the justice of the peace started to intervene, only narrowly to escape a blow himself. Outnumbered, the rope workers somehow managed to fend off the soldiers, who retreated once again to their barracks. This was not the end of the episode. Both sides swore to continue the battle after the weekend.[3]

The journeyman had insulted not just an occupying soldier and representative of British power but a competitor for scarce employment, a widely held concern among Boston's working population; the soldiers' response had been not just to a loud-mouth heckler, but to an entire population who underappreciated the hardships and sacrifices of military life.

Over the weekend there was at least one other minor skirmish and numerous rumors of an impending fight between soldiers and rope workers, one that threatened to escalate into large-scale violence. As three apprentices were spinning at McNeil's rope walk (near Gray's establishment) late Saturday afternoon, three grenadiers carrying bludgeons accosted them. "You damned dogs," they cried, "don't you deserve to be killed? Are you fit to die?" The apprentices, caught by surprise and unarmed, remained silent. A passerby, James Young, approached one of the grenadiers and taunted him with the riposte, "Damn it, I know what a soldier is." That prompted the grenadier to swing his club at Young and then at one of the apprentices. A nearby journeyman went to the tanhouse and brought out two bats. With the help of another bystander, he chased the soldiers from the site.[4]

Word of this episode fueled speculation about worse clashes to come. John Goddard was selling potatoes to soldiers at the barracks shortly after the grenadiers returned. He witnessed about twenty of the troops "much enraged; and one in a profane manner swore he would be revenged on them, if he fired the town." Through the communication system of a chimney sweep talking with his maid, John Gray heard that soldiers were planning to retaliate against the rope workers, and he determined to discuss the matter with Lieutenant Colonel William Dalrymple on Monday morning. Townspeople were not the only ones hearing rumors. When no one could account for the whereabouts of a Sergeant Chambers on Sunday morning, his commanding officer, Lieutenant Colonel Maurice Carr (a forty-year-old career officer with twenty-five years' service), assumed the worst. Accompanied by other officers, Carr hastened to Gray's rope walk and searched the premises but failed to locate his sergeant. Gray, who had not been at his workplace, soon learned of Carr's intrusion and immediately set out to see Dalrymple.[5]

The rope walk owner and the colonel civilly exchanged accounts of the previous day's events. On discovering the role his journeyman had played, Gray pledged to fire him the following day, promising to "do all in my power to prevent my people's giving them any affront in future." In return Dalrymple agreed to control his soldiers and to prohibit them from entering the rope walks. At this conciliatory juncture Lieutenant Colonel Carr entered the room, lamenting the abuse his men were receiving and expressing his fear that his sergeant had been murdered. Gray disdainfully suggested that Carr ask for his assistance before searching his property. If the situation had not been so dire and tempers so high, the two men might have shared a laugh the next morning, when the missing sergeant was found, unhurt, in a "House of Pleasure." But their suspicions inexorably suggested they were rushing toward a bloody Monday night.[6]

Boston still was locked in winter, and on that Monday, March 5, there was a foot of snow on the ground, covering the oyster shells that paved the streets. Frigid temperatures produced ice so thick as to hinder compaction, crusting the snow. Walking could be perilous, yet even those conditions probably seemed preferable to the slush of spring, still weeks away. Visibility remained good, even after sunset. It was a clear night, and the moon's reflection on the snow was bright enough to produce shadows. There would be no difficulty recognizing a friend—or an enemy. Henry Bass found it to be such a "pleasant" evening that he was surprised that at 9:15 there weren't more than fifteen people on King Street.[7] That would quickly change.

Had Bass been in the South End of town, he might have noticed more activity. As early as 7 o'clock and continuing for several hours, clusters of armed soldiers and bunches of town residents prowled the streets. County Coroner Robert Pierpoint observed two soldiers, one with a sword and the other with a club, rush by him. Joined by a third soldier with a bayonet, they passed him twice more, eventually riveting his attention with a bayonet slap and the threat that he soon would "hear more of it." Physician Richard Hirons noticed several soldiers with clubs and bayonets on the move near Murray's barracks. About 8 o'clock an officer and eleven soldiers gathered by the Liberty Tree. Their assignment apparently was to reconnoiter the area and to halt and question any group larger than two townspeople "with arms, clubs, or any other warlike weapons." Simultaneously there were angry residents in the streets, twelve of whom claimed that soldiers had attacked them. Several witnesses at subsequent trials later recalled groups of four or five Bostonians armed with sticks, more the size of bludgeons than walking sticks, hastening to and fro. Judge John Ruddock tried to put the best face on the situation by explaining, "They went so for several months before, they chused to do so, because they had been so often knocked down by the soldiers, some said the soldiers were going to fight with the people."[8]

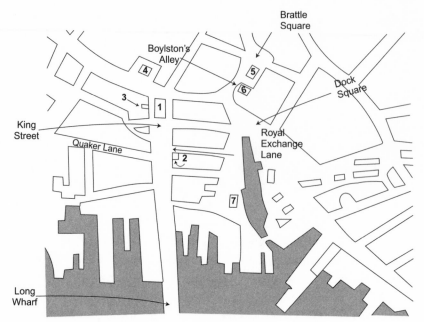

Map of central Boston. 1 is the Town House; 2 is the Custom House; 3 is the Main Guardhouse; 4 is the First or Old Brick Church; 5 is the Brattle Street Church; 6 is Murray's Barracks; and 7 is Faneuil Hall.

The posturing may have been more a show of bravado than malice, but the evidence still suggests that soldiers and residents were spoiling for a brawl. Unlike preliminaries on Pope's Day, the would-be combatants on this Monday night were armed and likely saw more at stake than fulfilling a ritual or winning annual bragging rights. The altercation at the rope walks had unleashed animosities that had been building for a year and a half.

The final series of events that led to the killings began innocently enough. A wigmaker's apprentice, Edward Gerrish, completed his day's work around 8 o'clock and went for a stroll. Along the way he met fellow apprentice Bartholomew Broader, who had just escorted Ann Green and Mary Rogers to the apothecary's and accompanied them back to the Custom House. Ann Green was the daughter of Bartholomew Green, a customs official who, with his family, including the maid Mary Rogers, resided there. In addition to housing the Greens, the Custom House served as a general facility for clearing vessels, storing records, and collecting duties. It enjoyed a central location on King Street, a few blocks west of the long wharf, a long block south of Dock Square near Faneuil Hall and Murray's barracks, and lay no more than a hundred yards east of the Town House and not much farther away from the main guard, which was across the street from the south door of the Town House. Because it housed valuable records and cash, a sentry was posted outside its door. While the apprentices chatted with the young women on the Custom House steps, they may have noticed the sentry, but flirting almost certainly held a higher priority. When Ann Green's brother suggested the women come inside, they all stepped into the warmth of the kitchen, where Gerrish and Broader lingered a brief time. Then they returned to King Street, the cold, and mischief.[9]

Whether to impress the young women, to vent youthful exuberance, to annoy an officer of the occupying force, or simply to repeat mistaken information, Gerrish shouted at Captain John Goldfinch of the 14th Regiment who was walking by, "There goes the fellow who hath not paid my master for dressing his hair." Wishing not to contribute to the unrest on that volatile night and fortified by a receipt for the wigmaker's services in his pocket, Goldfinch ignored the insult and continued on. About that time church bells throughout Boston pealed 9 o'clock. All was relatively but temporarily calm.[10]

The sentry, Hugh White, a private in the 29th Regiment, had overheard Gerrish's derision of the captain and lacked Goldfinch's restraint. White seethed at the disrespect shown to a British officer and lectured the apprentice, that Goldfinch "is a gentleman, and if he owes you any thing he will pay it." Gerrish retorted that there were no gentlemen in the regiment. At that, White left his post, stepped into the middle of the street, and challenged the apprentice to reveal himself. When Gerrish replied that he was not "ashamed to show his face," the sentry struck him on the side of the head with his gun. The apprentice, still in many ways a boy, immediately started crying and tearfully asked White why he was abusing people. As the sentry threatened to strike Gerrish again, other apprentices, attracted by the shouts, gathered and taunted the sentry with "scoundrel," "lobster," "bloody back," and errant snowballs. White became increasingly alarmed and called out for guards.[11]

Just a few blocks to the northwest, outside Murray's barracks, which housed part of the 29th Regiment, another altercation was in progress. A few minutes after 9 o'clock four teenage boys approached the covered passageway, called both Draper's Alley and Boylston's Alley, that connected Cornhill Street to Brattle Street and Brattle Square. The main entrance to the barracks was at the top of the alley, close by Brattle Street Church, and two soldiers, one with a sword and the other with a "large cudgel," bounded down the passageway and confronted the boys. After a brief scuffle, during which at least one boy was struck with a sword, the soldiers ran back for reinforcements. When additional soldiers brandishing tongs, shovels, and cutlasses appeared, Francis Archibald Jr. repeatedly hollered "Town born!" to catch the attention of some "lads" near the Town House and of anyone else who might lend assistance. Ensign Alexander Mall may have been trying to avert an escalation of hostilities or intending to retaliate against residents of the town (as Bostonians believed when they later indicted him), but in either case he raised additional troops. Seven to twelve grenadiers rushed out with drawn cutlasses, tongs, and shovels. They slashed indiscriminately at anyone in their path, wounding an oysterman, among others, and received blows in return. One soldier was knocked down and suffered a broken wrist. A group of soldiers then set out from Dock Square, near the barracks, in the direction of the Town House. When they heard the sentry's calls for help, they stormed down to the Custom House and chased fifteen to twenty young men and boys away.[12]

Captain Goldfinch, having ignored Gerrish's taunts, continued his evening stroll, eventually pausing at the intersection of Draper's Alley and Cornhill. There the sight of angry soldiers and cursing, snowball-throwing townspeople raised the specter of a full-scale riot. Though he was an officer of the 14th Regiment and the men and officers at Murray's barracks were of the 29th, Goldfinch pulled rank. He ordered the soldiers back into the barracks and called on the junior officers to assist him. In the midst of this confusion, Richard Palmes, a merchant sea captain and Son of Liberty, approached Goldfinch and pointedly commented that he "was surprised they suffered the soldiers to go out of the barracks after eight o'clock." One of the harried officers shot back, "Pray do you mean to teach us our duty?" "I did not," Palmes replied, "only to remind them of it." Wearily, an officer pleaded, "You see that the soldiers are all in their barracks, and why do you not go to your homes." Having accomplished his purpose with the officers, Palmes sought to defuse the situation further and, together with James Lamb, urged the crowd to go home. With shouts of "Home, home," many of the participants began to disperse.[13]

Brattle Street Church. In Samuel Adams Drake, *Old Landmarks and Historic Personages of Boston*, revised ed. (Boston, 1906), 123.

A few minutes later, when it seemed that the worst was over, a soldier dashed out of the barracks. At the head of Draper's Alley he dropped to one knee, raised his musket, and roared, "G. damn your Blood I'le make a Lane thro you all." One of the junior officers—Ensign Mall, Lieutenant Hugh Dickson, or Lieutenant Paul Minchin—quickly grabbed him and shoved him back into the barracks. Moments later, when the soldier repeated the performance, officers confiscated his weapon and again dragged him to the barracks and shut the gates.[14]

And then, about 9:15, in quick succession, the sounds of bells from the Old Brick, Brattle Street, and the Old South churches filled the night air. Ordinarily church bells rang at irregular times to alert the populace to a fire. In response to that imagined danger some Bostonians pulled two fire engines to the Town House and others carried fire buckets. But they soon learned that there was no fire. To the minds of those responsible for the pealing bells (one witness spotted "2 or 3 Lads" at the Old Brick "trying to open the Windows, in order to ring the Bell") the peril wore red coats. Soon hundreds of citizens gathered in the moonlit streets. At Dock Square, near Murray's barracks and within shouting distance of the Custom House, as many as two hundred people, including twenty-five to thirty merchant sailors led by the "tall Molatto" Crispus Attucks, crowded together before scattering in various directions. Some who walked toward the Town House began breaking windowpanes of the house of the nonimportation violator William Jackson, until stopped by Andrew Cazneau, a lawyer who attended the 1769 Sons of Liberty celebration but who later became a loyalist.[15]

The boys and young men who earlier had been chased away from the Custom House now believed it safe to return and resumed their tormenting of the sentry, Private Hugh White. A small number carried staves they had pulled off stalls at Market Square, but most only hurled snowballs and insults. Altogether there were as many as thirty people now on King Street near the sentry, a few of them older men standing among the youths. At times the crowd drew close to Private White and then ebbed back as he jabbed his bayonet at those closest to him. The boys kept up the attack of snowballs and an occasional oyster shell, but none struck the sentry. Harrison Gray Jr. warned the youths to desist, but White grew increasingly agitated, loaded his gun, and pointed it at his adversaries. Aware that soldiers could fire on the populace only following the order of a civil magistrate, but perhaps unaware that defending one's life was an exception to the rule, the boys and young men dared the sentry to shoot at them. "Fire! Damn you, fire!" they jeered. Edward Gambleton Langsford, one of the town watch, attempted to calm the soldier. They were "only a parcel of rude Boys," he soothed. There was no reason to be afraid. Don't fire, he cautioned. Henry Knox, a bookseller and future revolutionary general, was less tactful, telling White "if he fired he died." Despite being armed, White was but a single person facing a hostile crowd. He called for the guard, and someone inside the Custom House hastened to the main guardhouse for help.[16]

When the church bells began to ring, some members of the guard went to Captain Thomas Preston, the captain of the day, and informed him that the townspeople "were assembling to attack the troops." The forty-year-old Preston, a veteran of fifteen years' service, immediately rushed to the main guard and met with the officer in charge, Lieutenant

James Bassett, who, though only twenty years old, already had eight years of military experience. Learning of the sentry's plight, a flustered Bassett asked Preston, "What shall I do in this case?" Impatiently the captain told him to take six or seven men, but then, taking matters into his own hands, he hollered, "Damn you! Turn out, guard!" Led by Corporal William Wemms six grenadiers surged out of the guardhouse. They may not have been the best and the brightest, but they were among the biggest and burliest the 29th Regiment had to offer. They seemed in a great rage as they thundered down King Street, shouting "Make way" and pushing and slashing with their raised bayonets. The hatter Nathaniel Fosdick was caught in their path and foolishly refused to budge. He was fortunate, for the grenadiers parted around him and only nicked him with their bayonets as they passed.[17]

They reached the Custom House and the embattled sentry. Wemms formed his men into a half circle from the corner of the building where Royal Exchange Lane ran into King Street to the sentry's box. There he ordered the soldiers to load their muskets. Preston trailed behind. Before the captain reached the troops, Henry Knox literally pulled him aside by the coat. "For God's sake take care of your Men for if they fire your life must be answerable," Knox pleaded. "I am sensible of it," Preston peevishly replied and then hurried on to take command.[18]

Worried by what they perceived to be the intentions of the swelling crowd, the eight soldiers were already growing anxious about their situation. From the perspective of the grenadiers, their backs to the Custom House, Private Hugh Montgomery stood to the far right, nearest Royal Exchange Lane. His wife at the time of the incident may have feared for her husband's well-being, particularly after a neighbor in a dispute with her that evening wished he would be killed, but she confidently asserted that he "is able and will stand his ground." Immediately to Montgomery's left was Private James Hartigan, with Private John Carroll to his left. Carroll had been one of the soldiers tussling at the rope walks on Saturday, two days earlier. Spotting James Bailey, a sailor who had sided with the rope workers and now a bystander at the Custom House, he pressed his bayonet against Bailey's chest and then moved into formation. Next to Carroll was Private Matthew Kilroy, who also held a grudge. Kilroy had participated in the fray at the rope walks on the previous Friday, and his anger was still evident on Monday night, when he thrust his bayonet at the unsuspecting block maker James Brewer while marching with the other grenadiers toward the Custom House. Private William McCauley, who as he was loading swore and pushed his bayonet at John Adams's clerk, Jonathan Williams Austin, was the next soldier. Private William Warren stood to McCauley's left. Warren, like Kilroy and Carroll, had fought with the rope makers on Friday. The last two were the sentry Private Hugh White and Corporal William Wemms, who stood on the far left of the semicircle.[19]

Subsequent testimony about Captain Preston's position seemed hopelessly contradictory. Witnesses placed him both in front of the soldiers and behind them, to the left and to the right, even in between. It is entirely possible that Preston was moving during the event and that observers recalled his place at different moments, but the key question remains: Where was Preston at the time the first shot rang out? Days later he claimed that he was between the soldiers and the crowd, an assertion that seemed somewhat self-serving in that it supported his defense that he would not have given the suicidal order to fire when he stood in front of his men.[20] Although his statement probably was true, it still allowed for the possibility that he was in front of the soldiers but between their lengthy musket barrels—a chink in his argument.

As soon as Preston arrived at the Custom House, he began cajoling the belligerent crowd, the bulk of which was at the head of Royal Exchange Lane, not directly in front of all the soldiers. According to Robert Goddard, "The Captain told the Boys to go home least there should be murder done." They responded with more snowballs. Catcalls, whistles, and cheers increased in volume. "Bloody backs, you lobster scoundrels, fire if you dare," the boys and young men shouted in derision. They pressed near the soldiers, occasionally striking their muskets with sticks, but then fell back as the grenadiers thrust their bayonets at them. Amid the confusion, three townspeople drew near Preston. The young carpenter Theodore Bliss taunted him, "Why do you not fire? God damn you, fire!" Still acting as a conciliator, Richard Palmes stepped between the two and placed his left hand on Preston's right shoulder. John Hickling joined them and completed the portrait with his hand on Palmes's shoulder. Palmes inquired whether the guns were loaded, and Preston informed him they were, "with powder and ball." "I hope you do not intend they shall fire upon the inhabitants," Palmes remarked. Just as politely, the captain replied, "By no means."[21] This brief show of civility was soon lost among the growing cacophony.

As Preston concluded the conversation, a white object was thrown in their direction. It might have been a snowball, a chunk of ice, or a piece of white birch cordwood. Whatever its composition, the missile struck the muzzle of Private Montgomery's musket. Montgomery stepped back, recovered his balance, and discharged his weapon. Many scurried for cover or ducked down. Surprisingly, quite a few remained frozen in place, unable to believe that a shot had been fired. There was a pause, punctuated incredibly by renewed shouts of "Fire!"[22]

Estimates of the elapsed time between the first and next shots varied, but most observers agreed that there had been sufficient time, somewhere between a few seconds and half a minute, for Preston to have commanded the men to halt. Prompted by the first shot and without any prohibition from Preston, several of the other soldiers then fired at the crowd. At this point Palmes, standing between Preston and Montgomery, used his walking stick to knock the gun out of the grenadier's hands and then, with adrenaline pounding, swung to his other side, where he inadvertently hit Preston. The captain wasn't certain whether the blow had been intended for him, but he was sure that he would have been fatally injured had he not thrown up his arm in defense. As it was, his arm was briefly incapacitated. Palmes in his frenzy slipped to the ground, and as he regained his feet he saw Montgomery attempting to spear him with his bayonet. Throwing his stick at the soldier's head, he gained a reprieve and quickly escaped down Royal Exchange Lane. Montgomery made one last lunge for Palmes but lost his footing on the slippery snow and fell. By then other grenadiers had fired their muskets; seven or eight weapons were discharged. As the soldiers prepared to reload, Preston finally took charge and prevented further havoc "by striking up their fire-locks with [his] hand." Three persons were dead, two more lay dying, and six others had been wounded.[23]

Most of the victims were boys, young men, or sailors. Crispus Attucks, a sailor born in 1723 near Framingham, was the oldest of those killed. His parentage was Natick Indian and African American, and he may have been a slave in his early years. Only a temporary resident of Boston, he was set to sail for North Carolina. At six feet two inches, Attucks was unusually tall, and he was a leader of the sailors who earlier had been seen at Dock Square. He had been leaning on a stick as he stood on King Street, ten to fifteen feet from the soldiers and close to the head of Royal Exchange Lane, when two musket balls entered his chest.[24]

Boston Massacre, an engraving by Henry Pelham. This was the original creation after which Paul Revere made his famous print. (Courtesy of the American Antiquarian Society)

Close by Attucks and probably shot in the same volley was the rope maker Samuel Gray—no relation to John Gray—who had engaged in the Friday scuffle with the soldiers. Walking along Green Street as the bells tolled, he had asked Benjamin Davis Jr. where the fire was. Davis told him there was no fire but rather "the Soldiers fighting," and Gray excitedly exclaimed, "Damn it, I'm glad of it, i'le knock some of them in the Head." A small stick under his arm, he ran off in the direction of the commotion. On Quaker Lane near the Custom House, he encountered fellow rope maker Nicholas Ferriter, and together they walked the remaining way to King Street. Finding no action, Ferriter left with the understanding that Gray, who by then seemed calmer and without his stick, was going to return home as well. Gray must not have followed Ferriter's advice; for when the grenadiers arrived, he ran among the other spectators, clapping them on the back, urging them to stay, and advising them that the soldiers "dare not fire." He seriously misjudged the situation, apparently viewing it as merely a repeat of Friday's frolic. When the musket ball pierced his head, he was standing peacefully with his hands inside his coat.[25]

James Caldwell, the third victim to die at the scene, also was a mariner, a mate on Captain Morton's ship. He quite likely had been among the sailors at Dock Square. He was standing diagonally across King Street from the Custom House near Warden and Vernon's barbershop when two bullets struck him in the chest.[26]

Attucks, Gray, and Caldwell died almost immediately, but two others lingered a short while. Seventeen-year-old Samuel Maverick had been eating dinner with the keg maker Jonathan Cary and his family, when they heard the bells ring. They surmised there was a fire, and Maverick departed to see for himself. He was an apprentice to a joiner, "a promising youth," as newspaper accounts put it, and the half-brother of Ebenezer Mackintosh's wife. His promising future probably had little to do with his brother-in-law, for by 1770 Mackintosh had lost his political prominence as well as his town position of sealer of leather and was experiencing financial difficulties. There is no evidence that Mackintosh was present to witness any of the events and thus was spared the sight of Maverick being hit by an errant bullet. After the first shot, Maverick ran from the soldiers toward the Town House. According to the physician Richard Hirons, who examined the wound and was with Maverick when he died the following morning, the shape of the ball and the angle of entry indicated that the fatal shot had ricocheted before striking its victim. Only a bystander, he simply had been at the wrong place at the wrong time.[27]

Like Maverick, thirty-year-old Irish immigrant Patrick Carr had been attracted by the bells. At the home of his employer, a leather breeches maker, he learned that there was "an affray with the soldiers" rather than a fire and hurriedly put on an overcoat, hiding a sword between it and his ordinary coat. The breeches maker and a neighbor persuaded Carr to leave the sword behind before he rushed off. As he crossed King Street, near where Caldwell would be killed, to better view the soldiers, a musket ball "enter'd near his hip and went out at his side." He hung on for ten days. While on what would become his deathbed and with the prompting of the attending physician and future loyalist John Jeffries, Carr stated that the soldiers had shot in self-defense and that he "did not blame the man whoever he was, that shot him."[28]

Boston newspapers reported fears that two more of those who had been shot might die, but the remaining six victims ultimately recovered. Christopher Monk's wound was one of the more serious. Turned away from the soldiers, he was shot in the back "about 4 inches above the left kidney, near the spine," the ball traversing his torso and terminating in his chest, from where a physician removed it. He had been standing ten to fifteen feet from the grenadiers, above Royal Exchange Lane, with a "Catstick" (a stick used in the game tip-cat) in his hand. The first shot from Montgomery's gun didn't hit him, but it may explain why he was turned away from the soldiers when he was struck. Soon thereafter "he seemed to faulter," and James Brewer, a block maker who was next to him, asked if he had been wounded. Monk thought he had, but Brewer couldn't comprehend such an occurrence and initially tried to persuade the "lad" that he was mistaken; they were only firing powder.[29]

The merchant Edward Payne initially also suspected that only powder was being fired, but after the last burst from the muskets, he said, "I perceived I was wounded" in the arm. Along with Harrison Gray Jr. and George Bethune, he had been standing on the steps of his home, across King Street and slightly east of the Custom House and the soldiers. An important member of the popular movement, Payne sat on the merchants' committee that enforced the nonimportation agreement.[30]

Another victim, sailor Robert Patterson, had been more fortunate weeks before at the Christopher Seider tragedy, when pellets from Ebenezer Richardson's gun only passed through his clothing. As Patterson now stood in the middle of King Street about to place a hat on his head, musket balls pierced his right arm. With assistance, he trudged home in search of help.[31]

Two more apprentices, David Parker and seventeen-year-old John Clark, also received wounds. Parker was shot in the thigh, and Clark suffered a ball that entered "just above his groin and came out at his hip." The final victim was the tailor John Green, who had a bullet extracted from his thigh.[32]

Why the grenadiers fired remains a perplexing question. Almost everyone agreed that the soldier on the far right nearest Royal Exchange Lane, Montgomery, fired the first shot, probably reflexively, after an object struck the barrel of his musket. Montgomery was not responding to a command to fire or to threats that required self-defense. He accidentally pulled the trigger as he regained his balance and brought the weapon back up.

That may explain the initial shot, but what about those that followed? Twelve different deponents and witnesses stated or implied that Captain Thomas Preston had ordered the soldiers to fire, but eleven others swore either that someone other than Preston had given the order or that there had been no order at all. An additional eleven, including Richard Palmes, who stood next to Preston, testified that there had been an order but didn't know who had given it. Preston countered that he would not have stood in front of the muskets had he given such a command. Fellow officer Captain James Gifford concurred and defended Preston by testifying under oath that an officer would not order soldiers to fire when their bayonets were charged. He added that had such an order been made all of the soldiers would have fired at once rather than sporadically.[33] Gifford's testimony reduced the likelihood of Preston being directly responsible for the disaster, and the fact that the soldiers had not fired in unison cut against the claim that they had responded to shouts of "Fire!" regardless of the source. In short, it is unlikely that Preston gave the command or that the soldiers were merely following orders.

Preston declared that his men had acted in self-defense. After Montgomery discharged his weapon, the captain asserted, the men came under a barrage of "heavy clubs and snowballs . . . by which all our lives were in imminent danger."[34] It was a potentially risky line of defense. If their lives had been endangered, he should have commanded the soldiers to fire. If he had not given the order, he was either negligent and should have been reprimanded or there was no mortal threat.

In either case, Preston implied that their lives had not been threatened before the first shot. That may have been true, but there was no corroborative evidence that thrown objects endangered the men's lives *after* that shot either. If anything, fewer objects were flung and the soldiers were at less risk immediately after Montgomery pulled the trigger. Many of the people in the streets fled for safety or ducked for cover. Some stayed where they were, immobilized by disbelief or a bullfighter's daring, and a foolhardy few strode forward to see who had fired. The grenadiers may have been afraid and angry and perhaps they did feel in mortal peril, but they should have known that insults and taunts as well as snowballs, ice, oyster shells, and sticks emanating from a relatively small crowd, especially when its ranks were thinning, did not place their lives in jeopardy.

The original assemblage before the sentry was not larger than thirty people, primarily teenagers. As it marched to the Custom House, Preston's contingent attracted a larger throng, nearly doubling in size by the time the soldiers loaded their muskets. The crowd continued to grow, and at the time of the first shot probably numbered around 125 persons. Out of thirty-six deponents and trial witnesses, thirty-three estimated the size of the crowd at a hundred or fewer. The depositions and testimonies make it possible to identify and position on King Street and at the intersections near the Custom House sixty-eight different people. There was doubtless a substantial underrepresentation of sailors and apprentices, as well as some bystanders, so that an additional fifty to fifty-five people certainly falls within the range of possibility. Most of the crowd stood to the sides of the soldiers—the densest cluster at the head of Royal Exchange Lane where it met King Street—rather than directly in front of them. Paul Revere's diagram of where the victims were shot reinforces that testimony. The number of people still facing the troops after Montgomery's folly was significantly smaller than it had been earlier.[35] Eight armed men, with nearly a thousand reinforcements close by, deployed in front of an unarmed crowd of 125 that was rapidly diminishing were not in danger of their lives.

There looms the possibility that some of the soldiers killed or attempted to kill particular people deliberately. Sailors and soldiers had fought with each other nearly from the first day of the occupation, and Friday's rope walk fray still was fresh in the minds of soldiers of the 29th Regiment. Even in the moonlight, the sailors' attire distinguished them from the rest of the population. Two of the five men who died in the massacre were sailors, and one was a rope maker who had fought

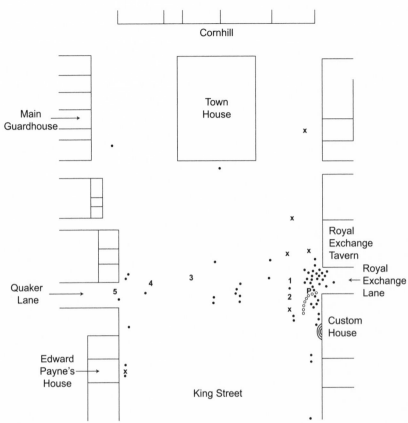

Map of people at the Boston Massacre. This diagram is modeled after Paul Revere's plan of the Massacre, but there are eight soldiers and Thomas Preston rather than Revere's seven soldiers, and Patrick Carr, the fifth victim who died later, is added. 1 is Crispus Attucks, 2 is Samuel Gray, 3 is James Caldwell, 4 is Patrick Carr, 5 is Samuel Maverick, and P is Thomas Preston. O represents each soldier, X represents each wounded person, and the solid dot represents spectators and participants. See chapter 11, n. 35 for sources.

with British troops on March 2. Another sailor was among the six who were wounded but recovered. It is equally possible that the victims were shot randomly. After all, the proportion of sailors and the rope maker who died approximated the proportion of sailors and rope makers in the crowd. Most of those who were killed or wounded were shot from a distance where visibility, even with moonlight, was limited and the accuracy of muskets was imperfect.

The deaths of Attucks and Gray, however, require special attention. Both of those men stood in close proximity to the grenadiers, and they would have been recognized as a sailor and a rope maker. The unusually tall, dark Crispus Attucks stood out still more, particularly at a distance of no more than fifteen feet. Two bullets, from one or two muskets, simultaneously struck him in the chest. Whether the responsible soldier or soldiers intended to kill him may never be known, but there can be little doubt that one or two aimed at him. Perhaps it is only a coincidence, but the only other victims who received two bullets were the sailors James Caldwell and Robert Patterson.[36]

The evidence that Samuel Gray was intentionally killed is stronger still. In a deposition Charles Hobby claimed that one of the grenadiers "at the distance of about four or five yards, pointed his piece directly for the said Gray's head and fired. Mr. Gray, after struggling, turned himself right round upon his heel and fell dead." Edward Gambett Langford, in his testimony at the soldiers' trial, identified the shooter as Matthew Kilroy, one of the grenadiers from the 29th Regiment who had participated in the March 2 brawl. Langford was confident of his identification of Kilroy but less certain that Gray had been the soldier's exclusive target. "Did not see that Kilroy aimed at Gray any more than me," he testified. "He designed to kill both of us I suppose."[37]

Edward Hill, Ebenezer Bridgham, and Joseph Hilyer all testified that one of the soldiers aimed at a "lad that was running down the middle of the street, and kept the motion of his gun after him a considerable time, and then fired," but missed. Hilyer stated that the culprit was the "last Man upon the left but one," presumably the sentry Hugh White. The sailor Robert Patterson also identified White as the man who wounded him, but he didn't indicate whether he thought the sentry purposefully shot him; the fatally wounded Patrick Carr believed that either White or Wemms was responsible.[38]

In none of these cases can we know with certainty what a soldier was thinking when he fired his weapon. Montgomery most likely had inadvertently pulled the trigger. The impulse of the others is murkier. Perhaps some did believe they were defending their lives or obeying a command, and perhaps a few discharged their weapons immediately after an adjacent comrade had fired. It is just as likely that several of them, without any premeditation, seized the opportunity to vent their frustration and anger at the hostile residents or to attain revenge. Whatever the case, the massacre on King Street was a soldiers' riot.

An additional ingredient makes the story even more complex. All who recounted how many muskets had been fired—except for Francis Read, who thought there had been eight to ten—reported that they heard and saw no more than eight of the soldiers' guns discharge, and yet there were more musket balls flying that night than there were grenadiers' weapons. Physicians extracted five balls from four of the victims. Additionally, two bullets struck James Caldwell and another two Robert Patterson, and one bullet each wounded the five other persons—a grand total of fourteen possible bullets. Some of the bullets may have struck more than one victim, but it is equally likely that other bullets hit no human target.[39] The conclusion that there were more than eight musket balls seems irrefutable.

There are three possible explanations for the surfeit of musket balls: the soldiers double-loaded their guns; they reloaded their guns and fired a second time; or people other than the soldiers, perhaps located in the second floor of the Custom House, also fired at the crowd. With three of the victims being hit by multiple bullets, Patterson's statement that the sentry brought up "his gun and fired, balls going through my lower right arm," and John Danbrook's testimony that two balls came from Montgomery's gun support the interpretation that a single round contained two musket balls. That alone would account for as many as sixteen bullets. The explanation that soldiers reloaded and fired again has little evidentiary basis. Only William Wyat saw such an activity, when, according to his description, Corporal William Wemms fired a second time after his gun only flashed with its first round. The near consensus that no more than eight guns had been fired discredits the reloading thesis. The last possibility, that gunfire also came from the second floor of the Custom House, is intriguing but, in the final analysis, inconclusive if not unconvincing. Five people, one of whom later committed perjury, deposed that they had witnessed weapons being discharged from the Custom House, and the physician Benjamin Church Jr. believed that the bullets he extracted from Crispus Attucks had a downward trajectory. But the simple fact that none of these witnesses claimed more than three shots came from the Custom House leaves the hypothesis with only limited explanatory power. It simply cannot account for all the extra bullets. More critically, although people asserted that they saw guns or flashes coming out of Custom House windows, no credible witness could identify who fired the weapons. Four men were charged; all were acquitted. There might have been guns blazing from the Custom House, but without evidence of who was firing them this interpretation lacks credible support.[40]

Church bells rang again, and news of the atrocity spread quickly through Boston that night. As shocked people rushed to help the victims, other residents, some of them armed, poured into King Street. At first the soldiers, perhaps misinterpreting the movement toward nearby fallen bodies as a threat to themselves and still filled with rage, thrust their bayonets at whoever came close, but then they regained their composure and drew back. Preston, alarmed by the possibility of a second massacre—this time of the grenadiers and himself—marched the men to the safety of the main guardhouse. He commanded them to seal off the narrow street from assaults. Hearing cries of "To arms! To arms!" and the town drums beating, Preston ordered that their own drums should sound to call out the 29th Regiment. The small street between the main guard and the Town House soon was filled with redcoats ready for battle. The first row of soldiers kneeled to maximize their firepower. The 14th Regiment armed itself in readiness but remained in its barracks.[41]

Town leaders sent expresses to neighboring towns informing them of what had occurred and alerting them to potential trouble, and they prepared to light the beacon on Beacon Hill as a signal for help. Thousands of armed men in the countryside were prepared to march to Boston.[42] If ever there was a moment during the occupation when a full-scale battle between colonists and British soldiers was imminent, that moment had arrived. One nervous soldier or one foolhardy colonist could have pulled a trigger leading to the deaths of hundreds that night; it could have been the shot heard 'round the world.

At his home in the North End about 10 o'clock, Acting Governor Thomas Hutchinson heard church bells close by and assumed there was a fire, but local residents informed him of the potentially greater threat. Hutchinson knew immediately that he had to intervene "or the town would be all in blood." Out on the street on his way to the Town House, he encountered the clamor of citizens, some with clubs and cutlasses, "all calling for their firearms." Fearing for his own safety, he ducked into a house and then snaked his way to King Street. He immediately called for Preston and rebuked him, "How came you to fire without Orders from a Civil Magistrate?" At Preston's trial months later, Hutchinson couldn't, or wouldn't, recall Preston's possibly incriminating response. Witnesses to the conversation, however, remembered the captain saying he did it to save his sentry or his men.[43] Their recollections weren't exact, and it is unclear to what specific action Preston may have been referring (perhaps he meant sending the troops to the Custom House, or perhaps he was covering for his men), but it was the closest to an admission of responsibility for the order to fire that he ever made.

Before entering the Town House, Hutchinson conferred with Colonel Maurice Carr, commander of the 29th Regiment, and they agreed to retire the troops to their barracks. But Hutchinson still needed to convince the townspeople to disperse. Following conversations in the packed Council Chamber with a few members of the Council, some of the justices, and other residents of the town, he went to the window and told the crowd that the soldiers were returning to their barracks. He also pledged that there would be an immediate inquiry concerning the conduct of Preston and the grenadiers. People below were satisfied for the time being, and at 1 o'clock in the morning most of them departed for their homes. Popular leaders relayed word to neighboring towns that the immediate crisis had ended, and they removed the unlit tar barrel from the beacon. Whatever desire there may have been for revenge was put aside for the restoration of peace, the hope for justice, and the likelihood of the soldiers leaving Boston.[44]

Roughly one hundred people stood vigil until the conclusion of the initial investigation. The justices began an inquest on the spot, interviewing witnesses as well as Captain Preston. By 3 a.m. they decided that there was sufficient reason to indict the captain and his men. The sheriff escorted Preston to jail, and the soldiers were forced to join him in the morning.[45] Hutchinson had skillfully guided negotiations to a temporary truce, but after a brief night's rest would be tested again the next day.

As the acting governor wearily arrived at the Town House the following morning, he might have seen blood still staining the snow, a grim reminder of the previous night and of how volatile the situation remained. Before the 11 o'clock meeting with the hastily assembled Council began, Boston's selectmen and several justices warned Hutchinson that there would be further bloodshed were the soldiers not removed from the town. There was to be a town meeting at Faneuil Hall that very morning, and the people would not be appeased "whilst the Troops were among them." Some of the justices resided outside of Boston, and they delivered the same message on behalf of the countrymen.[46]

When the formal Council meeting commenced with only Hutchinson and Council members present, those members reiterated the selectmen's and justices' concerns. Needing military advice, consent, and cover, Hutchinson with the Council's concurrence requested Colonels Dalrymple and Carr's presence. In the midst of their conversation, a committee of fifteen "respectable Gentlemen" representing the town meeting "waited" on the acting governor with the "opinion . . . that the inhabitants and soldiery can no longer live together in safety." They called on Hutchinson to order the troops out of town "to prevent further blood & carnage."[47]

After the committee from the town meeting left the room, the Council unanimously seconded the recommendation. When Hutchinson maintained that he had no authority to order the regiments away, eyes turned toward the military officers. Dalrymple, however, was adamantly opposed to removing the troops—at least that was what he wrote to Thomas Gage, his superior. He argued that if a rebellion against the soldiers was imminent, that was all the more reason to keep the regiments in place. He also contended that the "Officers of the Revenue" would be left unprotected. Hutchinson looked for a compromise that would end the crisis and proposed that the 29th, the more "obnoxious" regiment, be sent to Castle William, the main guard be removed, and the 14th stay in town but under restraints. Dalrymple reluctantly accepted the proposition, with the qualification that the location of the 29th was subject to Gage's approval. The acting governor invited the town committee back into the Council chamber and presented them with a written version of the offer.

To accommodate nearly four thousand people eagerly waiting for the committee's report, leaders moved the afternoon town meeting to Old South Church. There Hutchinson's proposal satisfied only one citizen; everyone else voted it unsatisfactory. The meeting created a new committee of its leading citizens—John Hancock, Samuel Adams, William Molineux, William Phillips, Joseph Warren, Joshua Henshaw, and Samuel Pemberton—to convey to the acting governor their demand for "a total and immediate removal of the Troops." When Hutchinson convened the afternoon session of the Council, Dalrymple, Carr, and Captain Caldwell of HMS *Rose* sat with them. He wanted other "Crown officers" there as well but didn't press his luck. Hutchinson had been prepared for a rejection from the town meeting and was not surprised when the seven-man committee informed him of the decision.

After the committee delivered the meeting's demand and left the room, the Council, Hutchinson, and the military officers resumed their earlier debate. Dire predictions came from each of the Council members. Royall Tyler foresaw ten thousand men from Boston and outlying areas battling the troops until the last soldier was vanquished. James Russell from Charlestown and Samuel Dexter from Dedham supported Tyler's grim vision, insisting that men from neighboring towns would take up arms. Another Council member cautioned that if either Hutchinson or Dalrymple refused to comply, the blame for the bloody consequences would fall on his shoulders. For his part, Hutchinson was skeptical that any such uprising would occur. It was one thing to respond to military atrocities and quite another to initiate a wholesale rebellion. But he didn't want to risk being wrong. Dalrymple reiterated his earlier analysis but was concerned that he had no more than "600 effective men" and that he could bring no more than four hundred to any one place in response to an uprising.

Facing a unanimous Council and a hostile town and countryside, Hutchinson concluded that both regiments must go to Castle Island. Master of finesse and protector of his own future, the acting governor put a quasi-order to Dalrymple in writing. "I am sensible I have no power to order the Troops to the Castle," he penned, "but under the present circumstances of the Town and Province I cannot avoid in consequence of this unanimous advice of the council desiring you to order them there which I must submit to you." Dalrymple, also watching out for his own interests, gave his word that he would comply, though in his letter to Gage he sought to avoid responsibility, claiming, "Being subservient to the Civil authority prevented me from doing what I could have wished."

The townspeople of Boston greeted the news happily but took the precaution of posting their own military watch each night until the troops were gone. They looked forward to a return to normality. "The town is quiet, the Troops preparing to leave it, Guards and Centuries at an end," the future loyalist and Hutchinson kin Andrew Oliver Jr. wrote on March 7. With relief and lament he noted, "Thus has an unarmed multitude in their own opinion gained a complete victory over two Regiments of his Majesty's regular Troops."[48]

Chapter 12

Aftermath

More than ten thousand mourners attended the funeral of Crispus Attucks, James Caldwell, Samuel Gray, and Samuel Maverick in the late afternoon of March 8. Most shops closed, and church bells in Boston, Charlestown, and Roxbury pealed as the procession began. Relations and friends brought the caskets of Gray and Maverick from family homes and townspeople accompanied those of the nonresidents Attucks and Caldwell from Faneuil Hall. The contingents met at King Street, the "Theatre of that inhuman tragedy," and, with family members and town residents so numerous as to have to walk six abreast, proceeded to the burying ground, where the bodies were placed in a single vault. Patrick Carr died six days later, and a similarly well-attended funeral commemorated the consequences of the soldiers' riot.[1] That, of course, was the point of such a public ritual: to be a reminder of the occupation, an instrument of solidarity, and last (and probably least) a remembrance of the victims.

The day before Carr's funeral the last of the troops left Boston. For more than a week they had dribbled out, a few companies at a time. By March 16 the remnants of the 14th Regiment joined their fellow soldiers at the barracks of Castle Island. They may have evacuated the town proper, but they still were only a few miles by sea away. Though Lieutenant Colonel Dalrymple delayed as long as he could, ultimately he had to keep his word. General Gage's initial reaction on hearing the news of the shooting of citizens and the agreement to remove all the troops was to approve what already had been determined; but when he learned on March 13 that some of the soldiers remained and not fully understanding the severity of the crisis, he quickly urged renegotiating the arrangement. He hoped that the removal of the despised 29th might satisfy Bostonians.[2] By the time his letter reached Dalrymple, both regiments were on Castle Island.

Provincial militiamen already occupied Castle William, the fort protecting Boston Harbor. British soldiers therefore had no choice but to reside in the barracks outside the fort, a space sufficient for a single regiment but inadequate for two. Recognizing the difficulty of the situation and the impossibility of the regiments fulfilling their purpose of assisting "the Civil Magistrates in the due Execution of the Laws," Gage proposed to Hutchinson that both regiments be sent out of the province, "one of them as Soon as Possible for, the Castle Barracks will not contain them both." The acting governor, trying to reduce his exposure, patiently explained that he lacked the power to order the troops from Massachusetts. In fact, he preferred that the regiments stay. "I am absolutely alone, no single person of my Council or any other person in authority affording me the least support and if the people are disposed to any measure nothing more is necessary than for the multitude to assemble, for nobody dares oppose them or call them to account," Hutchinson complained. "I could not justifie, at such a time, moving to send the Kings Troops out of the Province."[3]

Gage believed the health hazard posed by overcrowding outweighed Hutchinson's concerns, and he only waited for word from England to dispatch one of the regiments. Despite Hutchinson's cheerful account a month later of conditions on Castle Island that generated "so little complaint from Officers or Privates," Gage was unmoved. In mid-May the general ordered the 29th from Castle Island to New Jersey, and on May 17 all of the regiment except Thomas Preston, the soldiers in jail, and potential witnesses gladly left the boundaries of Boston. With the 14th in futile isolation, Dalrymple sought a better posting, but feared his career was ruined.[4]

Although British soldiers were nearby and could return as a police force in the unlikely event a civil magistrate would request them, Boston no longer was an occupied city. The first of the popular movement's two primary goals had been achieved. The second, the complete repeal of the Townshend Acts, proved elusive. In late April 1770 Bostonians received word that the ministry had revoked all the Townshend duties except for the one on tea. The removal of the tax on paper, glass, lead, and painters' colors helped British manufacturers who faced competition from colonial producers of those commodities. There were no tea plantations in North America, on the other hand, and the revenue from the tax was substantial. Had there been little or no colonial resistance, members of Parliament claimed they would have rescinded the tax on tea as well, but there had been opposition and Parliament felt once again compelled to demonstrate its power. Similar to the Declaratory Act in 1766, proclaiming Parliament's right to tax the colonies, the duty on tea in effect maintained the constitutionality of Parliament's sovereignty.[5]

The merchants' committee, by this point nearly synonymous with the town meeting, had made clear that nonimportation would continue until there was total repeal of the Townshend duties. But in 1766, when the ministry reduced the tax on sugar and molasses to a level at which merchants could prosper, Bostonians, like other colonists, pragmatically relented rather than adhering absolutely to the principle of no taxation without representation. Would they accept less than total victory this time? Tea was a discretionary consumer product that could be boycotted rather than an essential part of the economy, as was molasses for rum distillers, but the populace still was enflamed from the occupation and the Massacre. Some members of the Boston community, such as well-stocked merchants and artisans and manufacturers who made goods that also were produced in Britain, would profit from a continuation of nonimportation; other merchants, shopkeepers, and unemployed mechanics and laborers favored the economic opportunity that restored normal trade would provide. Some believed that the principles at stake demanded ongoing sacrifice, whereas others were willing to settle for a compromise.[6]

The ships that brought news of the partial repeal of the Townshend duties also carried cargo prohibited under the Nonimportation Agreement. A few sea captains in London, with orders to ship goods as soon as the duties were lifted, may have mistakenly assumed that the curtailing of levies on four out of the five categories of commodities fulfilled colonial expectations, or they may have exploited (or been ordered to exploit) a perceived opportunity to restore full trade. Whatever the motives, the Body of the merchants' committee was not yet willing to halt nonimportation without the nullification of all taxes on commerce. After vigorous debate at several heavily attended meetings, the Body "bro't the importers to a due reflection on their own mistaken conduct, and a free consent under their hands to reship all their goods for London immediately." John Hancock, "so nobly generous and disinterested," provided without charge his own ship to transport the goods back to England. For an undisclosed reason, culpable merchants professed that tea couldn't be reshipped and voluntarily stored it in the cellar of the Custom House with the promise that they wouldn't sell it. The Body found those conditions unsatisfactory yet also recognized that seizing the contraband from the Custom House was politically unwise. With the hope of finding a means to break the impasse, it held more meetings.[7]

Boston newspapers created the impression of near unanimity for the vigorous maintenance of nonimportation until Parliament repealed all duties, but there were signs of growing disaffection. John Rowe, a leading merchant and smuggler who had been in the forefront of opposition to British trade restrictions, confided in his diary that he "did not approve much of their Proceedings—think them too severe." Nathaniel Rogers, one of the well-publicized violators and a nephew of Thomas Hutchinson, went well beyond muttering in his diary. He hastened to New York City with the hope of enlisting that city's merchants in a coalition of importers who dared to resist nonimportation. New York was fertile ground for undermining the Nonimportation Agreement, but Rogers's scheme was premature. On the evening of May 10 several thousand New York "spectators" witnessed an effigy of Rogers dangling from a gallows. The crowd paraded the effigy and gallows through the city's streets until they arrived at the visiting merchant's lodgings "in order to pay their respects to himself." When the crowd discovered that he was not in residence (fortunately for him, he was dining out of town), it took the pageantry to the Common and burned it "amidst the joyful acclamations of the people." The crowd dispersed, but friends warned Rogers of what had transpired. About 2 o'clock in the morning, Rogers's servant surreptitiously gathered his belongings, and they fled the city for Boston, where they were only slightly more welcome.[8]

Although New Yorkers thwarted Rogers on this occasion, his venture highlighted the precarious alliance of Boston, New York, and Philadelphia merchants. Should any one of those groups capitulate, the entire colonial Nonimportation Agreement was jeopardized. Economic and political leverage to repeal the last of the trade taxes would diminish should British manufacturers, workers, and merchants increase their business, and no merchant wanted to watch helplessly as trade was diverted to competitors in another city that had abandoned nonimportation. In mid-May, when letters from New York and Philadelphia inquired whether Boston merchants had decided to break the agreement (rumors had been floating of such an action), the Body at Faneuil Hall voted "nearly unanimously" to hold steady and quickly informed the public and concerned persons in other cities that Boston would not import British goods until all duties were repealed. Once again, impassioned letters focusing on first principles appeared in Boston newspapers. Should colonists accept taxation without their consent, if only for the single item of tea, "Better Security" cautioned, they would be opening the door to their own enslavement. "Will you be freemen or slaves? Will you purchase an inheritance for yourselves and your posterity? Will you purchase a goodly dwelling, or lie doom'd to a dungeon?"[9]

The crowd as an enforcer of nonimportation reappeared. On June 1 a large throng visited the storehouse, lodgings, and shop of the McMasters brothers. For nearly a year James and Patrick McMasters's names had been advertised in Boston papers and flyers as import violators, and it is likely that they owned some of the tea secured in the Custom House cellar. This occasion went well beyond efforts to deter commerce. The boisterous assembly demanded that the McMasters close their business and leave town by June 4 to "avoid the consequences of the public resentment." Sufficiently intimidated, the brothers agreed to shut down their enterprise and negotiated an extension of their residence, until at least the meeting of the Body on June 7. They failed to appear, but the popular leader William Molineux presented an application from Nathaniel Rogers, who, "in the most suppliant manner," promised "to do everything in his power to satisfy the people and recover their esteem." Molineux urged acceptance, but others suspected Rogers's transformation merely a ploy to win him favor before he became secretary of the province. After "a very full debate," the application was tabled, never to be considered again.[10]

Rogers was denied the town's respect, but he fared better than one of the McMasters, who was caught in town on June 19. Placed in a cart with a barrel of tar and a bag of feathers, he began to panic as it approached King Street, the site designated for his humiliation. Fearing he might faint, some in the crowd allowed McMasters to rest in a house before undergoing "the indignity of this modern Punishment." Severely shaken, he promised to leave the town never to return were he spared being tarred and feathered. All accepted the proposal on the condition that he return to the cart and be hauled to the town's boundary with Roxbury. After departing Boston another of the brothers was ostracized again, being forced to leave both Marblehead and Salem.[11]

None of the commissioners suffered physical injury, but some assailants broke windows at Henry Hulton's country home. Hulton, believing "the town is little short of a state of Anarchy," stayed away from Boston for the first three months after the Massacre, then fled for Castle William after the broken window incident. The remaining commissioners, customs officials, and their families also sought the safety of the Castle. They may have been overreacting, just as they had in 1768, and perhaps hoped for a repeat performance from the ministry, but Bostonians were pleased that the board had stopped meeting. Brattle Street Church minister Samuel Cooper, in a letter to former governor Thomas Pownall, declared himself "an enemy to all Disorders, and wish they c'd be prevented." He added, however, that the circumstances of a government enforcing unconstitutional measures perhaps warranted the behavior.[12]

Rowdy crowds, calls for protecting colonial rights, fearful commissioners at Castle William, and efforts to compel support of nonimportation: all were reminiscent of summer 1768. Yet there were some important differences as well. The only objectionable tax was on tea; there was little likelihood of troops soon returning to patrol Boston streets; and there were sharper divisions within Boston and between the major cities.

New York turned out to be the weak link. In late June New York merchants sent a letter proposing that trade with Great Britain should be restored except for tea. The Body in Boston remained absolutists—at least to outside eyes—and resolved to boycott all British commodities until Parliament repealed the tax on tea. Despite both Boston and Philadelphia residents rejecting their proposition, New York merchants broke the coalition, and on July 11 the *Earl of Halifax*, a packet boat, sailed for England with orders for all goods but tea. Months later Samuel Adams concluded that the New York defection killed the Nonimportation Agreement.[13]

Bostonians' immediate reaction was to pretend that nothing had changed. One *Boston Evening-Post* writer blustered that they didn't need New York. The growth of domestic manufacturing and disciplined consumption would deliver them from British impositions. The pageantry of flags, drums, and a French horn provided a prelude to the meeting of the Body on July 24 and perhaps energized flagging spirits. One committee traveled to Salem, Marblehead, Newbury, and Haverhill to combat breaches of the Agreement, and another committee deliberated on how to hold "the Union of the Colonies" together. But they must have known they were merely postponing the time until they must make a bitter decision. When Philadelphia merchants went the way of New York on September 20, even fleeting hopes died. Within weeks the fraying Body voted "to open the Importation of Goods from Great Britain, except Teas, and such other Articles as are, or may be subject to Duties for the Purpose of raising a Revenue in America," and the committee of inspection returned stored property to its owners.[14]

Neither the House as a body nor Acting Governor Thomas Hutchinson entered into these debates and decisions. Power had shifted to Boston, its leaders and its people, and the influence of the province's central institutions had weakened. That certainly was the assessment of Hutchinson, Gage, Dalrymple, and the commissioners. In April 1770 Gage complained, "Government is at End in Boston, and in the hands of the People, who have only to assemble to execute any Designs." His solution, as he told Hutchinson and members of the ministry, was force. He may have based his conclusion on Dalrymple's post-Massacre opinion that the acting governor "has no weight or power here." Henry Hulton agreed and blamed the government's decline on the "fanatic rage of independent levellers."[15] All three men shared a hierarchical view of governance, and the increased power of popular voices appalled them.

Hutchinson similarly was an elitist, but he must have understood that his limited authority resulted from more than a rising democracy. As lieutenant governor and acting governor, he had had to enforce policy with which he sometimes disagreed. His ambitions were both a strength that drove him to excel and part of his problem. He could disagree privately and obliquely with his superiors; but if he didn't want to damage his career he had to support the king, the ministry, and Parliament publicly. After the Massacre he felt the Council and other allies (he had long since given up on the House) had abandoned him. He was caught in the grip of a vise—the surging popular movement on one side, the British government on the other—and felt alone, isolated. Perhaps experiencing the return of a depression that had incapacitated him previously, and for once questioning his own abilities, in late March he sent a letter of resignation to the Earl of Hillsborough. After all his years yearning to be governor and after all his compromises, he finally decided he no longer could continue. He didn't realize that Francis Bernard had resigned as governor; and while his letter was in transit, a letter from Hillsborough offering him the position crossed his somewhere on the Atlantic. He was embarrassed and possibly chagrined, but wavered from accepting. Eventually, as the passions provoked by the occupation receded, he changed his mind, and late in the year officially became governor.[16]

With a prickly and depressed acting governor and a partisan House, little was accomplished in the provincial government. They had been moved to the periphery of power, and their own pettiness and focus on small victories made them nearly irrelevant. When Hutchinson raised the issue of his unpaid salary, the House grudgingly approved reduced funds. When the House nominated John Hancock as speaker pro tempore during Thomas Cushing's illness, the acting governor rejected the choice. After learning of his possible appointment as governor, Hutchinson became marginally more conciliatory, but he still reveled in frustrating the assembly.[17]

The chief issue of contention was the location of the General Court. Hutchinson had inherited Bernard's decision to move the Court across the Charles River from Boston to Cambridge. The ostensible reason for the relocation was to separate the House from the influence of Boston, but near the end of his administration Bernard delighted in inflicting any irritation he could. Although the Earl of Hillsborough instructed Hutchinson to place the Court at Cambridge, he still allowed the acting governor latitude to use his own best judgment. Seeking to establish his and the British government's authority, Hutchinson led House members to believe that he was acting only on instructions. When the assembly argued that this was all an inconvenience to itself and to Harvard College, where it sat, partially because of the difficulty of being apart from records, Hutchinson responded that his hands were tied; he must not depart from his duty to the king. The House countered that there was a law, dating from King William's reign, establishing the colony's capital at Boston. The acting governor retorted that its reference was to a "form" (Boston was named only because it was the capital at the time, not necessarily forever), not to an imperative. With that, the House, reacting to the move as an intended insult, resolved not to do business until it was reconvened in Boston.[18] Each side tried to believe it was fighting for principle, when in fact all that was at stake was pride and partisan advantage.

The provincial government remained stalled until mid-September 1770, when the House learned that the acting governor had authorized the removal of provincial troops from Castle William and had replaced them with redcoats. In the spring the Earl of Hillsborough had alerted both Hutchinson and Gage of the king's desire to transfer possession of the fort to the Crown. Hutchinson worried that the action would stir unrest, or worse, in Boston and postponed shifting power as long as he could. When he received an express message from Gage on September 8 with an accompanying order from Hillsborough commanding the transfer, he faced yet another dilemma. Massachusetts's charter specified that all of the colony's forts were under the command of the governor. Replacing the province's force with British soldiers appeared a violation of that stipulation. Hutchinson reconciled himself to Hillsborough's order with the belief that as commander in chief he still controlled the fort regardless of who occupied it. As long as he was the one to make the decision, it complied with the charter. His perception of diminishing tensions in Boston as well as the benefit to his own career made the judgment all the easier.[19]

Hutchinson and Dalrymple met the next day to work out the arrangements. To perpetuate the charade of command, the future governor offered the lieutenant colonel a commission. Dalrymple hesitated until he consulted with Gage. Hutchinson at first was willing to delay for Gage's instructions, but something bothered him. Perhaps he feared how the ministry would view his hesitation, or perhaps he trusted that everyone would agree that the charter must be obeyed. In any case, without any further negotiation he decided to order the transfer. On the morning of September 10 he so informed the Council. There was a brief debate, during which he convinced most of the members that he had no options. In the afternoon, after a ceremonial exchange of keys, the provincial troops under the leadership of a disgusted John Phillips marched out of Castle William and were replaced by several companies of the 14th Regiment.[20]

For Hutchinson the timing was as good as it could be. Distracted by the unraveling Nonimportation Agreement, Bostonians' outrage was muted. As Gage put it, there was "consternation" but no "commotion." In late November the House belatedly registered its displeasure. Hutchinson

216 | As If an Enemy's Country

had violated the charter by relinquishing control of Castle William, a fort built by provincial funds; but there was nothing they could do, and their constituents yearned for a return to normality. No matter how much Hutchinson protested that he still was in control, he wasn't.[21] Dalrymple reported to Gage, not to the acting governor. British regulars, not the Massachusetts militia, occupied Castle William. Hutchinson had complained of his decreasing power in March. He contributed to its diminution in September, rationalized the outcome in November, and became governor soon thereafter.

Although Boston's mood mellowed during the course of 1770, immediately after the Massacre passions ran high. According to John Adams's account in his *Autobiography*, on the morning of March 6, roughly twelve hours after the soldiers' riot on King Street, the prosperous merchant and future loyalist James Forrest, "with tears streaming from his eyes," came into his law office and lamented that no lawyer would defend Captain Thomas Preston. Forrest already had met with the Admiralty Court judge Robert Auchmuty and with the promising young attorney Josiah Quincy Jr., and neither man would agree to take on the case unless joined by Adams. Adams replied that every man deserved a fair trial, but also that he would use no artifice. He would only present a straightforward case, nothing "more than Fact, Evidence and Law would justify." Should Preston accept those terms, he would serve as his lawyer. The deal was made. Reflecting back on his decision three years later, Adams wrote in his diary, "The Part I took in Defence of Captn. Preston and the Soldiers, procured me Anxiety, and Obloquy enough. It was, however, one of the most gallant, generous, manly and disinterested Actions of my whole Life, and one of the best Pieces of Service I ever rendered my Country."[22]

Adams was a man on the rise. Born in Braintree on October 19, 1735, of a pious and moderately well-off country family, he attended Harvard College to fulfill his father's wish that he become a clergyman. But the ministry was not for him, and after graduating from college he read law while teaching school in Worcester. In 1758 he was admitted to the Boston bar. He was immensely ambitious, seeking not merely fame and fortune but immortality, as he told his close friend Jonathan Sewall, and the law and public service were his means. As complex a man as any of the future founding fathers, Adams was principled, committed to helping his "country" as well as himself, intelligent, hardworking to

John Adams, 1765, a pastel on paper portrait by
Benjamin Blyth. (Courtesy of the Massachusetts
Historical Society / The Bridgeman Art Library)

the point of exhaustion, introspective but capable of self-delusion, quick
to imagine slights, and consumed by his reputation. He was sometimes
tormented by the conflict between principle and personal advantage.
The *Autobiography* was begun after he left the presidency, and it, and to
a certain extent his diary, was written with posterity (and immortality)
in mind.[23] Adams revealed flaws and honest depictions, but he also
constructed the person he wanted future generations to admire.

Adams's description of his meeting with Forrest and his assessment of
his decision to defend Preston reveal how he wished to be remembered
and in part who he was. On March 6 he was thirty-four years old, married,
a father, and on the threshold of prominence. He was becoming one of
Boston's leading lawyers. A cousin of Samuel Adams and a participant in
the popular movement, he nonetheless was in the second tier of Boston
leaders. He was not yet someone whom Auchmuty—more distinguished
than Adams in the Boston legal community, a member of the court
faction, and a future loyalist—or the young Quincy would follow without

other inducements. Weeks later Quincy explained to his father, who had chastised him for taking on a seemingly career-killing assignment, that he had accepted the post only after receiving the encouragement of "an Adams [Samuel], a Hancock, a Molineux, a Cushing, a Henshaw, a Pemberton, a Warren, a Cooper, and a Phillips."[24]

John Adams must have had a similar arrangement, and his election as one of Boston's four representatives in June may have been part of his compensation. Rather than being rejected for defending Preston and the soldiers, he was rewarded with the trust and confidence of his fellow citizens. Nor did he work for free. At a period when the "Bar and the Clerks universally complain of the Scarcity of Business," a condition Adams attributed to the Nonimportation Agreement and the "declension of trade," he had landed a large, important, and highly publicized case.[25]

Boston leaders had more to do than secure defense lawyers who were friendly to the town. Unsure whether Attorney General Jonathan Sewall would pursue convictions vigorously, they hired Robert Treat Paine, a Taunton attorney and former Boston resident, to augment the prosecution. Although the town paid for Paine's services, it presented him as a representative of the victims' families to mask its involvement. The selectmen and other leaders rapidly collected testimonies deposed in public meetings before justices of the peace, a setting that provided openness and intimidation. They wanted to obtain evidence while memories were still fresh so as to assist the prosecution and to fuel the public relations war in England. They suspected Hutchinson, the commissioners, and the military would attempt to shape the ministry's and the English public's view of the incident, and hastened to spin their version.[26]

Crown officials in Boston and the military were indeed secretly gathering their own firsthand accounts. They sought to convince British authorities that the soldiers had been provoked to fire after the maltreatment of the previous year and a half. Their immediate goal, however, was to delay the trials. They already were fearful that Bostonians might take the law into their own hands and kill Preston and the soldiers, and they were certain that fair trials were not possible until emotions had cooled. Attorney General Sewall helped postpone the trial by leaving town soon after indicting Preston and the soldiers. He generally focused on legal matters elsewhere and avoided involvement in cases in which he would alienate his superiors with convictions or anger the town with acquittals. Nor was there a functioning chief justice. As soon as he became acting governor, Hutchinson had recused himself from the Superior Court but did not resign. The remaining four justices used the attorney general's absence as an excuse for not hearing criminal cases.[27]

Boston leaders, at one point invading the courtroom, pressured the court to begin the trials. Reluctantly the justices negotiated a compromise whereby they would sit for the trial of Ebenezer Richardson, the customs informer who had killed Christopher Seider, but postpone the trial of the Massacre defendants until late May. Much to the justices' chagrin and contrary to its instructions, the jury found Richardson guilty of murder. The judges deferred sentencing him, and nearly two years later the Crown pardoned him. When the court reconvened in late May, two of the judges failed to appear—one was sick and the other had fallen from his horse, or so it was said—and the Massacre trial was delayed again until late August.[28]

Despite his role in the shootings on King Street, Preston generally was well regarded. John Rowe, when entering into his diary the events of March 5, noted that Preston "bears a good Character." Only a week after the fatal episode, William Palfrey, John Hancock's clerk and an important person in the popular movement, wrote that Preston "before this unfortunate event . . . always behav'd himself unexceptionably & had the character of a sober, honest man & a good officer." Apparently wanting to reinforce such opinions, from the confines of the Boston jail Preston placed a notice in the *Boston Gazette* praising "the Inhabitants in general of this Town—who throwing aside all Party and Prejudice, have with the utmost Humanity and Freedom stept forth Advocates for Truth, in Defence of my injured Innocence, in the late unhappy Affair that happened on Monday Night last: And to assure them, that I shall ever have the highest Sense of the Justice they have done me." General Gage concluded that Preston was premature in his gratitude and predicted that his words would be used against him. Privately Preston also wrote his version of the events of March 5—his "case" was published and distributed widely in England—but Gage declined to print it in the colonies for fear that it would provoke the population.[29]

Unfortunately for Preston, Gage was accurate on both counts. After three months in jail, the captain grew increasingly anxious. He wrote

Dalrymple of "his great fears that the people were so enraged as to force the Gaol that night and make him a sacrifice, several of his friends having informed him this was their intention." A few days later the side-by-side publication in Boston newspapers of his flattering advertisement and his case, in which he charged Bostonians with aiding desertions and having a "malicious Temper," made him out to be a hypocrite and must have raised his concerns about the actions townspeople would take. Some residents at the subsequent town meeting were outraged, and one of them made a motion to print Boston's narrative of the Massacre along with the depositions. Wishing Preston a fair trial, a majority of those present voted against the motion. Instead the town wanted either clarification of the captain's meaning or a retraction, and it formed a committee to interview the prisoner.[30]

On July 10 the powerful group of Thomas Cushing, Richard Dana, Samuel Adams, John Hancock, William Phillips, William Molineux, and Ebenezer Storer asked Preston for an explanation of the discrepancies. He asserted that others had rewritten the case and that the published version was different from his own, though he declined to indicate the specific changes. The following day, the committee sent Preston a letter requesting him to give an instance of a Bostonian aiding desertion and to substantiate his claim that there had been a plan for the town's residents and militias from outside Boston to attack the troops on March 5 or 6. Preston wisely, and much to Gage's relief, refused to respond.[31]

For most of the summer Preston remained fretful (a death threat didn't help), but as August came to a conclusion and the weather finally began to cool, so did the captain's emotions. Preston petitioned the court "to bring him to trial," and Dalrymple was optimistic that there would be a fair outcome. Hutchinson was encouraged, too, but had a strategy originally suggested by Hillsborough should there be a guilty verdict. He would ask the court for a reprieve from delivering sentences until their next session the following March. During that time he would write the ministry for pardons, which would arrive before sentencing. The Superior Court arraigned the nine prisoners on September 7 and set the trial for October 23. Hutchinson regretted the delay, for that would provide less time for the potentially life-saving pardons to be issued in London and applied in Boston.[32]

At some point between the arraignment and the beginning of the trial, it was decided that Preston should be tried separately from the men. That was an advantage for him, because he was the only one of the nine who demonstrably had not pulled a trigger. The actions of the soldiers, who were significantly less popular than their captain, should not increase his vulnerability. Were the key question whether he had given the order to fire, and were the men not present to claim that they had only followed orders, Preston had a far better chance of a not guilty verdict. The division into two trials was a setback for the soldiers. Were Preston found not guilty prior to their trial, they would be much less likely to escape responsibility. Three of the soldiers—Hugh White, James Hartigan, and Matthew Kilroy—petitioned the court to join the trials but were unsuccessful.[33]

Preston's long-awaited trial ran from Wednesday, October 24, to Tuesday, October 30, breaking only for Sunday. It had been nearly eight months since the soldiers had killed and wounded the people on King Street. Samuel Quincy, solicitor general of the colony, Josiah's older brother and a future loyalist, replaced the absent Jonathan Sewall and, with Robert Treat Paine, served as the Crown's prosecutor. John Adams, Josiah Quincy, and Robert Auchmuty defended Preston, although Quincy took no public part at the trial.

In the course of the six days there were erudite and lengthy opening and closing arguments and the examination of nearly fifty witnesses. The most important and determining portion of the trial, however, was the jury selection of the first day. Adhering to provincial law, Boston officials placed in a box the names of all freeholders who had not served on a jury in the previous three years and withdrew thirty-six. Illness or other cause, such as Phillip Dumaresq's request to be excused because he already had decided that Preston was innocent, reduced the pool. Defense lawyers challenged so many would-be jurors that the sheriff had to solicit bystanders to fill the panel. Five of the twelve jurors were future loyalists, including the previously excused Dumaresq, who just happened to be available. Conviction for a capital offense required unanimity; only one dissenting voice was needed to prevent a verdict of guilty. With a packed jury, Preston's fate was settled on the first day; the rest of the trial was a formality, important only for public consumption.[34]

The central question was whether Preston had ordered the soldiers to fire. Both teams of lawyers focused their arguments, their choice of witnesses, and their cross-examinations on that key point. The prosecution's witnesses had either heard Preston or a man they took to be him give the command, while the defense's witnesses swore the opposite. The conflicting evidence plagued Samuel Quincy and Robert Treat Paine. In his closing Paine acknowledged, "There is some little Confusion in the Evidence"; he tried to put the best spin on it by asserting that it "must certainly operate as much to their [the defense's] Disadvantage, as ours," but few in the courtroom would have concurred. The popular movement partisan William Palfrey wrote, "Even in my own mind there still remains a doubt whether Capt Preston gave the orders to fire." To no one's surprise, the jury found Preston not guilty, and the town accepted the verdict without commotion. A free man, Thomas Preston rushed to Castle William, where he resided until the conclusion of the soldiers' trial and then sailed for London.[35]

Jury selection for the grenadiers' trial began on Tuesday, November 27. Twenty-one potential jurors were challenged, leaving not a man from Boston. None of the jurors had experienced a year and a half of military occupation. Even so, the trial proved to be far more complicated than Preston's, and the outcome was far less certain. There was no doubt that the eight soldiers on trial had stood before the Custom House on the evening of March 5, that some, if not all, had fired their muskets, and that five people died. The common impression was that seven or eight shots were discharged. That was the easy part. The difficulty, at least for the prosecution, was that there were eight soldiers and five victims. Attucks and Caldwell had each been struck by two musket balls, and the other three had been hit by one each. At most, seven of the eight soldiers had killed someone on King Street; more likely only five had. Quincy and Paine would have to prove who killed whom and develop a strategy that would convict soldiers who hadn't killed or may not have even fired.[36]

As if the prosecution didn't already have a demanding assignment, Samuel Quincy made matters worse in his opening statement. Rather than describe the horror of the crime and call for justice, he instructed the jury on the need for a fair trial and reminded them of the defendants' humanity ("whether eight of your fellow subjects shall live or die!") rather than of the victims' deaths. After the prosecution witnesses appeared, Quincy summed up the evidence. Citing fatigue for his disorganization, he again was mediocre at best. After identifying each of the prisoners as having been present at the event, he singled out Kilroy and Montgomery as shooters of specific persons, but then surprisingly drew back with the disclaimer, "Who they were that killed those several persons, may not be precisely ascertained, except in the case of Killroy, against whom I think you have certain evidence." He attempted to recover with the stricture that it was "immaterial" who had fired the fatal bullets, for all who were present "are in the eye of the law, principals."[37]

Josiah Quincy opened for the defense. He acknowledged the obvious—five persons had been killed—and raised questions as to whether those deaths constituted "any homicide," who had committed the killings, and whether there were extenuating circumstances that reduced the charge from murder to manslaughter. He followed his brother's lead, reminding the jury that soldiers were entitled to the same protections of the law as were other subjects of the Crown. Last, he challenged the quality of the prosecution's evidence. The defense then used its witnesses to try to establish that the crowd had incited the soldiers to fire in self-defense or, at least, in response to provocation.[38]

In his review of the evidence, Josiah Quincy focused on the crowd as the source of the problems, though he cannily reduced Bostonians' responsibility by claiming that the provocateurs were primarily sailors. He also distinguished between the soldiers outside the barracks, an unlawful assembly, and the troops who had been ordered to the protection of the sentry at the Custom House, a lawful assembly. That was a key distinction. Were it an unlawful assembly, all participants in the incident were equally liable for the deaths. Were it a lawful assembly, only those individuals who could be proved to have killed a particular person could be held legally accountable. Should the jury accept the argument that the soldiers were lawfully present before the Custom House, only the two soldiers who had been identified as killers, Montgomery and Kilroy, were in jeopardy. Had they fired in self-defense, Quincy emphasized, it was justifiable homicide, and they should be found not guilty. He finished with a fallback. Had Montgomery and Kilroy not acted in self-defense, they had committed manslaughter, not murder. Their acts had not been premeditated with malice. They had not sought out the people on King Street but had been ordered to the scene. They may have fired in anger provoked by the crowd's assaults, but it was spontaneous, not planned.[39]

More elegantly, John Adams presented the same line of reasoning in his closing for the defense. "We are to look upon it as more beneficial, that many guilty persons should escape unpunished," he proclaimed, "than one innocent person should suffer." In this simple way he indirectly reminded the jury that there was no way to know who had killed specific victims. There was no evidence that all of the soldiers had fired their muskets. Clearly some of the soldiers who had killed would go free, but better that outcome than that an innocent person be executed. If the soldiers were in front of the Custom House lawfully, they could not be convicted as a group, only as individuals. He then turned his attention to Montgomery and Kilroy, the two men who had been identified as killers. Like Josiah Quincy, Adams reviewed the various forms of homicide—justifiable and excusable, which were not criminal offenses, and murder and manslaughter, which were. "A motley rabble of saucy boys, negroes and molattoes, Irish teagues and out landish jack tars" had confronted the soldiers. By implication, the solid citizens of Boston were not to blame for the assaults of sticks and snowballs, and the soldiers were justly alarmed. And even if the grenadiers weren't responding to a life-threatening attack, they still had been provoked. They had not marched to the Custom House with the intent of killing people; they had fired in the midst of a melee. At worst, Montgomery and Kilroy had committed manslaughter.[40]

Robert Treat Paine for the prosecution had the last words before the judges issued their instructions. He honed in on the two most vulnerable soldiers. He was certain Montgomery had killed Crispus Attucks. There was sufficient evidence to maintain the charge of murder, but Paine wavered. If the jurors believed Montgomery had been knocked down before he fired, "his Crime I acknowledge can amount no higher than Manslaughter." Why Paine so readily reduced the severity of the crime is difficult to understand, for Richard Palmes, whose testimony had been central to the defense in Preston's trial and whom Adams had characterized as "the most material Witness in the Case," had testified that Montgomery had discharged his musket after something struck its barrel but before he fell down. Other witnesses disagreed with Palmes's account, but Paine need not have capitulated to them. He was certain, however, that Kilroy had killed Samuel Gray. Here Paine held firm. He depicted the soldier as a cold-blooded murderer who had shot Gray "deliberately and after Caution not to fire."[41]

Proving to the jury that the other six soldiers deserved punishment was a harder task, and Paine proved no more capable than Samuel Quincy. He seemingly exonerated Wemms as the soldier who hadn't fired and admitted that "which of the other 5 prisoners killed the other 3 of the deceased appears very uncertain" and that the soldiers lawfully marched to the Custom House and lawfully stood before it. The jurors already had learned that persons in a lawful assembly were not responsible for the criminal activity of those in their midst; only the specific perpetrators were liable. Paine tried to persuade them that once the shots were fired "without just Cause" the soldiers no longer were a lawful assembly and that each of them became criminally accountable at that point, regardless of who discharged a weapon or killed a victim. That was as strong a case as he could make.

The judges—John Cushing, Benjamin Lynde, Peter Oliver, and Edmund Trowbridge—were remnants of a hierarchy seemingly under siege. They supported authority and distrusted the people. Royal governors had appointed each of them. Although Oliver was the only member of the group to become a loyalist, none of the others later took the patriot side, avoiding exile by neutrality. One by one they instructed the jury in the meaning, if not the exact words, of the defense. Oliver recommended that all eight of the soldiers should be acquitted, while the others agreed that Kilroy was guilty of manslaughter but split on whether Montgomery should be found not guilty because of justifiable homicide or guilty of manslaughter. The jury deliberated for two and a half hours and decided that Kilroy and Montgomery were guilty of manslaughter and that the other soldiers were not guilty. The two convicted soldiers remained in jail until December 14, when, pleading benefit of clergy (by this period, a means open to everyone for reducing a death sentence to a lesser punishment), they had their thumbs branded and then left to rejoin their free comrades.[42]

Five people died and six others were wounded, but the punishment for Preston and the eight soldiers, beyond incarceration until the conclusion of their trials, was two branded thumbs. The citizens of Boston could take pride that there had been a fair and open trial. There had been no vigilante justice, but neither had there been justice. Had the victims been more prominent, such as the wounded merchant Edward Payne, rather than transient or poor, there might have been more of an outcry. As it was, there was some grumbling, an inflammatory broadside that was pulled down off the door of the Town House, and a series of lengthy newspaper articles by Samuel Adams.[43] Most Bostonians settled for returning to a life without soldiers and with fewer duties on commerce.

Conclusion

A Revolutionary Legacy

After a decade of political turbulence, economic depression, and social disruption, prospects were improving for Bostonians. It was not a perfect world, but it was much better than it had been for some time. Soldiers no longer patrolled the streets, there were no guard stations or sentries scattered throughout the town, and cannon weren't directed at the south Town House door. There was no stamp tax or duties placed on lead, glass, paper, and painters' colors.

Trade exploded with the collapse of nonimportation. In 1771 imports from Great Britain to New England increased sixfold over 1769, the only full year of nonimportation, and more than three times the total for 1770.[1] Merchants and shopkeepers once again stocked their shelves with irresistible items, and sailors and maritime workers found employment. The popular movement dominated Boston and held majorities in both the House and Council; the court faction, with Thomas Hutchinson at its head, still controlled the executive and judicial branches of the provincial government but was much weaker than before the Stamp Act crisis. Bostonians and other colonists almost regained the quasi-autonomy that had existed prior to the conclusion of the Seven Years' War.

Detractors of this view of a reinvigorated climate could point to many exceptions. The 14th Regiment was only three miles away and could be reinforced with other regiments and reoccupy the town. The commissioners had returned from their second retreat to Castle William and, along with their customs service colleagues, were still capable of renewing mischief. There still were taxes on tea and sugar that Parliament had imposed without the consent of colonists. The Declaratory Act, loudly proclaiming Parliament's sovereignty and its right to tax, remained in place. A few, such as Samuel Adams, already had decided that there must be independence from Great Britain, but they were realistic enough to recognize that for the moment they didn't have adequate support either in Boston or throughout the colonies for any chance of success. Most Bostonians resented the impositions but yearned for some semblance of their earlier lives and grudgingly accepted the status quo.

Merely because they were willing to settle for an imperfect present didn't mean that the years of turmoil hadn't profoundly changed the people of Boston. It had been a gradual process of alienation from British authority. There had long been rivalries between royal governors and legislatures, between a court faction and other political interests, and between those in power and those on the outside. For the most part, these were partisan competitions within the province of Massachusetts.

There also had long been dissatisfaction with some British trade policies, though regulations had been circumvented, particularly by smuggling and bribery. Following the Seven Years' War, however, the British government began reforming its customs service to better enforce their law and imposing duties with the purpose of raising revenue. When colonists petitioned Parliament to rescind the Sugar Act and the Stamp Act on the basis that they violated the constitutional protection of no taxation without representation and because they inflicted economic duress, British authorities didn't respond; they didn't even officially read the documents. It became clear that the ministry and Parliament viewed colonists as a subordinate class of subjects. With legal channels exhausted or ignored, Boston took the colonial lead and resorted to extralegal measures--nonimportation, street demonstrations, and intimidation of officials. Parliament nullified the Stamp Act and modified the Sugar Act, but it also institutionalized its sovereignty over the colonies with the Declaratory Act, a statement that trumpeted the position that colonists did not have full rights of British citizenship.

Bostonians and others resented the distinction but tried to live within the system until the Townshend Acts. British authorities once again initiated tax bills on an unrepresented people (this time as much to put colonists in their place as to raise revenue), and they also located customs commissioners in the most unruly colonial city. The residents of Boston opposed new duties and a strengthened customs service and directed a campaign of intimidation at the newly arrived officials. The commissioners, in turn, brought with them the same disdain for Boston citizens held by the ministry and Parliament (and George III, for that matter); and when they were greeted by nighttime serenades, street demonstrations, and resistance to their sometimes overzealous efforts to enforce trade laws, they, reinforced by a battered Governor Francis Bernard, beseeched officials in England to send them military support.

The stationing of the troops was the turning point in the radicalization of Boston opinion. Earlier responses had contained anger and frustration, but also the determination to find a solution within the confines of the imperial system. The colonists made excuses. British officials must not understand the financial and personal sacrifices people had made in the war against the French and their allies. They must not comprehend the economic and social disruption in the war's aftermath. They would respond reasonably once they discovered the mistakes they had made. When instead ministries and Parliament ignored colonial conditions and pleas and imposed more taxes without consent and with an even stronger apparatus for enforcement, the impact on Boston was greater than in other colonial cities, and hence there was greater alienation.

The placing of four regiments in Boston as a police force to support British officials rather than as an army to protect the population certified that the town was being occupied as a hostile country and that Bostonians were viewed as an enemy people. That certainly was the impression of the citizens of Boston. The townspeople could not escape checkpoints, drills, thrust bayonets, angry and profane words, whippings on the Common, scuffles, competing laborers, assaults by drunken officers and men, redcoats with their wives, children, camp followers, and hangers-on cluttering the streets, and ultimately musket balls and death. They were hardly innocent themselves, often provoking the soldiers. They had not, however, invited the regiments. Just like a bayonet, the standing army was thrust at them. In their minds, they became not a subordinate but a separate people. They increasingly perceived themselves as Americans rather than British. The first American revolution was in Bostonians' sense of their identity.

With the departure of the troops, the town largely autonomous of British authority, and the Massachusetts countryside and other colonies less inclined to act, thoughts of separation were put on hold. That situation could have remained indefinitely; but when Britain resumed more aggressive policies in 1773 and particularly in 1774 with the

Intolerable Acts, the latent revolutionary fervor of Bostonians returned, not to be dampened until independence was achieved.

Each year from 1771 to 1783 a commemoration of the Massacre on King Street was held. The annual tribute was a reminder of the perils of a standing army, the violations of colonial rights, the arrogance and perfidy of the royal government, and the existence of Bostonians and other colonists as a people apart, a population with unraveling ties to the British empire. Beginning at noon on March 5, 1771, church bells rang for an hour in Boston. In the evening Thomas Young gave an oration at the Manufactory, "being the Place where the first Effort of Military Tyranny was made within a few Days after the Troops arrived." Paul Revere placed window displays at his home in the North End. One window illustrated "the Ghost of the unfortunate young Seider, with one of his Fingers in the Wound," and listed the names of those who had died at the Massacre. A second window depicted the soldiers firing their muskets at the people: "the Dead on the Ground—and the Wounded falling, with the Blood running in Streams from their Wounds." The third window showed a woman "representing America" with the "Cap of Liberty" on her head, "one Foot on the head of a Grenadier lying prostrate grasping a Serpent—Her Finger pointing to the Tragedy." The bells tolled again from 9 o'clock until 10, when the "Exhibition was withdrawn" and thousands of spectators returned to their homes.[2]

The next year Joseph Warren gave the oration in the afternoon at the Old South Church. An illuminated lantern with bloody memories of the fallen five (Seider no longer was mentioned) was displayed on a balcony on King Street that evening, and church bells pealed from 9:15 until 10:00. That was the pattern until 1776, when British troops again occupied Boston. By necessity, Peter Thacher of Malden gave the oration at the meetinghouse in nearby Watertown. In 1777, with the end of the second military occupation, the oration returned to Boston. There still was a political and psychological need for the citizens to remember. And so it went through 1783, until the Treaty of Paris recognized the United States as an independent country.[3] The realization that had come with the landing of the occupying soldiers on October 1, 1768—that Bostonians and their countrymen were a separate people—had become a reality.

Acknowledgments

The research and writing of history often is a solitary endeavor—perhaps that's part of its appeal—but conversations with friends and colleagues, insights that pop from the pages of strangers' books, and the comradery in libraries and archives temper any sense of isolation. This book has benefited from the advice, suggestions, and encouragement of others; in fact, it would not exist without such help.

Anyone who knows Gary Nash must marvel at his many kindnesses. Despite a busy schedule, he answered many questions, provided wise counsel, and read several of the chapters. Once again, I am grateful for his assistance and friendship. From the days when we were young faculty members semi-seriously pondering the possibility of forming an intentional community to the present, Norm and Emily Rosenberg have offered warm support, laughter, and good advice. Together they helped me weigh some options at a critical stage of the project, and Norm carefully read two pivotal chapters, making them much stronger. David Fischer not only urged me to examine depositions of British soldiers, but also generously shared his copies with me. The library and staff of the Bonnie Bell Wardman Library at Whittier College during the years of Phil O'Brien's leadership were an invaluable resource. Particular thanks to Michele Anderson, Cindy Bessler, Joe Dmohowski, Steve Musser, Mike Polifka, Ann Topjon, Shelley Urbizagastegui, and Mary Ellen Vick. The Huntington Library is one of the world's great treasures, and I am fortunate to live nearby. Everyone on its staff is helpful, but I especially want to thank Chris Adde for his tireless assistance.

Tim Bent at Oxford University Press offered helpful suggestions and encouragement throughout the process of bringing this book to life. I'm particularly appreciative of his skillful and imaginative line editing. Dayne Poshusta graciously answered endless questions patiently and promptly and was invaluable in shepherding the many parts along. Christine Dahlin, with professional skill and sympathy for an author's concerns, supervised the book through production.

Many others contributed by a timely inquiry, a brilliant idea, a high five, or, more commonly now, a fist bump. I happily thank Don Archer, Lauren Baxter, Megan Baxter, Bill Bulger, Barbara and Terry Douglass, Joe Fairbanks, Bill Geiger, Sandy and Jim Jordan, Dave and Beth Macleod, Bob Marks, Bob Middlekauff, Dick and Jan Potter, Mary Lou and Joe Sortais, Lori Slater, Hal Sweet, and Dennis Thavenet. Derek Mayo and Jason Mayo helped me see the world fresh again, in ways that only grandchildren can do.

My mom insisted on my reading drafts to her and, even after hearing a clumsy paragraph or a series of garbled pages, offered praise. Thank goodness for moms. In the study we share, Ginny was captive to each completed sentence and responded, as she does in all things, with encouragement, kindly phrased suggestions (even using nonthreatening green ink), and affection.

Notes

INTRODUCTION

1. Frey, *British Soldier in America*, 3.
2. Fischer, *Washington's Crossing*, 33; Maier, *From Resistance to Revolution*, 18; Reid, *In Defiance of the Law*, 89; the Quartering Act is at www.ushistory. org/declaration/related/quartering.htm.
3. *Boston Evening-Post*, May 27, 1765; *Boston Gazette*, June 16, 1766, Sept. 21, 1767; Thomas Hutchinson to Richard Jackson, Oct. 28, 1767, Hutchinson Correspondence, Massachusetts Archives (microfilm), vol. 25, page 206; Andrew Eliot to Thomas Hollis, Sept. 27, 1768, in "Letters from Andrew Eliot to Thomas Hollis," 428.
4. Rowe, *Diary*, 175; *Boston Chronicle*, Sept. 29, Oct. 3, 1768; *Boston Evening-Post*, Oct. 3, 1768; Drake, *Old Landmarks,* 9, 114; Everard, *Thomas Farrington's Regiment,* 60
5. *A Report of the Record Commissioners of the City of Boston, Containing the Selectmen's Minutes from 1764 Through 1768,* 311; *Boston Gazette*, Nov. 21, 1768.
6. *Selectmen's Minutes*, 170.
7. C. Shaw, *Topographical and Historical Description,* 57; Kulikoff, "Progress of Inequality," 393–94; Drake, *Old Landmarks,* 9, 18, 22.
8. A. Gordon, "Journal," 449; Thomas Gage to Earl of Hillsborough, Sept. 26, 1768, in Gage, *Correspondence,* 1:196; Francis Bernard to Earl of Hillsborough, Oct. 1, 1768, in *Letters to the Ministry,* 68; Samuel Adams to Dennys De Berdt, Oct. 3, 1768, in H. A. Cushing, *Writings of Samuel Adams*, 4:248; Andrew Eliot to Thomas Hollis, Oct. 17, 1768, in "Letters from Eliot to Hollis," 432; Dickerson, *Boston under Military Rule,* Oct. 3, 1768, 2; Council to Earl of Hillsborough, Apr. 15, 1769, in *Journals of the House of Representatives of Massachusetts* [hereafter *JHR*], 46:38.
9. Warren, *History,* 1:65.

CHAPTER 1

1. Jensen, *Founding of a Nation,* 41; Middlekauff, *Glorious Cause,* 53; F. Anderson, *Crucible of War,* 487–94, 503–4, 511–12; Lawson, *George Grenville*, 140-41; Johnson, *Prologue to Revolution*, 111, 115.

2. F. Anderson, *Crucible of War*, 505–6; Marks, *Origins of the Modern World*, 90–92.

3. Jensen, *Founding of a Nation*, 4, 41; Middlekauff, *Glorious Cause*, 57–58; F. Anderson, *Crucible of War*, 562, 811 n.5; Gould, *Persistence of Empire*, 70–71.

4. Jensen, *Founding of a Nation*, 288; Middlekauff, *Glorious Cause*, 51–52; F. Anderson, *Crucible of War*, 560–61; Bullion, "'The Ten Thousand in America,'" 651, and "Security and Economy," 502; Knollenberg, *Origin of the American Revolution*, 92–94; Reid, *In Defiance of the Law*, 51–53, 59; Shy, *Toward Lexington*, 62, 67, 69, 81–82.

5. F. Anderson, *Crucible of War*, 562–63; Bullion, "Security and Economy," 502; Knollenberg, *Origin of American Revolution*, 87–88, 94; Shy, *Toward Lexington*, 52.

6. F. Anderson, *Crucible of War*, 563; Barrow, *Trade and Empire*, 177–78; Dickerson, *Navigation Acts*, 169–70.

7. F. Anderson, *Crucible of War*, 573–74; Johnson, "Passage of the Sugar Act," 507–14.

8. The Sugar Act is available at www.ushistory.org/declaration/related/sugaract.htm.

9. Sugar Act; F. Anderson, *Crucible of War*, 577–78, 579; Tyler, *Smugglers and Patriots*, 68–69; Bullion, *Great and Necessary Measure*, 91.

10. Sugar Act.

11. Nash, *Urban Crucible*, 241–43; F. Anderson, *People's Army*, 3–6; Bridenbaugh, *Cities in Revolt*, 76; Kulikoff, "Progress of Inequality," 381; Tyler, *Smugglers and Patriots*, 72; "The Answer of Francis Bernard Esq. Governor of his Majesty's Province of Massachusetts Bay to the Queries proposed by the Right Honorable The Lords Commissioners for Trade & Plantations," September 5, 1763, in Benton, *Early Census Making*, 49.

12. Nash, *Urban Crucible*, 242; Young, "Women of Boston," 183; Francis Bernard to the Council and House, May 26, 1763, *JHR*, 40:9–10.

13. Nash, *Urban Crucible*, 252; Tyler, *Smugglers and Patriots*, 72; Thomas Hutchinson to William Bollan, July 14, 1760, in *Jasper Mauduit*, 7–8; F. Anderson, *Crucible of War*, 317; Pencak, *War, Politics and Revolution*, 154–55; Francis Bernard to the Lords of Trade, August 1, 1764, in W. Gordon, *History*, 1:138–39.

14. Shaw, *Topographical and Historical Description of Boston*, 92–93; Boyle, "Boyle's Journal," 151–52; *Boston Evening-Post*, Mar. 24, 1760; *Boston Gazette*, Jan. 19, 1761, Jan. 30, 1764.

15. *Selectmen's Minutes*, June 30, 1764; *JHR*, Jan. 17, 1764, 40:196–97 and June 8, 1764, 41:56–57; *Boston Gazette*, Feb. 13, 1764; *Boston Evening-Post*, Apr. 2, 30, 1764.

16. *Boston Gazette*, Mar. 19, 1764.

17. *Boston Gazette*, Feb. 27, 1764; *Boston Evening-Post*, Mar. 26, Apr. 16, 1764; Boyle, "Boyle's Journal," 164.

18. Middlekauff, *Glorious Cause*, 84–85; Francis Bernard to Richard Jackson, Aug. 3, 1763, in Nicolson, *Papers of Francis Bernard,* 390; Francis Bernard to the Queries of the Board of Trade, Sept. 5, 1763, *Papers of Bernard*, 401; Francis Bernard to John Pownall, Oct. 30, 1763, Dec. 30, 1763, *Papers of Bernard*, 428, 451; Francis Bernard to the Lords Commissioners for Trade and Plantations, Dec. 26, 1763, in Bernard, *Select Letters,* 8; Francis Bernard to the Earl of —, Nov. 10, 1764, in *Select Letters*, 13–14. For a full political biography, see Nicolson, *"Infamas Govener."*

19. Shipton, *Sibley's Harvard Graduates,* 8:149–217; Thomas Hutchinson to Peter Leitch, July 13, 1764, Hutchinson Correspondence, Massachusetts Archives (microfilm), vol. 26, pages 88, 90, 112; Jensen, *Founding of a Nation*, 74–76; Bailyn, *Ordeal of Thomas Hutchinson,* 50; Middlekauff, *Glorious Cause*, 85–86.

20. Thomas Hutchinson to —, July 11, 1764, and Hutchinson to —, Nov. 4, 1764, Hutchinson Correspondence, Massachusetts Archives (microfilm), vol. 26, pages 88, 90, 112; Knollenberg, *Origin of American Revolution*, 185.

21. Waters, *Otis Family,* 116–20; Waters and Schutz, "Patterns of Massachusetts Colonial Politics," 560–61; Middlekauff, *Glorious Cause*, 84–86; Nash, *Urban Crucible*, 274–75; Adair and Schutz, *Peter Oliver's Origin,* 48; Edmund Trowbridge to William Bollan, July 15, 1762, in *Jasper Mauduit*, 66–67; James Otis, *Boston Gazette*, Apr. 4, 14, 1763.

22. Wroth and Zobel, "Editorial Note" on Petition of Lechmere, in Wroth and Zobel, *Legal Papers of John Adams* [hereafter *LPJA*], 2:106–15; *Boston Gazette*, Nov. 23, 1761; Waters, *Otis Family*, 121–24.

23. Wroth, and Zobel, "Editorial Note," in *LPJA*, 2:106–15; *Boston Gazette*, Nov. 23, 1761; Waters, *Otis Family*, 121–24.

24. Middlekauff, *Glorious Cause*, 87–88; Wroth and Zobel, "Editorial Note," in *LPJA*, 2:116–22; Waters, *Otis Family*, 132–35; *JHR*, Feb. 1, 1765, 41:205–6.

25. Francis Bernard to Thomas Pownall, August 28, 1761, in *Papers of Bernard*, 145; Francis Bernard to Richard Jackson, June 8, 1763, in *Papers of Bernard*, 375–76; J. Adams, *Diary,* 1:271.

26. For a transcript of the charter of 1691 on which the government was based, see http://avalon.law.yale.edu/17th_century/mass07.asp.

27. *Boston Evening-Post*, Nov. 21, 28, 1763, Jan. 30, Feb. 6, 1764; *Boston Gazette*, Apr. 30, 1764.

28. Thomas Cushing to Jasper Mauduit, Oct. 28, Nov. 11, 1763, Jan. 1764, in *Jasper Mauduit*, 130–33, 138–39, 145–46.

29. *Boston Gazette*, May 14, 1764; Instructions to Boston Representatives from the town, May 24, 1764, in *A Report of the Record Commissioners of the City of Boston , Containing the Boston Town Records, 1758 to 1769,* 120–22.

30. *JHR*, June 13, 1764, 41:72–77.

31. *Boston Gazette*, Aug. 20, 1764; Thomas Hutchinson to William Bollan, Oct. 4, 1764, Hutchinson Correspondence, Massachusetts Archives (microfilm), vol. 26, page 102.

32. *Boston Evening-Post*, Sept. 24, Oct. 8, 1764; *Boston Gazette*, Sept. 24, Oct. 1, 8, 22, 1764.

33. *JHR*, Oct. 18, 24, Nov. 1–3, 1764, 41:94–95, 111, 129, 132–33, 135; Thomas Cushing to Jasper Mauduit, Nov. 17, 1764, in *Jasper Mauduit*, 170–71.

CHAPTER 2

1. Morgan, "Postponement of the Stamp Act," 353–76; Morgan and Morgan, *Stamp Act Crisis,* 77–92; Jensen, *Founding of a Nation*, 59–63; Middlekauff, *Glorious Cause*, 70–74; Bullion, *Great and Necessary Measure*, 122-25, 200.

2. Morgan and Morgan, *Stamp Act Crisis*, 92–96; Jensen, *Founding of a Nation*, 62–65; Middlekauff, *Glorious Cause*, 74–76; Thomas Whately to John Temple, June 12, 1765, in *Bowdoin-Temple Papers*, 60.

3. The Stamp Act is at www.ushistory.org/declaration/related/stampact.htm.

4. Warden, *Boston,* 161; Rowe, *Diary*, Jan. 21, 1765, 75; Knollenberg, *Origin of American Revolution*, 169; John Hancock to Barnard and Harrison, Jan. 21, 1765, in A. E. Brown, *John Hancock,* 61–62.

5. John Hancock to Barnard and Harrison, Apr. 1765, in A. E. Brown, *John Hancock*, 69; *Boston Gazette*, May 20, 27, June 3, 1765; *Boston Evening-Post*, May 27, 1765.

6. Thomas Hutchinson to Richard Jackson, June 4, 1765, Hutchinson Correspondence, Massachusetts Archives (microfilm), vol. 26, page 139; John Adams, "Dissertation on the Canon and the Feudal Law," *Boston Gazette*, Oct. 21, 1765; *JHR*, Oct. 24, 1765, 42:133–36, and Oct. 29, 1765, 42:151–53; Francis Bernard to the Lord of —, Nov. 23, 1765, in *Select Letters*, 31–32.

7. Conser, "Stamp Act Resistance," 59; Hoerder, *Crowd Action,* 90.

8. *JHR*, June 25, 1765, 42:108–10.

9. *Newport Mercury*, June 24, 1765, reprinted in *Boston Gazette*, July 1, 1765; Morgan and Morgan, *Stamp Act Crisis*, 121–32; Jensen, *Founding of a Nation*, 103–5; Middlekauff, *Glorious Cause*, 79–83.

10. *Boston Gazette*, July 8, 1765.

11. Boyle, "Boyle's Journal," Aug. 14, 1765, 169; Rowe, *Diary*, Aug. 14, 1765, 88–89; John Avery to John Collins, Aug. 19, 1765, in Stiles, *Extracts,* 436–37; A. Z. to the editors, *Boston Evening-Post*, Aug. 19, 1765; *Boston Gazette*, Aug. 19, 1765; Morgan and Morgan, *Stamp Act Crisis*, 164; Nash, *Urban Crucible*, 292–94; Young, *Liberty Tree,* 327–38.

12. *Boston Gazette*, Aug. 19, 1765, including watchmen's report of Aug. 15.

13. *Boston Gazette*, Sept. 2, 1765; Proclamation by Francis Bernard, Aug. 28, 1765, in *Boston Evening-Post*, Sept. 2, 1765; Thomas Hutchinson to Richard Jackson, Aug. 30, 1765, Hutchinson Correspondence, Massachusetts Archives (microfilm), vol. 26, pages 146–47; Nash, *Urban Crucible*, 294.

14. Hutchinson's Superior Court Address, Aug. 27, 1765, in Quincy Jr., *Reports of Cases,* 171–73.

15. Thomas Hutchinson to Richard Jackson, June 4, 1765, Hutchinson Correspondence, Massachusetts Archives (microfilm), vol. 26, page 139; Thomas Hutchinson to —, Oct. 1, 1765, Hutchinson Correspondence, Massachusetts Archives (microfilm), vol. 26, page 155; T. Hutchinson, *History of Massachusetts Bay,* 3:89–90; Conser, "Stamp Act Resistance," 33–34; Nash, *Unknown American Revolution,* 48–49.

16. *Boston Evening-Post*, Aug. 15, 28, Sept. 2, 1765; P. O. Hutchinson, *Diary and Letters,* 1:71–72; *Boston Gazette*, Oct. 7, 1765; Nash, *Unknown American Revolution*, 49–50; Hoerder, *Crowd Action,* 110–12; Zobel, *Boston Massacre,* 37; Reid, *In a Rebellious Spirit,* 18–19.

17. Francis Bernard to Thomas Gage, Aug. 29, 1765, in Channing and Coolidge, *Barrington-Bernard Correspondence,* 229–30.

18. Thomas Gage to Francis Bernard, Gage to Lieutenant Coninghame, Gage to Lord Colville, Sept. 6, 1765, in Channing and Coolidge, *Barrington-Bernard Correspondence*, 230–35.

19. *Boston Gazette*, Sept. 9, 1765; Francis Bernard to Thomas Gage, Sept. 12, 1765, in Channing and Coolidge, *Barrington-Bernard Correspondence*, 236–38.

20. Nash, *Urban Crucible*, 298; *Boston Town Records*, Aug. 27, 1765, 152; *Boston Gazette*, Sept. 2, 1765; *Boston Evening-Post*, Sept. 16, 1765; House to Francis Bernard, Oct. 24, 1765, *JHR*, 42:137.

21. *Boston Evening-Post*, Sept. 16, 1765; *Boston Town Records*, Sept. 27, 1765, 157–58.

22. Pauline Maier, "Samuel Adams," *American National Biography Online*, www.anb.org/articles/01/01–00008.html; Maier, "New Englander as Revolutionary: Samuel Adams," in *The Old Revolutionaries,* 3–50; Drake, *Old Landmarks*, 309; Adair and Schutz, *Peter Oliver's Origin*, 41; J. Adams, *Diary*, Dec. 30, 1772, 2:74.

23. Bernard's speech, Sept. 25, 1765, *JHR*, 42:118–23; Bernard to Council and House, Sept. 25, 1765, *JHR*, 42:124–25; *Boston Gazette*, Sept. 30, 1765.

24. B. W. to the Inhabitants of the Province of the Massachusetts-Bay, *Boston Gazette*, Oct. 7, 1765.

25. *Boston Gazette*, Sept. 23, 1765.

26. House to Francis Bernard, Oct. 25, 1765, *JHR*, 42:131–38.

27. Grey Cooper to Francis Bernard, Oct. 8, 1765, in Channing and Coolidge, *Barrington-Bernard Correspondence*, 239–40; Francis Bernard to —, Oct. 28, 1765, in *Select Letters*, 27; *Boston Gazette*, Oct. 28, 1765.

28. Order of Selectmen of Boston, Oct. 29, 1765, in *Boston Evening-Post*, Nov. 4, 1765; Boyle, "Boyle's Journal," Nov. 1, 1765, 170–71; *Boston Evening-Post*, Nov. 4, 1765; *Boston Gazette*, Nov. 4, 1765.

29. *Boston Gazette*, Nov. 4, 1765; Tudor, *Life of James Otis,* 26–28; Rowe, *Diary*, Nov. 5, 1764, 67–68; Boyle, "Boyle's Journal," Nov. 5, 1764, 167; Young, *Liberty Tree*, 111.

30. *Boston Town Records*, Nov. 2, 1765, 158; Boyle, "Boyle's Journal," Nov. 5, 1765, 171; *Boston Evening-Post*, Nov. 11, 18, 1765. As often occurred, the *Boston Gazette* published identical articles.

31. New York, Nov. 7, 1765, *Boston Gazette*, Nov. 18, 1765; Philadelphia, Nov. 14, 1765, *Boston Evening-Post*, Nov. 25, 1765.

32. John Hancock to Barnards and Harrison, Oct. 14, 1765, in A. E. Brown, *John Hancock*, 86–88; *Boston Evening-Post*, Oct. 21, Nov. 25, 1765; *Boston Gazette*, Nov. 25, 1765.

33. *Boston Evening-Post*, Dec. 9, 1765; *Boston Gazette*, Dec. 16, 1765; James Murray to John Murray, Nov. 13, 1765, in Murray, *Letters,* 155.

34. *Boston Gazette*, Dec. 16, 23, 1765.

35. *Boston Gazette*, Dec. 16, 23, 1765; Henry Bass to Samuel P. Savage, Dec. 19, 1765, *Proceedings*, 688–89; Morgan and Morgan, *Stamp Act Crisis,* 174–81; Hoerder, *Crowd Action,* 125.

36. Morgan and Morgan, *Stamp Act Crisis*, 181; John Hancock to Barnards and Harrison, Dec. 21, 1765, in A. E. Brown, *John Hancock*, 99; Henry Bass to Samuel P. Savage, Dec. 19, 1765, *Proceedings*, 689.

37. Morgan and Morgan, *Stamp Act Crisis*, 217–18; J. Adams, *Diary*, Dec. 18–19, 1765, 1:263–65.

38. J. Adams, *Diary*, Dec. 19, 25, 1765, 1:266, 274.

39. J. Adams, *Diary*, Dec. 20, 1765, 1:266–67; Morgan and Morgan, *Stamp Act Crisis*, 182–83; Jensen, *Founding of a Nation*, 143–45; Thomas Hutchinson to Benjamin Franklin, Jan. 1, 1766, Hutchinson Correspondence, Massachusetts Archives (microfilm), vol. 26, page 192; *Boston Gazette*, Dec. 23, 1765.

40. Morgan and Morgan, *Stamp Act Crisis*, 183–86; Jensen, *Founding of a Nation*, 145; *Boston Gazette*, Mar. 17, 1766.

CHAPTER 3

1. Thomas Hutchinson to Thomas Pownall, Mar. 8, 1766, Huchinson Correspondence, Massachusetts Archives (microfilm), vol. 26, pages 207–14.

2. J. Adams, *Diary*, Feb. 1763, 1:238; Tyler, *Smugglers and Patriots*, 5.

3. *Boston Town Records*, Sept. 27, 1765, 157–58; Tyler, *Smugglers and Patriots*, 8.

4. Henry Bass to Samuel P. Savage, Dec. 19, 1765, *Proceedings*, 688–89; J. Adams, *Diary*, Dec. 19, 1765, 1:265.

5. G. P. Anderson, "Note on Ebenezer Mackintosh," 357–61; J. Adams, *Diary*, Jan. 15, 1766, 1:294; Bullock, *Revolutionary Brotherhood,* 107; Day and Day, "Another Look," 32–33; Carp, *Rebels Rising,* 41.

6. Warden, *Boston*, 156, 217; Fischer, *Paul Revere's Ride,* 19–20, 27–28; Bullock, *Revolutionary Brotherhood*, 107; Cary, *Joseph Warren,* 55–56; Rowe, *Diary*, Nov. 23, 1768, 180; Miller, *Sam Adams,* 40; J. Adams, *Diary*, 1:*passim*.

7. Carp, *Rebels Rising*, 29; Adair and Schutz, *Peter Oliver's Origin,* 43; W. Gordon, *History,* 1:178–79.

8. Shipton, "John Avery," in *Sibley's Harvard Graduates*, 14:384–89; G. P. Anderson, "Ebenezer Mackintosh," 30; Hoerder, *Crowd Action,* 112, 125; Hutchinson, *Diary,* Aug. 27, 1765, 1:71–72; Nash, *Unknown American Revolution*, 52–53, *Boston Gazette*, Nov. 11, 1765; Thomas Hutchinson to Thomas Pownall, Mar. 8, 1766, Hutchinson Correspondence, Massachusetts Archives (microfilm), vol. 26, page 211, Adair and Schutz, *Peter Oliver's Origin,* 43; W. Gordon, *History,* 1:54–55. Masaniello (1622–47) was a Neopolitan who led rebels against the Hapsburgs in 1647.

9. G. P. Anderson, "Ebenezer Mackintosh," 22–25.

10. G. P. Anderson, "Ebenezer Mackintosh," 26–27; Young, *Liberty Tree,* 339–42; *Boston Town Records*, Mar. 12, 1765, 132.

11. G. P. Anderson, "Ebenezer Mackintosh," 28; Young, *Liberty Tree,* 341–42.

12. Nash, *Unknown American Revolution*, 57–58; Gilje, *Liberty on the Waterfront,* 104–5.

CHAPTER 4

1. Morgan and Morgan, *Stamp Act Crisis*, 328; Middlekauff, *Glorious Cause*, 107–8; Jensen, *Founding of a Nation*, 159–60.

2. Langford, "First Rockingham Ministry," 96; F. Anderson, *Crucible of War*, 698–701; Middlekauff, *Glorious Cause*, 111–13; Jensen, *Founding of a Nation*, 167–68.

3. Langford, "First Rockingham Ministry," 106, 110–11; F. Anderson, *Crucible of War*, 701–2; Middlekauff, *Glorious Cause*, 110, 115; Jensen, *Founding of a Nation*, 162–63.

4. Langford, "First Rockingham Ministry," 96; F. Anderson, *Crucible of War*, 703–5; Middlekauff, *Glorious Cause*, 109, 114; Jensen, *Founding of a Nation*, 169–72. The Declaratory Act is available at www.ushistory.org/declaration/related/declaratory.htm.

5. J. Adams, *Diary,* Jan. 15, 1766, 1:294; *Boston Evening-Post*, Apr. 7, 28, 1766; *Boston Town Records*, Apr. 21, 1766, 175–76; *Boston Gazette*, Apr. 21, 1766; *Selectmen's Minutes*, May 16, 1766.

6. *Boston Evening-Post*, May 19, 26, 1766; *Boston Gazette*, May 19, 26, 1766; Rowe, *Diary,* May 19, 1766, 95.

7. *Boston Gazette*, Mar. 24, 1766; *Boston Evening-Post*, Mar. 31, Apr. 28, May 5, June 9, 16, 1766.

8. *Boston Gazette*, Apr. 7, 1766; Jensen, *Founding of a Nation*, 194.

9. Boston Gazette, Mar. 31, Apr. 14, 1766; Jensen, *Founding of a Nation*, 194.

10. Francis Bernard to Lord Barrington, July 5, 1766, in Channing and Coolidge, *Barrington-Bernard Correspondence*, 110; Bernard to the House, May 28, 29, 1766, *JHR*, vol. 43, pt. 1, 5, 10; *JHR*, May 28, 1766, vol. 43, pt. 1, 7, 8; Lynde, *Diaries,* 191.

11. Francis Bernard to the House and Council, May 29, 1766, *JHR*, vol. 43, pt. 1, 11–13.

12. House to Francis Bernard, June 3, 1766, *JHR*, vol. 43, pt. 1, 21–28.

13. *JHR*, June 3, June 11, 1766, vol. 43, pt. 1, 35, 74; W. Gordon, *History*, 1:209.

14. Francis Bernard to the House and Council, June 3, 1766, *JHR*, vol. 43, pt. 1, 29–33.

15. House to Francis Bernard, June 5, 1766, *JHR*, vol. 43, pt. 1, 41–46.

16. *JHR*, June 10, 13, 17, 24, 25, 1766, vol. 43, pt. 1, 67, 78, 90, 118, 126; Francis Bernard to House, June 20, 25, 27, 1766, *JHR*, vol. 43, pt. 1, 111–12, 124, 133–34; House to Francis Bernard, June 25, 26, 28, 1766, *JHR*, vol. 43, pt. 1, 124–25, 131–32, 143–44.

17. *Boston Gazette*, June 16, 1766.

18. Alden, *General Gage in America*, 113–15.

19. Thomas Gage to Lord Barrington, Jan. 16, 1766, in Gage, *Correspondence*, 2:334.

20. Gilje, *Road to Mobocracy*, 53; Tiedemann, *Reluctant Revolutionaries*, 109; New York, July 14, 1766, *Boston Evening-Post*, July 28, 1766; New York, July 14, 1766, *Boston Gazette*, July 28, 1766.

21. New York, Aug. 18, 1766, *Boston Evening-Post*, Aug. 25, 1766; New York, Aug. 18, 1766, *Boston Gazette*, Aug. 25, 1766; Thomas Gage to Richmond, Aug. 26, 1766, in Gage, *Correspondence*, 1:103–4.

22. New York, Aug. 25, Oct. 23, Nov. 3, 1766, Mar. 26, 1767, *Boston Gazette*, Sept. 1, Nov. 3, 17, 1766, Apr. 6, 1767; New York, Sept. 1, 1766, *Boston Evening-Post*, Sept. 8, 1766.

23. Extract of letter from Jasper Mauduit, Mar. 28, 1766, *Boston Evening-Post*, May 19, Aug. 11, 1766; *Boston Gazette*, Sept. 8, 1766.

24. Jensen, *Founding of a Nation*, 177–79; Barrow, *Trade and Empire*, 214.

25. This and the following paragraphs on the Malcom episode are based on declaration of William Sheaffe and Benjamin Hallowell, Sept. 25, 1766, in Wolkins, "Daniel Malcom," 26–29; declaration of John Tudor, Sept. 25, 1766, in Wolkins, 30–31; deposition of Nathaniel Barber, Sept. 25, 1766, in Wolkins, 32–33; declaration of Stephen Greenleaf, Oct. 1, 1766, in Wolkins, 34–39; declaration of Daniel Malcom, Oct. 21, 1766, in Wolkins, 39–42; declaration of William Mackay, Oct. 20, 1766, in Wolkins, 43–45.

26. Zobel, *Boston Massacre*, 56–57; town letter to Dennys De Berdt, *Boston Town Records*, Oct. 8, 22, 1766, 187, 192–94.

27. Francis Bernard to the House, Oct. 29, 1766, *JHR*, vol. 43, pt. 1, 148; *JHR*, Oct. 30, 31, Nov. 4, 5, 6, 7, 1766, vol. 43, pt. 1, 155–56, 158, 159, 168–69, 170–71, 178–80, 182; House to Francis Bernard, Nov. 11, 1766, *JHR*, vol. 43, pt. 1, 191–92.

28. *JHR*, Dec. 4, 1766, vol. 43, pt. 1, 207–8; Jensen, *Founding of a Nation*, 210–11.

29. J. Adams, *Diary*, Dec. 4, 1766, 1:329.

CHAPTER 5

1. Thomas Cushing to Dennys De Berdt, May 9, 1767, in "Letters of Thomas Cushing," 348–49.

2. Jensen, *Founding of a Nation*, 216–20; Middlekauff, *Glorious Cause*, 145–47.

3. Jensen, *Founding of a Nation*, 223–25; Middlekauff, *Glorious Cause*, 149–50; Barrow, *Trade and Empire*, 216.

4. Townshend Act is available at www.ushistory.org/declaration/related/townshend.htm; Jensen, *Founding of a Nation*, 225–26; Middlekauff, *Glorious Cause*, 150–51; Barrow, *Trade and Empire*, 217–18.

5. *Boston Evening-Post*, July 6, Aug. 10, Sept. 14, 28, Nov. 9, 1767; *Boston Gazette*, Sept. 21, Oct. 12, 26, Nov. 16, 1767; Thomas Hutchinson to Richard Jackson, Oct. 28, 1767, Hutchinson Correspondence, Massachusetts Archives (microfilm), vol. 25, pages 206–8; *Boston Town Records*, Dec. 22, 1767, 227–30; Alden, *General Gage,* 154; Andrew Eliot to Thomas Hollis, Dec. 10, 1767, in "Letters from Eliot to Hollis," 419.

6. *Boston Evening-Post*, Mar. 30, 1767; Andrew Eliot to Thomas Hollis, Dec. 10, 1767, in "Letters from Eliot to Hollis," 414.

7. *Boston Town Records*, July 13, 1767, Mar. 14, 22, 1768, 216–17, 218–19, 241, 242–43; Rowe, Mar. 13, 1768, *Diary*, 183.

8. Francis Bernard to Earl of Shelburne, Jan. 30, 1768, in *Letters to the Ministry*, 5–6; *Boston Gazette*, Sept. 21, 1767; *Boston Evening-Post*, Sept. 28, 1767; Thomas Hutchinson to Richard Jackson, Oct. 28, 1767, Hutchinson Correspondence, Massachusetts Archives (microfilm), vol. 25, page 206.

9. *Boston Town Records*, Nov. 20, 1767; *Boston Evening-Post*, Nov. 23, 30, 1767.

10. *Boston Gazette*, Aug. 31, 1767; *Boston Evening-Post*, Sept. 7, Oct. 12, 1767; Hoerder, *Crowd Action,* 162.

11. *Boston Gazette*, Sept. 28, 1767.

12. *Boston Town Records*, Oct. 28, 1767, 221–22; Middlekauff, *Glorious Cause*, 157.

13. *Boston Gazette*, Nov. 2, Dec. 14, 1767; *Boston Evening-Post*, Dec. 28, 1767.

14. *Boston Evening-Post*, Nov. 23, 1767; Andrew Eliot to Thomas Hollis, Dec. 10, 1767, in "Letters from Eliot to Hollis," 418–19; Breen, *Marketplace of Revolution,* 70–71.

15. *Boston Chronicle*, Dec. 21, 1767–Mar. 7, 1768; *Boston Evening-Post*, Dec. 21, 1767–Feb. 8, 1768; *Boston Gazette*, Dec. 21, 1767–Feb. 8, 1768; Middlekauff, *Glorious Cause*, 154–56.

16. Francis Bernard to Earl of Shelburne, Jan. 21, 1768, in *Letters to the Ministry*, 4–5.

17. House to Dennys De Berdt, Jan. 12, 1768, *JHR*, 44:241–50.

18. House to Earl of Shelburne, Jan. 15, 1768, *JHR*, 44:219–24; Petition of House to George III, Jan. 20, 1768, *JHR*, 44:217–19; House to the Marquis

of Rockingham, Jan. 22, 1768, *JHR*, 44:228; House to Henry Seymour Conway, Feb. 13, 1768, *JHR*, 44:224–26; House to the Right Honorable the Lords Commissioners of the Treasury, Feb. 17, 1768, *JHR*, 44:233–36.

19. House to Earl of Shelburne, Jan. 15, 1768, *JHR*, 44:219–24; Petition of House to George III, Jan. 20, 1768, *JHR*, 44:217–19; House to the Marquis of Rockingham, Jan. 22, 1768, *JHR*, 44:228; House to Henry Seymour Conway, Feb. 13, 1768, *JHR*, 44:224–26; House to the Right Honorable the Lords Commissioners of the Treasury, Feb. 17, 1768, *JHR*, 44:233–36; Francis Bernard to Lord Barrington, Jan. 28, 1768, in Channing and Coolidge, *Barrington-Bernard Correspondence*, 134, 136–37.

20. A Circulatory Letter, Feb. 11, 1768, *JHR*, 44:236–39.

21. *JHR*, 44:164; Bernard to House, Feb. 16, 1768, *JHR*, 44:171; House to Bernard, Feb. 18, 1768, *JHR*, 44:176–78, 190, 191, 194; Bernard to House, Mar. 1, 1768, *JHR*, 44:206, 207; Bernard to House, Mar. 4, 1768, *JHR*, 44:213–14; Jensen, *Founding of a Nation*, 279–80; Barrow, *Trade and Empire*, 222; *Boston Gazette*, Jan. 26, 1767.

22. Ann Hulton to Mrs. Adam Lightbody, Dec. 17, 1767, Feb. 15, 1768, in Hulton, *Letters,* 8, 10; *Boston Evening-Post*, Nov. 23, 1767; James Otis to the Printers, *Boston Gazette*, Nov. 30, 1767; Rowe, *Diary*, Feb. 10, 1768, 150.

23. Commissioners of the Customs to Lords of the Treasury, Feb. 12, 1768, in Wolkins, "Seizure," 264–65, 267.

24. Francis Bernard to Earl of Shelburne, Mar. 21, 1768, in *Letters to the Ministry*, 17–19.

25. Francis Bernard to Earl of Shelburne, Mar. 19, 1768, in *Letters to the Ministry*, 12–17; Francis Bernard to Lord Barrington, Mar. 4, 1768, in Channing and Coolidge, *Barrington-Bernard Correspondence*, 148; Thomas Hutchinson to Thomas Pownall, Mar. 26, 1768, Hutchinson Correspondence, Massachusetts Archives (microfilm), vol. 26, page 297.

26. Francis Bernard to Lord Barrington, Mar. 4, 1768, in Channing and Coolidge, *Barrington-Bernard Correspondence*, 148–49.

27. Rowe, *Diary*, Mar. 1, 4, 1768, 152–53, 153–55; Tyler, *Smugglers and Patriots*, 16–17, 30; Fowler, *Baron of Beacon Hill,* 91.

28. Thomas Gage to Lord Barrington, Mar. 10, 1768, in *Correspondence of Gage*, 2:462; Francis Bernard to Earl of Shelburne, Mar. 21, 1768, in *Letters to the Ministry*, 18–19.

29. Thomas Cushing to Dennys De Berdt, Apr. 18, 1768, in "Letters of Cushing," 350–51; Rowe, *Diary*, Mar. 4, 1768, 153–55.

30. Tyler, *Smugglers and Patriots*, 18; Nash, *Urban Crucible*, 354; Egnal and Ernst, "Economic Interpretation," 21; Hoerder, *Crowd Action,* 161–62; Francis Bernard to Earl of Hillsborough, Aug. 9, 1768, in *Letters to the Ministry*, 49–50.

31. *Boston Gazette*, June 9, Aug. 18, 1766, Mar. 23, June 8, Aug. 17, 1767, June 6, 1768.

32. Rowe, *Diary*, Mar. 18, 1768, 156–57; Francis Bernard to Earl of Shelburne, Mar. 19, 1768, in *Letters to the Ministry*, 12–17; *Boston Gazette*, Mar. 21, 1768; Commissioners of the Customs to Lords of the Treasury, Mar. 28, 1768, in Wolkins, "Seizure," 269–71.

33. *Boston Gazette*, Mar. 23, 1767, Mar. 21, 1768.

34. Rowe, *Diary*, Mar. 18, 1768, 156–57; Francis Bernard to Earl of Shelburne, Mar. 19, 1768, in *Letters to the Ministry*, 12–17; *Boston Gazette*, Mar. 21, 1768; Commissioners of the Customs to Lords of the Treasury, Mar. 28, 1768, in Wolkins, "Seizure," 269–71; Drake, *Old Landmarks*, 98, 236; Thomas Hutchinson to Richard Jackson, Mar. 23, 1768, Hutchinson Correspondence, Massachusetts Archives (microfilm), vol. 26, page 296.

35. Francis Bernard to Earl of Shelburne, Mar. 19, 1768, in *Letters to the Ministry*, 12–17; Commissioners of the Customs to Lords of the Treasury, Mar. 28, 1768, in Wolkins, "Seizure," 269–71.

CHAPTER 6

1. Dickerson, "Opinion of Attorney General Sewall," 501–2.

2. Berkin, *Jonathan Sewall*; Calhoon, *Loyalists,* 68–69; J. Adams, *Diary*, 3:278.

3. Dickerson, "Opinion of Sewall," 502–4.

4. *Boston Town Records*, May 4, 1768, 250; *Selectmen's Minutes*, May 11, 1768, 292; Jensen, *Founding of a Nation*, 281.

5. Fowler, *Baron of Beacon Hill*; Baxter, *House of Hancock,* 148–49, 284; A. E. Brown, *John Hancock*, 37; T. Hutchinson, *History of Massachusetts Bay*, 3:214–15.

6. William De Grey, Case of the "Liberty," July 25, 1768, in Wolkins, "Seizure," 273.

7. Commissioners of Customs to Samuel Hood, Feb. 12, 1768, in Wolkins, "Seizure," 278; Samuel Hood to John Corner, May 2, 1768, in Wolkins, "Seizure," 271.

8. Hood to Corner, May 2, 1768, in Wolkins, "Seizure," 271–72; Thomas Hutchinson to Richard Jackson, June 16, 1768, in Wolkins, "Seizure," 283; *Boston Town Records*, June 14, 1768, 254; *JHR*, June 2, 1768, 45:25; *Boston News-Letter*, June 16, 1768.

9. Deposition of Thomas Kirk, in *Letters to the Ministry*, 90–91; Boyle, "Boyle's Journal," May 10, 1768, 254.

10. William De Grey, Case of the "Liberty," July 25, 1768, in Wolkins, "Seizure," 274; Joseph Harrison to Lord Rockingham, June 17, 1768, in Watson, "Joseph Harrison," 589.

11. Joseph Harrison to Lord Rockingham, June 17, 1768, in Watson, "Joseph Harrison," 589–90; Thomas Hutchinson to Richard Jackson, June 16, 1768, in Wolkins, "Seizure," 281; Lemisch, "Jack Tar," 391–92; Reid, *In a Rebellious Spirit*, 93.

12. Harrison to Rockingham, June 17, 1768, in Watson, "Joseph Harrison," 590–91; Francis Bernard to Earl of Hillsborough, June 11, 1768, in *Letters to the Ministry*, 20–21.

13. Harrison to Rockingham, June 17, 1768, in Watson, "Joseph Harrison," 591–92; Francis Bernard to Earl of Hillsborough, June 11, 1768, in *Letters to the Ministry*, 20–21.

14. Francis Bernard to Earl of Hillsborough, June 13, 14, 1768, in *Letters to the Ministry*, 21–22, 24.

15. Commissioners of the Customs to Lords of the Treasury, Mar. 28, 1768, in Wolkins, "Seizure," 269–71; Joseph Harrison to Lord Rockingham, June 17, 1768, in Watson, "Joseph Harrison," 592; *Boston Evening-Post*, June 20, 1768; Reid, *In a Rebellious Spirit*, 104, 107.

16. Joseph Harrison and Benjamin Hallowell to John Robinson, June 12, 1768, in *Letters to the Ministry*, 97–98; Joseph Harrison and Benjamin Hallowell, June 14, 1768, in *Letters to the Ministry*, 101; Joseph Harrison to Lord Rockingham, June 17, 1768, in Watson, "Joseph Harrison," 592.

17. Joseph Harrison to Lord Rockingham, June 17, 1768, in Watson, "Joseph Harrison," 592–94.

18. *Boston News-Letter*, June 16, 1768; Francis Bernard to Earl of Hillsborough, June 16–18, 1768, in *Letters to the Ministry*, 25–28; *Boston Town Records*, June 14, 1768, 254–55; Rowe, *Diary*, June 14, 1768, 165–66.

19. *Boston Town Records*, June 15, 1768, 256; Francis Bernard to Earl of Hillsborough, June 16–18, 1768, in *Letters to the Ministry*, 25–28; *Boston Evening-Post*, June 20, 1768.

20. Earl of Hillsborough to Thomas Gage, June 8, 1768, in *Correspondence of Gage*, 2:68–69.

21. Earl of Hillsborough to Thomas Gage, July 30, 1768, in *Correspondence of Gage*, 2:72–74; Reid, *In a Rebellious Spirit*, 69.

22. Francis Bernard to House of Representatives, *JHR*, 45:68–69; *JHR*, 45:104–12.

23. *JHR*, June 22, 23, 1768, 45:70–72; Francis Bernard to House of Representatives, June 24, 1768, *JHR*, 45:75–76.

24. *JHR*, June 29, 1768, 45:86; Francis Bernard to House of Representatives, June 28, 29, 1768, *JHR*, 45:85, 88.

25. House of Representatives to Francis Bernard, June 30, 1768, *JHR*, 45:91–94; Rowe, *Diary*, June 30, 1768, 167–68; *JHR*, June 30, 1768, 45:94–96; House to Earl of Hillsborough, June 30, 1768, *JHR*, 45:99–104.

26. Thomas Gage to Earl of Hillsborough, June 17, 1678, in *Correspondence of Gage*, 1:180; Thomas Gage to Commissioners of Customs, June 21, 1768, in *Letters to the Ministry*, 107.

27. Thomas Gage to Earl of Hillsborough, 28, 1678, in *Correspondence of Gage*, 1:182–83; Thomas Gage to Lord Barrington, June 28, 1768, in *Correspondence of Gage*, 2:479–80.

28. Francis Bernard to Earl of Hillsborough, July 9, 1768, in *Letters to the Ministry*, 40; Francis Bernard to Lord Barrington, July 11, 1768, in Channing and Coolidge, *Barrington-Bernard Correspondence*, 165; Thomas Gage to Francis Bernard, July 11, 1768, quoted in *Correspondence of Gage*, 2:77n.

29. Francis Bernard to Earl of Hillsborough, July 30, 1768, in *Letters to the Ministry*, 36–37; Francis Bernard to Lord Barrington, July 20, 30, 1768, in Channing and Coolidge, *Barrington-Bernard Correspondence*, 167–69, 169–70; Abstract of Council Minutes, July 27, 29, 1768, *JHR*, 46:54–60; Rowe, *Diary*, July 29, 1768, 171.

30. *Boston Town Records*, June 17, 1768, 258–59; *JHR*, June 18, 1768, 45:63–64; Francis Bernard to Lord Barrington, July 11, 1768, in Channing and Coolidge, *Barrington-Bernard Correspondence*, 165; F. F. to the printers, *Boston Gazette*, Aug. 8, 1768; *Boston Gazette*, Aug. 15, 1768.

31. Francis Bernard to Earl of Hillsborough, July 9, 18–19, 1768, in *Letters to the Ministry*, 38–41, 44–46; Rowe, *Diary*, July 16, 1768, 170; *Boston Gazette*, July 18, 1768.

32. Francis Bernard to Earl of Hillsborough, July 9, 11, 1768, in *Letters to the Ministry*, 39–40, 41; Thomas Gage to Earl of Hillsborough, August 19, 1768, in *Correspondence of Gage*, 1:189.

33. Rowe, *Diary*, July 28, Aug. 1, 1768, 171; *Boston Evening-Post*, Aug. 1, 15, 1768; Francis Bernard to Earl of Hillsborough, Aug. 9, 1768, in *Letters to the Ministry*, 49–50; *Boston Gazette*, Aug. 22, 1768; Shepherd and Walton, *Shipping*, 135; Tyler, *Smugglers and Patriots*, 140.

34. *Boston Evening-Post*, Aug. 22, 1768; Rowe, *Diary*, Aug. 15, 1768, 172; Nash, *Unknown American Revolution*, 57–58.

35. Thomas Gage to Earl of Hillsborough, Sept. 9, 10, 1768, in *Correspondence of Gage*, 1:191, 195; Zobel, *Boston Massacre*, 89; Thomas Gage to Lord Barrington, Sept. 10, 1768, in *Correspondence of Gage*, 2:487.

36. *Boston Gazette*, Sept. 5, 1768.

37. *Boston Gazette*, Aug. 6, 1768; Francis Bernard to Earl of Hillsborough, Sept. 16, 1768, in *Letters to the Ministry*, 52–56, 48; Rowe, *Diary*, Sept. 9, 1768, 174.

38. *Boston Gazette*, Sept. 19, 1768; Drake, *Old Landmarks*, 349; T. Hutchinson, *History of Massachusetts Bay*, 3:147.

39. Francis Bernard to Earl of Hillsborough, Sept. 16, 1768, in *Letters to the Ministry*, 53–56; *Boston Gazette*, Sept. 19, 1768.

40. Francis Bernard to Boston town committee, Sept. 13, 1768, in *Boston Town Records*, 261.

41. *Boston Gazette*, Sept. 19, 1768; *Boston Town Records*, Sept. 13, 1768, 264.

42. *Boston Gazette*, Sept. 19, 1768; *Boston Town Records*, Sept. 13, 1768, 264.

43. *Boston Gazette*, Sept. 19, 1768; *Boston New-Letter*, Sept. 22, 1768.

44. *Boston Gazette*, Sept. 26, Oct. 3, 1768; R. D. Brown, "Massachusetts Convention," 101–4, and *Revolutionary Politics,* 29–30.

45. *Boston Gazette*, Sept. 26, 1768.
46. *Boston Gazette*, Sept. 26, 1768.
47. *Boston Gazette*, Oc. 3, 1768.

CHAPTER 7

1. *Journal of the Times*, Sept. 29, 1768, 1; *Selectmen's Minutes*, Oct. 1, 1768, 311.
2. Thomas Gage to Lord Barrington, Sept. 26, 1768, in *Correspondence of Gage*, 2:488; Francis Bernard to Earl of Hillsborough, Oct. 1, 1768, in *Letters to the Ministry*, 68.
3. Francis Bernard to the House, May 28, 1767, *JHR*, 44:9; F. Anderson, *People's Army*, 111–20.
4. Frey, *British Soldier in America*, 3, 6, 118, 137; F. Anderson, *People's Army*, 27; *A Short Narrative of the Horrid Massacre in Boston,* 45; Shy, *Toward Lexington*, 309.
5. Everard, *Thomas Farrington's Regiment*, 59–60, 61, 72, 73; Frey, *British Soldier in America*, 136; Fischer, *Washington's Crossing*, 34.
6. Everard, *Thomas Farrington's Regiment*, 55, 60, 73.
7. Everard, *Thomas Farrington's Regiment*, 58–60; *Boston Gazette*, June 26, 1769.
8. Francis Bernard to Earl of Hillsborough, Sept. 23, 1768, in *Letters to the Ministry*, 56–57; Proceedings of the Council, Sept. 19, 1768, in *Bowdoin-Temple Papers*, 101. The Quartering Act is available at www.ushistory.org/declaration/related/quartering.htm.
9. Francis Bernard to Earl of Hillsborough, Sept. 23, 1768, in *Letters to the Ministry*, 57–58; *Journal of the Times*, Sept. 30, 1768, 1; *Boston Evening-Post*, Oct. 3, 1768.
10. Francis Bernard to Earl of Hillsborough, Sept. 23, 1768, in *Letters to the Ministry*, 58–60; *Proceedings of the Council*, Sept. 21, 1768, in *Bowdoin-Temple Papers*, 102–3; *Selectmen's Minutes*, Sept. 21, 1768, 310.
11. Francis Bernard to Earl of Hillsborough, Sept. 23, 1768, in *Letters to the Ministry*, 60–61; Drake, *Old Landmarks*, 302–4; *JHR*, Feb. 9, 1768, 44:155, and Sept. 24, 1768, 46:60–63.
12. Francis Bernard to Earl of Hillsborough, Oct. 1, 1768, in *Letters to the Ministry*, 66–67.
13. Francis Bernard to Earl of Hillsborough, Oct. 1, 1768, in *Letters to the Ministry*, 68.
14. Francis Bernard to Earl of Hillsborough, Oct. 1, 1768, in *Letters to the Ministry*, 68.
15. Drake, *Old Landmarks*, 305–6.
16. *Boston Evening-Post*, Oct. 3, 1768.
17. *Boston Evening-Post*, Oct. 3, 1768; *Selectmen's Minutes*, Oct. 1, 4, 5, 1768, 311, 312; Rowe, *Diary*, Oct. 1, 7, 16, 1768, 175–76, 177.
18. *Boston Chronicle*, Oct. 3, 1768.

19. Francis Bernard to Earl of Hillsborough, Oct. 5, 1768, in *Letters to the Ministry*, 70–71.

20. Francis Bernard to Earl of Hillsborough, Oct. 5, 6, 1768, in *Letters to the Ministry*, 71–72; Council to Francis Bernard, Oct. 5, 1768, *JHR*, 46:65; *Boston Gazette*, Apr. 17, 1769.

21. Thomas Gage to Earl of Hillsborough, Oct. 10, 31, 1768, in *Correspondence of Gage*, 1:201, 202–3; *Boston Chronicle*, Oct. 17, 1768; Francis Bernard to Earl of Hillsborough, Nov. 1, 1768, *JHR*, 46:3; Advice of Council, Oct. 17, 1768, *Boston Evening-Post*, Oct. 31, 1768.

22. *Boston Gazette*, Oct. 24, 1768; Francis Bernard to Earl of Hillsborough, Nov. 1, 1768, *JHR*, 46:4; Thomas Hutchinson to —, June 2, 1767, Hutchinson Correspondence, Massachusetts Archives (microfilm), vol. 26, page 276.

23. *Boston Gazette*, Oct. 24, 1768; Francis Bernard to Earl of Hillsborough, Nov. 1, 1768, *JHR*, 46:4.

24. *Boston Gazette*, Oct. 24, 1768; Francis Bernard to Earl of Hillsborough, Nov. 1, 1768, *JHR*, 46:4.

25. Francis Bernard to Earl of Hillsborough, Nov. 1, 1768, *JHR*, 46:5–7; Thomas Gage to Earl of Hillsborough, Oct. 31, 1768, in *Correspondence of Gage*, 1:202–3, 205.

26. Francis Bernard to Earl of Hillsborough, Nov. 1, 1768, *JHR*, 46:5–7; *Selectmen's Minutes*, Oct. 27, 1768, 313; Rowe, *Diary*, Oct. 29, 1768, 178; *Boston Evening-Post*, Oct. 31, 1768.

27. Thomas Gage to Earl of Hillsborough, Oct. 31, 1768, in *Correspondence of Gage*, 1:204; Francis Bernard to Earl of Hillsborough, Nov. 1, 1768, *JHR*, 46:5–6; Lord Barrington to Francis Bernard, Oct. 3, 1768, in Channing and Coolidge, *Barrington-Bernard Correspondence*, 171.

28. Thomas Gage to Earl of Hillsborough, Oct. 31, 1768, in *Correspondence of Gage*, 1:204.

29. Andrew Eliot to Thomas Hollis, Oct. 17, 1768, in "Letters from Eliot to Hollis," 432; Thomas Hutchinson to Thomas Whately, Oct. 17, 1768, Hutchinson Correspondence, Massachusetts Archives (microfilm), vol. 25, page 283; Thomas Gage to Lord Barrington, Sept. 13, 1766, in *Correspondence of Gage*, 2:373; *Journal of the Times*, Oct. 3, 1768; depositions of John Croker and James Corkrin, July 24, 1770, British National Archives [hereafter BNA], CO5/88 XC1580. I thank David Hackett Fischer for generously sharing his copies of the entire file of depositions with me.

30. *Journal of the Times*, Oct. 8, 9, 12, 31, 1768, 4–5, 17; Shy, *Toward Lexington*, 305–6; T. Hutchinson, *History of Massachusetts Bay*, 3:161; *Boston Evening-Post*, Oct. 31, 1768; *Boston Gazette*, Oct. 31, 1768.

31. *Journal of the Times*, Oct. 6, 14, 29, 31, 1768, 3, 6, 16–17; Rowe, *Diary*, Nov. 1, 1768, 178; *Selectmen's Records*, Oct. 31, 1768, 314; *Boston Gazette*, Nov. 7, 1768.

32. Greene, *Negro,* 16–17; McManus, *Black Bondage,* 6, 39; Wood, *Origins of American Slavery,* 103; Archer, *Fissures in the Rock,* 127–28, 155.

33. Greene, *Negro,* 63, 126–27, 177, 179, 187, 262, 268; McManus, *Black Bondage,* 59, 106; Moore, *Notes on the History of Slavery,* 11; Jordan, *White Over Black,* 125; Twombly and Moore, "Black Puritan," 226–27; Zilversmit, *First Emancipation,* 19; Higginbotham, *In the Matter of Color,* 72; Horton and Horton, *In Hope of Liberty,* 26; Fredrickson, *White Supremacy,* 72–73; Fields, "Slavery, Race, and Ideology," 95–118; Piersen, *Black Yankees,* 49–51; Breen, "Covenanted Militia," 41; Melish, *Disowning Slavery,* 4–6; *A Report of the Record Commissioners of the City of Boston, 1660 to 1701,* Nov. 5, 1661, 5.

34. Piersen, *Black Yankees,* 18; Berlin, *Many Thousands Gone,* 178; McManus, *Black Bondage,* 14, 199–206; Moore, *Slavery in Massachusetts,* 50–51; Nash, *Urban Crucible,* 107.

35. Sewall, "Selling of Joseph," in *Diary,* 2:1117–21; Sweet, *Bodies Politic,* 58–60, 62–64.

36. *A Report of the Record Commissioners of the City of Boston, 1701 to 1715,* May 26, 1701, 5; Jordan, *White over Black,* 139; Greene, *Negro in New England,* 208; Frederickson, *White Supremacy,* 107–8, 125–26.

37. *A Report of the Record Commissioners of the City of Boston, 1700 to 1728,* Apr. 19, 1723, 173–75; *JHR,* June 7, 17, 20, 21, 1723, Aug. 13, 15, 22, 27, 1723, Dec. 4, 5, 7, 10, 14, 17, 1723, 5:18–19, 36, 43, 48, 114, 121, 138, 145, 258, 259, 264, 274, 286, 292.

38. *Boston Town Records,* May 4, 1723, June 24, 1728, 176–77, 223; *A Report of the Record Commissioners of the City of Boston, 1729 to 1742,* Apr. 28, 1736, 139; *A Report of the Record Commissioners of the City of Boston, 1742 to 1757,* Aug. 1, 1757, 315; *Boston Town Records,* Mar. 12, 1759, 20.

39. *Boston Gazette,* Aug. 19, July 18, 1765; Desrochers, "Slave-for-Sale Advertisements," 623–64.

40. Nash, *Unknown American Revolution,* 62–63; *JHR,* Jan. 7, Feb. 2, 1764, 40:170, 263–64, June 10, 1766, vol. 43, pt. 1, 110, Mar. 13, 14, 16, 1767, vol. 43, pt. 2, 387, 390, 393; *Boston Town Records,* May 10, 1766, Mar. 16, 1767, 183, 200.

41. Humphrey Ploughjogger [John Adams] to the *Boston Gazette,* Oct. 14, 1765, in Taylor, Kline, and Lint, *Papers of John Adams,* 1:147.

CHAPTER 8

1. Council's Address to Thomas Gage, Oct. 27, 1768, *JHR,* 46:66–68.

2. Thomas Gage to Council, Oct. 28, 1768, *Boston Evening-Post,* Oct. 31, 1768; Thomas Gage to Earl of Hillsborough, in *Correspondence of Gage,* 1:204–5.

3. *Journal of the Times,* Oct. 26, 1768, 12; Thomas Gage to Earl of Hillsborough, Oct. 31, 1768, in *Correspondence of Gage,* 1:205.

4. Rowe, *Diary*, Nov. 13, 1769, 179; Henry Hulton to Robert Nicholson, Apr. 6, 1769, in W. Brown, "Englishman Views the American Revolution," 14–16; Ann Hulton to Mrs. Adam Lightbody, Apr. 10, 1769, in *Letters of a Loyalist Lady*, 17–19.

5. Ann Hulton to Mrs. Adam Lightbody, Apr. 10, 1769, in *Letters of a Loyalist Lady*, 19; Homosum, "To the Young Ladies of Boston," Dec. 10, 1768, *Boston Evening-Post*, Jan. 30, 1769; *Journal of the Times*, Dec. 14, 1768, 34–35.

6. Wroth and Zobel, "Editorial Note" to Sewall v. Hancock, *LPJA*, 2:173–83; *Journal of the Times*, Nov. 3, 7, 28, Dec. 5, 14, 1768, Jan. 2, 5, 7, 28, 30, Feb. 11, 21, 24, Mar. 2, 26, 1769, 18, 19, 28, 31, 34, 43, 44–45, 46, 56, 57, 64, 67, 68, 72, 83–84; Thomas Gage to Earl of Hillsborough, Mar. 5, 1769, in *Correspondence of Gage*, 1:220.

7. Dickerson, "Editorial Introduction," *Journal of the Times*, vii–xiii; T. Hutchinson, *History of Massachusetts Bay*, 3:162.

8. *Journal of the Times*, Oct. 19, Nov. 2, 9, 30, 1768, 8, 17–18, 21, 28.

9. *Journal of the Times*, Nov. 30, Dec. 2, 31, 1768, 28–29, 30, 42–43; T. Hutchinson, *History of Massachusetts Bay*, 3:161; Vindex, *Boston Gazette*, Dec. 5, 1768.

10. *Journal of the Times*, Dec. 13, 1768, 34.

11. *Journal of the Times*, Nov. 25, 1768, 26.

12. *Journal of the Times*, Nov. 9, 1768, Jan. 22, 24, Feb. 8, 27, May 2, June 22, 1769, 21, 53–54, 63, 71, 94, 111–12; *Selectmen's Minutes*, Nov. 28, 1768, 317; *A Report of the Record Commissioners of the City of Boston, 1769 through April, 1775,* Jan. 21, 1769, 3.

13. Archer, *Fissures in the Rock*, 98–110, 144–45; *Journal of the Times*, Oct. 14, 21, Nov. 27, Dec. 25, 1768, Jan. 8, Apr. 2, 9, 1769, 6, 8, 28, 39–40, 47, 86, 89; Hoerder, *Crowd Action,* 52.

14. *Journal of the Times*, Nov. 6, 20, Dec. 19, 31, 1768, Jan. 1, May 3, June 5, July 24, 1769, 19, 24–25, 37, 42, 43, 94, 106, 118–19; J. Adams, *Diary*, 3:289–90.

15. *Journal of the Times*, Nov. 1, Dec. 19, 1768, Mar. 6, 18, 27, Apr. 21, June 11, 1769, 17, 37, 74–75, 79, 84, 92, 107–8; *Boston Evening-Post*, Mar. 13, 1769; *Boston Gazette*, Mar. 13, 1769; deposition of John Norfolk, Aug. 25, 1770, BNA, CO5/88 XC1580.

16. *Journal of the Times*, Feb. 27, Apr. 19, June 13, 1769, 71, 91, 108; *Boston Evening-Post*, Feb. 27, 1769; *New England Historical and Genealogical Register*, 48:435.

17. *Journal of the Times*, Jan. 9, 31, Apr. 21, July 25, 28, 29, 30, 1769, 47, 57, 92, 119–23 (depositions of Edmund Quincy, Peter Barbour, Jeremiah Belknap, John Loring, Edward Jackson, and Stephen Greenleaf appear in the July issues); William Palfrey to John Wilkes, July 26, 1769, in Ford, "John Wilkes and Boston," 205–6; Wroth and Zobel, "Editorial Note" to Rex v. Ross, *LPJA*, 2:431–33; *JHR*, July 15, 1769, 45:192; depositions of Alexander Ross, Charles Fordyce, John Phillips, Samuel Heale, and Jonathan Stevenson, Aug. 25, 1770, BNA, CO5/88 XC1580.

18. *Journal of the Times*, Nov. 1, 9, Dec. 12, 1768, Feb. 8, 27, Mar. 6, 18, Apr. 15, May 1, 16, June 12, July 4, 21, 23, 1769, 17, 21, 34, 63, 71, 74–75, 79, 90, 94, 99, 108, 114, 118.

19. T. Hutchinson, *History of Massachusetts Bay*, 3:162; *Journal of the Times*, Apr. 30, May 17, July 3, 1769, 93–94, 100, 114; *Boston Evening-Post*, July 3, 1769; *Boston Gazette*, July 3, 1769.

20. Hoerder, *Crowd Action*, 191; Shy, *Toward Lexington*, 309; *Journal of the Times*, Dec. 5, 16, 29, 1768, Jan. 31, Mar. 18, 1769, 31, 37, 42, 58, 79; *Boston Chronicle*, Dec. 19, 1768; *Boston Evening-Post*, Dec. 19, 1768, Jan. 16, Feb. 13, 1769; *Boston Gazette*, Dec. 19, 1768, Jan. 16, Feb. 6, 13, 1769; Rowe, *Diary*, Jan. 31, 1769, 182; Boyle, "Boyle's Journal," Apr. 27, 1769, 258.

21. Depositions of Henry Cullin, John Eyley, Richard Henley, Thomas Light, Jessey Lindley, James McKaan, William Murray, Richard Ratcliff, Thomas Thornley, Thomas Todger, Samuel Unwin, John Woolhouse, July 24, 26, 28, Aug. 25, 1770, BNA, CO5/88 XC1580.

22. Deposition of Cornelius Murphy, July 24, 1770, BNA, CO5/88 XC1580.

23. Deposition of William Godson, July 24, 1770, BNA, CO5/88 XC1580.

24. Deposition of Thomas Smilie, July 24, 1770, BNA, CO5/88 XC1580.

25. Deposition of Thomas Smilie, July 24, 1770, BNA, CO5/88 XC1580.

26. Deposition of John Timmons, July 28, 1770, BNA, CO5/88 XC1580.

27. Depositions of William Banks, Robert Balfour, and William Lake, Aug. 25, 1770, BNA, CO5/88 XC1580.

28. Depositions of John Shelton, James Botham, William Mabbot, Aug. 25, 1770, BNA, CO5/88 XC1580.

29. Depositions of William Halam, Edward Osbaldistan, Gavin Thompson, Eustace Merryweather, William Henderson, and William Leeming, Aug. 25, 1770, BNA, CO5/88 XC1580.

30. Depositions of William Jones and Richard Pearsall, July 28, 1770, BNA, CO5/88 XC1580.

31. Depositions of William Jones, Richard Pearsall, John Arnold, John Shelley, Dennis Towers, Jacob Brown, Henry Cullin, John Dumphy, and John Timmons, July 24, 28, Aug. 25, 1770, BNA, CO5/88 XC1580.

32. Francis Bernard to —, Dec. 23, 1768, in Channing and Coolidge, *Barrington-Bernard Correspondence*, 253–58; Francis Bernard to Lord Barrington, Mar. 18, 1769, in Channing and Coolidge, *Barrington-Bernard Correspondence*, 197–98; Resolves of the House of Lords, *Boston Evening-Post*, Mar. 20, 1769.

33. Samuel Cooper to Thomas Pownall, May 11, 1769, in Tuckerman, "Letters of Samuel Cooper," 308; House to Francis Bernard, May 31, 1769, *JHR*, 45:117–18; Francis Bernard to House, May 31, June 1, 1769, *JHR*, 45:120, 122.

34. *JHR*, June 3, 1769, 45:122; *Boston Gazette*, June 12, 1769.

35. House to Francis Bernard, June 13, 1769, *JHR*, 45:130–31.

36. Francis Bernard to House, June 14, 1769, *JHR*, 45:132; William Palfrey to John Wilkes, June 13, 1769, in Ford, "Wilkes and Boston," 201; *Boston Chronicle*, June 19, 1769.

37. House to Francis Bernard, June 19, July 4, 1769, *JHR*, 45:135–36, 189; *JHR*, June 21, 1769, 45:138; Francis Bernard to House, June 21, 28, 1769, *JHR*, 45:139, 150–51; Francis Bernard to Lord Barringon, June 27, 1769, in Channing and Coolidge, *Barrington-Bernard Correspondence*, 205; Petition to the King, June 27, 1769, *JHR*, 45:197–99.

38. Francis Bernard to House, July 6, 12, 1769, *JHR*, 45:164, 180.

39. Francis Bernard to House, July 15, 1769, *JHR*, 45:196; *JHR*, July 14, 1769, 45:188; House to Francis Bernard, July 15, 1769, *JHR*, 45:192–94; Thomas Gage to Earl of Hillsborough, July 23, 1769, in *Correspondence of Gage*, 1:232.

40. Earl of Hillsborough to Thomas Gage, Mar. 24, 1769, in *Correspondence of Gage*, 2:87; Thomas Gage to Earl of Hillsborough, Oct. 31, 1768, in *Correspondence of Gage*, 1:204–5.

41. Thomas Gage to Earl of Hillsborough, June 10, July 22, 1769, in *Correspondence of Gage*, 1:227, 229; *Journal of the Times*, June 21, 1769, 111; Francis Bernard to Lord Barrington, June 27, 1769, in Channing and Coolidge, *Barrington-Bernard Correspondence*, 205.

42. *Boston Evening-Post*, June 26, July 10, July 31, 1769; Thomas Gage to earl of Hillsborough, July 22, 1769, in *Correspondence of Gage*, 1:228–29.

43. Boyle, "Boyle's Journal," Aug. 1, 1769, 259; Rowe, *Diary*, Aug. 1, 1769, 190; Thomas Young to John Wilkes, Aug. 3, 1769, in Ford, "Wilkes and Boston," 207; *Boston Gazette*, Aug. 7, 1769.

44. *Boston Gazette*, Aug. 7, 1769; Andrew Eliot to Thomas Hollis, Oct. 17, 1768, in "Letters from Eliot to Hollis," 433–34.

45. *Boston Evening-Post*, Aug. 21, 1769; *Boston Gazette*, Aug. 21, 1769; Rowe, *Diary*, Aug. 14, 1769, 191.

46. Hoerder, *Crowd Action,* 139; "An Alphabetical List," 140–42; Seybolt, *Town Officials,* 293–361; Shipton, *Sibley's Harvard Graduates*, vols. 7–17; Day and Day, "Boston 'Caucus,'" 32–33; *LPJA*, vols. 1–3; J. Adams, *Diary,* vols. 1–3; Drake, *Old Landmarks, passim*; Winsor, *Memorial History,* vol. 3; Rowe, *Diary, passim*; *JHR*, 45:122.

47. Shipton, *Sibley's Harvard Graduates*, vols. 7, 11, 13–15; Winsor, *Memorial History*, vol. 3; *LPJA*, vols. 2–3; J. Adams, *Diary,* vols. 1–2; Drake, *Old Landmarks, passim*; Rowe, *Diary, passim*; Andrew Eliot to Thomas Hollis, July 10, 1769, in "Letters from Eliot to Hollis," 442.

CHAPTER 9

1. Hoerder, *Crowd Action,* 161–62; Egnal and Ernst, "Economic Interpretation of Revolution," 21; Egnal, *Mighty Empire,* 163; Shepherd and Walton, *Shipping, Maritime Trade,* 115; Fowler, *Baron of Beacon Hill,* 91.

2. Hoerder, *Crowd Action,* 162; Tyler, *Smugglers and Patriots*, 137; *Boston Gazette*, Feb. 20, 1769.

3. See October 1768 and March 1769 issues of *Boston Chronicle*, *Boston Evening-Post*, *Boston Gazette*, and *Massachusetts Gazette*.

4. *Boston Evening-Post*, Apr. 24, May 1, 1769.

5. *Boston Evening-Post*, May 8, 1769; *Boston Gazette*, May 15, 1769; Samuel Cooper to Thomas Pownall, May 11, 1769, in Tuckerman, "Letters of Cooper to Pownall," 307; Schlesinger, *Colonial Merchants,* 158–59.

6. *Boston Chronicle*, June 1, 1769.

7. Alden, "John Mein," 571–99; J. Adams, *Diary*, Jan. 30, 1768, 1:338.

8. *Boston Chronicle*, Dec. 21, 1767; Americus to the Editors, *Boston Gazette*, Jan. 18, 1768.

9. *Massachusetts Gazette*, Jan. 21, 1768; Wroth and Zobel, "Editorial Note" for Gill v. Mein, *LPJA*, 1:151–54.

10. *Boston Evening-Post*, June 5, 1769.

11. *Massachusetts Gazette*, June 8, 1769.

12. *Boston Evening-Post*, July 3, 10, 31, 1769; *Boston Gazette*, July 3, 10, 17, 24, 31, 1769; *Massachusetts Gazette*, July 6, 13, 1769.

13. *Boston Evening-Post*, Aug. 14, 1769; *Boston Gazette*, Aug. 14, 1769; Rowe, *Diary*, Aug. 4, 1769, 190–91.

14. *Boston Chronicle*, Aug. 17, 1769.

15. *Boston Chronicle*, particularly Aug. 17, 21, 24, 28, 31, 1769; *Boston Gazette*, July 31, Aug. 14, 21, 1769; "Alphabetical List of Sons of Liberty," 140–42.

16. *Boston Evening-Post*, Aug. 21, 1769; *Boston Gazette*, Aug. 21, 1769.

17. *Boston Evening-Post*, Aug. 21, 1769; *Boston Gazette*, Aug. 21, 1769.

18. *Boston Chronicle*, Aug. 21, 1769; *Massachusetts Gazette*, Aug. 24, 1769.

19. *Boston Chronicle*, Aug. 28, 1769; John Hancock to Haley & Hopkins, Sept. 6, 1769, in A. E. Brown, *John Hancock*, 166.

20. *Boston Evening-Post*, Aug. 28, 1769; *Boston Gazette*, Aug. 28, 1769.

21. *Boston Evening-Post*, Aug. 28, 1769; *Boston Gazette*, Aug. 28, 1769; *Boston Chronicle*, Aug. 31, 1769.

22. *Boston Gazette*, Sept. 4, 1769.

23. *Boston Chronicle*, Sept. 4, 1769; *Boston Gazette*, Sept. 11, 1769; John Robinson's account, *Massachusetts Gazette*, Sept. 11, 1769; James Otis's rejoinder, *Boston Gazette*, Sept. 18, 1769.

24. J. Adams, *Diary*, Sept. 3, 4, 1769, 1:342–43; James Otis to the printers, *Boston Gazette*, Sept. 4, 1769; Robinson's account, *Massachusetts Gazette*, Sept. 11, 1769.

25. Rowe, *Diary*, Sept. 5, 1769, 192; Thomas Young to John Wilkes, Sept. 6, 1769, in Ford, "Wilkes and Boston," 209; *Boston Evening-Post*, Sept. 11, 1769; *Boston Gazette*, Sept. 11, 18, 25, Oct. 23, 1769; *Massachusetts Gazette*, Sept. 11, 18, 1769.

26. Rowe, *Diary*, Sept. 6, 1769, 192; Thomas Young to John Wilkes, Sept. 6, 1769, in Ford, "Wilkes and Boston," 209; James Murray to —, Sept. 30, 1769, in *Letters of Murray*, 159–62.

27. J. Adams, *Diary*, 2:48n. and Jan. 16, 1770, 1:348–49; *Boston Evening-Post*, Sept. 25, Oct. 9, 1769; Zobel, *Boston Massacre*, 149; Andrew Eliot to Thomas Hollis, Sept. 7, 1769, in "Letters from Eliot to Hollis," 444; *Selectmen's Minutes*, Oct. 7, 1769, 39.

28. All issues of *Boston Chronicle*, Sept., Oct. 1769; Hoerder, *Crowd Action*, 215.

29. *Boston Evening-Post*, Sept. 11, 1769; *Boston Gazette*, Sept. 11, 1769; *Boston Chronicle*, Sept. 14, 1769.

30. *Boston Gazette*, Sept. 4, 18, Oct. 2, 1769.

31. *Boston Gazette*, Aug. 21, Oct. 9, 16, 1769; *Boston Evening-Post*, Sept. 11, Oct. 2, 1769; Norton, *Liberty's Daughters*, 166; James Bowdoin to Thomas Pownall, Dec. 5, 1769, in *Bowdoin-Temple Papers*, 158; *Boston Town Records*, Oct. 4, 1769, 298.

32. See October issues of *Boston Chronicle*, *Boston Evening-Post*, *Boston Gazette*, and *Massachusetts Gazette*.

33. *Boston Evening-Post*, Oct. 9, 1769; *Boston Gazette*, Sept. 11, 18, Oct. 9, 16, 1769.

34. Shepherd and Walton, *Shipping, Maritime Trade*, 113, 115; Labaree, *Boston Tea Party*, 24, 35.

35. Rowe, *Diary*, Oct. 24, 1769, 194; *Selectmen's Minutes*, Oct. 25, 1769; *Boston Evening-Post*, Oct. 30, 1769; depositions of John Ness, Samuel Hickman, Mick McGrover, Robert Adamson, John Stevens, William Coleman, John Thorpe, William Fowler, John Park, Thomas Sherwood, Robert Holbrook, and William Marburn, Aug. 25, 1770, BNA, CO5/88 XC1580; Zobel, *Boston Massacre*, 139–43.

36. Alden, "John Mein," 589–90; *Boston Chronicle*, Oct. 26, 1769; D. Bayley to the editors, *Boston Evening-Post*, Oct. 16, 1769.

37. Boyle, "Boyle's Journal," Oct. 28, 1769, 260–61; Rowe, *Diary*, Oct. 28, 1769, 194; *Boston Evening-Post*, Oct. 30, Nov. 20, 1769; *Massachusetts Gazette*, Nov. 2, 1769; Thomas Hutchinson to Earl of Hillsborough, Nov. 11, 1769, Hutchinson Correspondence, Massachusetts Archives (microfilm), vol. 26, page 403.

38. Boyle, "Boyle's Journal," Oct. 28, 1769, 260; Rowe, *Diary*, Oct. 28, 1769, 194; *Boston Chronicle*, Oct. 30, 1769; *Boston Evening-Post*, Oct. 30, 1769; *Massachusetts Gazette*, Nov. 2, 1769 ; "Gailer v. Trevett," *LPJA*, 1:41–42.

39. *Boston Chronicle*, Nov. 2, 1769; *Massachusetts Gazette*, Nov. 2, 1769; William Palfrey to John Wilkes, Nov. 5, 1769, in Palfrey, *History of New England*, 5:415n.; Thomas Hutchinson to Lord ?, Oct. 30, 1769, Hutchinson Correspondence, Massachusetts Archives (microfilm), vol. 26, page 400.

40. *Boston Gazette*, July 31, 1769; *Boston Evening-Post*, Nov. 13, 20, 1769; John Hancock to Haley & Hopkins, Nov. 4, 1769, in A. E. Brown, *John Hancock*, 166–67.

41. *Boston Gazette*, Dec. 11, 1769, Mar. 9, 1761, Nov. 6, 1769; *Boston Chronicle*, 1767–70; *Boston Evening-Post*, 1761–70; *Boston Gazette*, 1761–70; *Massachusetts Gazette*, 1761–70; Cleary, *Elizabeth Murray*, 60, 101, 253n.

42. Norton, "Cherished Spirit," 51, 55; Cleary, *Elizabeth Murray*, 97, 134–35 (quote of "more custom" from 135).

43. Thomas Gage to Earl of Hillsborough, Dec. 4, 1769, in *Correspondence of Gage*, 1:242; *Boston Evening-Post*, Dec. 25, 1769; Andrew Eliot to Thomas Hollis, Dec. 25, 1769, in "Letters from Eliot to Hollis," 446–47.

CHAPTER 10

1. Tyler, *Smugglers and Patriots*, 144; Bernhard Knollenberg, *Growth of the American Revolution,* 74; *Boston Gazette*, Jan. 22, 1770; Civis, *Boston Gazette*, Feb. 5, 1770; Thomas Hutchinson to Earl of Hillsborough, Feb. 28, 1770, in *Documents of the American Revolution,* 51.

2. *Boston Gazette*, Jan. 1, 1770.

3. *Massachusetts Gazette*, Jan. 4, 1770; John Taylor, Jan. 8, 1770, *Massachusetts Gazette*, Jan. 11, 1770; *Boston Gazette*, Jan. 29, 1770. These sources of Taylor's account and the merchants association's response also apply to the following two paragraphs.

4. Theophilus Lillie, Jan. 9, 1770, *Massachusetts Gazette*, Jan. 11, 1770.

5. Theophilus Lillie, Jan. 9, 1770, *Massachusetts Gazette*, Jan. 11, 1770.

6. Theophilus Lillie, Jan. 9, 1770, *Massachusetts Gazette*, Jan. 11, 1770.

7. Determinatus to the Printers, *Boston Gazette*, Jan. 8, 1770.

8. *Boston Gazette*, Jan. 22, 1770; Rowe, *Diary*, Jan. 17, 1770, 196; Samuel Cooper to Thomas Pownall, Jan. 30, 1770, in "Letters from Cooper to Pownall," 314–15.

9. *Boston Gazette*, Jan. 22, 1770.

10. *Boston Gazette*, Jan. 22, 1770; Rowe, *Diary*, Jan. 18, 1770, 196; Samuel Cooper to Thomas Pownall, Jan. 30, 1770, in "Letters from Cooper to Pownall," 315; Nathaniel Rogers to Thomas Hutchinson, Jan. 19, 1770, Hutchinson Correspondence, Massachusetts Archives (microfilm), vol. 25, page 351.

11. *Boston Gazette*, Jan. 22, 1770; Rowe, *Diary*, Jan. 19, 1770, 196; Samuel Cooper to Thomas Pownall, Jan. 30, 1770, in "Letters from Cooper to Pownall," 315; Thomas Hutchinson to Francis Bernard, Jan. 27, 1770, Hutchinson Correspondence, Massachusetts Archives (microfilm), vol. 26, pages 434–35.

12. *Boston Gazette*, Jan. 29, 1770; Rowe, *Diary*, Jan. 23, 1770, 196; Samuel Cooper to Thomas Pownall, Jan. 30, 1770, in "Letters from Cooper to Pownall," 315; Thomas Hutchinson to Francis Bernard, Jan. 27, 1770,

Hutchinson Correspondence, Massachusetts Archives (microfilm), vol. 26, pages 434–35.

13. *Boston Gazette*, Jan. 29, 1770; Samuel Cooper to Thomas Pownall, Jan. 30, 1770, in "Letters from Cooper to Pownall," 315.

14. *Boston Chronicle*, Jan. 22, 1770; *Boston Gazette*, Jan. 29, 1770.

15. *Boston Chronicle*, Jan. 18, 1770.

16. *Boston Chronicle*, Jan. 22, Feb. 1, 5, 12, 1770.

17. *Boston Evening-Post*, Jan. 29, Feb. 5, 12, 1770; *Boston Chronicle*, Feb. 1, 22, 1770.

18. *Boston Evening-Post*, Feb. 12, 1770; *Boston Gazette*, Feb. 5, 12, 19, 1770.

19. Zobel, *Boston Massacre*, 172.

20. *Boston Gazette*, Jan. 1, 8, Feb. 19, 1770; *Massachusetts Gazette*, Jan. 29, Feb. 1, 1770; *Boston Chronicle*, Feb. 5, 1770; *Boston Evening-Post*, Feb. 5, 19, 1770.

21. *Boston Gazette*, Feb. 19, 1770; *Boston Evening-Post*, Feb. 19, 1770. This and the following paragraphs on the riots at Golden Hill and Nassau Street are informed also by Boyer, "Lobster Backs," 281–308; Countryman, *People in Revolution,* 63–66; Gilje, *Road to Mobocracy*, 55–58; Tiedeman, *Reluctant Revolutionaries*, 147–49.

22. *Boston Gazette*, Dec. 27, 1768, Feb. 19, 1770; *Boston Evening-Post*, Feb. 19, 1770; Shy, *Toward Lexington*, 309; *Journal of the Times*, Dec. 18, 1768, 37.

23. *Boston Evening-Post*, Feb. 26, 1770; Boyle, "Boyle's Journal," Feb. 22, 1770, 84:262; Wroth and Zobel., "Editorial Note" to Rex v. Richardson, *LPJA*, 2:396–98; Town Letter to Dennys De Berdt, in *Boston Town Records*, Oct. 22, 1766, 194.

24. *Boston Evening-Post*, Feb. 26, 1770; Wroth and Zobel., "Editorial Note" to Rex v. Richardson and "Paine's Minutes of the Trial," *LPJA*, 2:398, 416–21. These sources apply to the following paragraph as well.

25. *Boston Evening-Post*, Feb. 26, 1770; *Massachusetts Gazette*, Mar. 1, 1770.

26. *Boston Evening-Post*, Feb. 26, 1770; William Palfrey to John Wilkes, Mar. 5, 1770, in Elsey, "John Wilkes and William Palfrey," 417.

27. *Boston Evening-Post*, Feb. 26, 1770; *Boston Gazette*, Mar. 5, 1770; Rowe, *Diary*, Feb. 26, 1770, 197; Thomas Hutchinson to Earl of Hillsborough, in *Documents of American Revolution*, 2:51; Wroth and Zobel., "Editorial Note" to Rex v. Richardson, *LPJA*, 2:400.

CHAPTER 11

1. There is an abundance of primary sources for the Boston Massacre and events immediately preceding it. Well over a hundred depositions, witness testimonies at the trials, letters, and newspaper articles offer competing versions of what occurred. Apart from agreement on such basic facts as who were the victims and who were the soldiers and officer, there is a wide variety of accounts of key issues, from how many people were present to whether the soldiers' lives were imperiled and whether there was an order

to fire. In short, there are several plausible reconstructions. I, of course, consider my interpretation to be the most accurate, but more than usual the reader should carry a heavy load of skepticism at every step. For an alternative plausible reconstruction, see Zobel, *Boston Massacre*, 180–205; for a short perceptive account, see Allison, *Boston Massacre*, 9–18. Drake, *Old Landmarks*, 271, 273; *Short Narrative*, 39, 48; *LPJA*, 3:133–34; *Boston Evening-Post*, Mar. 5, 1770; deposition of Patrick Walker, July 28, 1770, BNA, CO5/88 XC1580.

2. *Short Narrative*, 39–40, 48; *LPJA*, 3:133–34; *Boston Evening-Post*, Mar. 5, 1770.

3. *Short Narrative*, 39–41, 48; *LPJA*, 3:133–34, 141; *Boston Evening-Post*, Mar. 5, 1770.

4. *Short Narrative*, 42 (quotes from this deposition); *Boston Evening-Post*, Mar. 5, 1770.

5. *Short Narrative*, 41, 59; *Boston Gazette*, Mar. 12, 1770; Thomas Hutchinson to Earl of Hillsborough, Mar. 12, 1770, in *Documents of American Revolution*, 2:58.

6. *Short Narrative*, 41; *Boston Gazette*, Mar. 12, 1770; William Dalrymple to Earl of Hillsborough, Mar. 13, 1770, in *Documents of American Revolution*, 2:60.

7. *Short Narrative*, 49, 58, 67, 78, 82, 83, 85, 90; *LPJA*, 3:57, 107, 117, 132, 135, 140, 171, 221.

8. *Short Narrative*, 46, 47, 57, 79; *LPJA*, 3:80, 169–70, 178, 200, 218; *Boston Gazette*, Mar. 12, 1770.

9. *Short Narrative*, 57, 99, 100; *LPJA*, 3:50, 217; Drake, *Old Landmarks*, 96–98; Zobel, *Boston Massacre*, 184–85.

10. *Short Narrative*, 48; *LPJA*, 3:50, 187.

11. *Short Narrative*, 48, 50, 57–58; *LPJA*, 3:50, 52–53.

12. *Short Narrative*, 49, 67–68, 83–84; *LPJA*, 3:111, 181, 183, 215, 220; Drake, *Old Landmarks*, 121; *Boston Gazette*, Mar. 12, 1770.

13. *Short Narrative*, 62–63, 70; *LPJA*, 3:182–83, 184–87, 215–16.

14. *LPJA*, 3:182.

15. *Short Narrative*, 79; *LPJA*, 3:58, 115, 117–18, 122, 123–24, 170–77, 178–79, 190, 216; J. Adams, *Diary*, 1:347n.; Winsor, *Memorial History*, 3:178n.

16. *Short Narrative*, 54, 73; *LPJA*, 3:53, 59, 60, 63, 64, 65, 69, 74, 109, 126, 127, 180, 195, 197, 207, 209.

17. Preston's account in Dalrymple to Hillsborough, Mar. 13, 1770, in *Documents of American Revolution*, 2:64–65; Everard, *Thomas Farrington's Regiment*, 72; *Short Narrative*, 58, 63–64, 65, 66, 67, 68–69, 73, 76, 87, 89; *LPJA*, 3:53, 55, 57, 58, 59, 70, 128–30, 196, 205–6, 211, 222–23.

18. *Short Narrative*, 58, 63–64, 65, 66, 67, 68–69, 73, 76, 87, 89; *LPJA*, 3:53, 55, 57, 58, 59, 70, 128–30, 196, 205–6, 211, 222–23.

19. *Short Narrative*, 47; *LPJA*, 3:102–3, 104, 107, 108, 110, 113, 115, 122, 145, 199.

20. Preston's account in Dalrymple to Hillsborough, Mar. 13, 1770, in *Documents of American Revolution*, 2:65.

21. *Short Narrative*, 49, 61–62, 65, 70–71, 86–88, 88–89; *LPJA*, 3:53, 54–55, 56, 57, 60, 64, 65–67, 69, 70–72, 74, 77, 102–3, 108–11, 118–19, 124, 130, 198, 203–5, 211–12; Preston's account in Dalrymple to Hillsborough, Mar. 13, 1770, in *Documents of American Revolution*, 2:65.

22. *Short Narrative*, 64, 65, 71; *LPJA*, 3:51, 71, 76, 106, 115, 118, 122, 127, 136; Preston's account in Dalrymple to Hillsborough, Mar. 13, 1770, in *Documents of American Revolution*, 2:65.

23. *Short Narrative*, 64, 65, 71, 74; *LPJA*, 3:51, 59, 60, 63, 71, 76, 78, 103, 106, 115, 118, 122, 124, 127, 136, 137, 181; Preston's account in Dalrymple to Hillsborough, Mar. 13, 1770, in *Documents of American Revolution*, 2:65–66.

24. *LPJA*, 3:46–47, 72, 73, 114–15, 117, 120, 127–28, 130; Henry M. Ward, "Crispus Attucks," American National Biography Online, www.anb.org/articles/01/01–00034.html; *Boston Gazette*, Oct. 2, 1750, Mar. 12, 1770.

25. *Short Narrative*, 63; *LPJA*, 3:105, 108–10, 120, 127–28, 133, 188, 207; *Boston Gazette*, Mar. 12, 1770.

26. *LPJA*, 3:127–28; *Boston Gazette*, Mar. 12, 1770.

27. *LPJA*, 3:141, 183, 185; G. P. Anderson, "Ebenezer Mackintosh," 46; Hoerder, *Crowd Action,* 141; *Boston Gazette*, Mar. 12, 1770.

28. *LPJA*, 3:212–14; Tom D. Crouch, "John Jeffries," American National Biography Online, www.anb.org/articles/20/20–00512.html; *Boston Gazette*, Mar. 12, 1770.

29. *LPJA*, 3:112–13; *Boston Gazette*, Mar. 12, 1770.

30. *Short Narrative*, 74; *LPJA*, 3:221–23; *Boston Gazette*, Mar. 12, 1770.

31. *Short Narrative*, 85; *Boston Gazette*, Mar. 12, 1770.

32. *Boston Gazette*, Mar. 12, 1770.

33. *Short Narrative*, 59, 61, 62, 63, 64, 65, 66, 67, 69, 70, 71, 72, 75, 77, 82, 85, 86, 87; *LPJA*, 3:54, 55, 57, 59, 61, 66–67, 69–70, 72, 74, 75, 76, 77, 78, 79, 105, 107, 112, 115, 118, 119, 125, 126, 128, 130, 135, 208; Preston's account in Dalrymple to Hillsborough, Mar. 13, 1770, in *Documents of American Revolution*, 2:65.

34. Preston's account in Dalrymple to Hillsborough, Mar. 13, 1770, in *Documents of American Revolution*, 2:66.

35. *Short Narrative*, 48, 49, 50, 54, 58, 60, 62, 63, 64, 67, 68, 71, 73, 74, 77, 78, 82, 83–84, 87, 102; *LPJA*, 3:50, 52, 53, 55, 57, 63, 64, 65, 79, 102–3, 106, 107, 108, 112, 124, 127, 129–30, 137, 180, 194, 198, 199–200, 207, 211–12; see Paul Revere's diagram in *LPJA*, 3: opposite 68. On the map of people at the Boston Massacre, fifty-seven spectators and participants, in addition to the eleven who were wounded or killed, have been identified and placed in approximate locations as of the first shot. That group consisted of Andrew (an African American designated in the records only by his given first name), Francis Archibald Jr., Jonathan Williams Austin, James Bailey,

Jedediah Bass, Theodore Bliss, William Botson, James Brewer, Ebenezer Bridgham, Benjamin Burdick, Thomas Cain, Daniel Calef, John Coburn, Daniel Cornwall, Peter Cunningham, John Danbrook, Benjamin Davis, James Dodge, Samuel Drowne, Nathaniel Fosdick, Benjamin Frizel, John Frost, Robert Fullerton, Robert Goddard, Harrison Gray Jr., John Gridley, Thomas Hall, Joseph Helyer, John Hickling, Ebenezer Hinkley, Joseph Hinkley, Charles Hobby, Joseph Hooton Jr., Patrick Keaton, Henry Knox, Edward Gambleton Langsford, John Leach Jr., Thomas Marshall, Diman Morton, Matthew Murray, Richard Palmes, Newton Prince, Francis Read, Nathaniel Russell, William Sawyer, Joseph Simpson, William Strong, William Tant, Daniel Usher, Jane Whitehouse, Thomas Wilkinson, Robert Williams, Charles Willis, John Wilson, James Woodall, and William Wyat. After the first shot, many in the crowd scattered and the pattern was different.

36. *Short Narrative*, 85, 97; *Boston Gazette*, Mar. 12, 1770.
37. *Short Narrative*, 63; *LPJA*, 3:108–9.
38. *Short Narrative*, 85; *LPJA*, 3:63, 79, 106, 131, 132, 133, 137, 213.
39. *Short Narrative*, 77, 85; *Boston Gazette*, Mar. 12, 1770; Wroth and Zobel, "Editorial Note to the Boston Massacre Trials," *LPJA*, 3:30n.; Dickerson, "Commissioners," 307–25.
40. *Short Narrative*, 72, 75–76, 79, 80, 84, 85, 97; *LPJA*, 3:121; Boston Gazette, Mar. 12, 1770; Wroth and Zobel, "Editorial Note" to the Boston Massacre Trials, *LPJA*, 3:30n.; Dickerson, "Commissioners," 307–25; Zobel, *Boston Massacre*, 211–12, 218, 295–98; Mayo, *Additions,* 19, 20–21.
41. Boyle, "Boyle's Journal," Mar. 5, 1770, 263; *Short Narrative*, 81, 93, 94; William Palfrey to John Wilkes, Mar. 13, 1770, in Elsey, "Wilkes and Palfrey," 480; Preston's account in Dalrymple to Hillsborough, Mar. 13, 1770, in *Documents of American Revolution*, 2:66; *Boston Evening-Post*, Mar. 12, 1770; *Boston Gazette*, Mar. 12, 1770; Thomas Hutchinson to Earl of Hillsborough, Mar. 12, 1770, in *Documents of American Revolution*, 2:58; Thomas Hutchinson to Francis Bernard, Mar. 12, 1770, Hutchinson Correspondence, Massachusetts Archives (microfilm), vol. 25, page 380.
42. Thomas Hutchinson to Earl of Hillsborough, Mar. 12, 1770, in *Documents of American Revolution*, 2:58; Thomas Hutchinson to Francis Bernard, Mar. 12, 1770, Hutchinson Correspondence, Massachusetts Archives (microfilm), vol. 25, page 380.
43. Thomas Hutchinson to Thomas Gage, Mar. 6, 1770, in R. G. Adams, *New Light on the Boston Massacre,* 14; Thomas Hutchinson to Earl of Hillsborough, Mar. 12, 1770, in *Documents of American Revolution*, 2:58; Thomas Hutchinson to Francis Bernard, Mar. 12, 1770, Hutchinson Correspondence, Massachusetts Archives (microfilm), vol. 25, page 380; *LPJA,* 3:61, 80–81; Preston's account in Dalrymple to Hillsborough, Mar. 13, 1770, in *Documents of American Revolution*, 2:66.

44. Boyle, "Boyle's Journal," Mar. 5, 1770, 263–64; Andrew Oliver Jr., to Benjamin Lynde Jr., Mar. 6, 1770, in Lynde, *Diaries*, 226–27; Thomas Hutchinson to Earl of Hillsborough, Mar. 12, 1770, in *Documents of American Revolution*, 2:58; Preston's account in Dalrymple to Hillsborough, Mar. 13, 1770, in *Documents of American Revolution*, 2:66; Thomas Hutchinson to Thomas Gage, Mar. 6, 1770, in R. G. Adams, *New Light*, 14; James Murray to Elizabeth Smith, Mar. 12, 1770, in *Letters of Murray*, 163; *Boston Evening-Post*, Mar. 12, 1770; *Boston Gazette*, Mar. 12, 1770; Maurice Carr to Thomas Gage, Mar. 7, 1770, in R. G. Adams, *New Light*, 20; William Palfrey to John Wilkes, Mar. 13, 1770, in Elsey, "Wilkes and Palfrey," 480.

45. Boyle, "Boyle's Journal," Mar. 5, 1770, 264; Thomas Hutchinson to Earl of Hillsborough, Mar. 12, 1770, in *Documents of American Revolution*, 2:58; Preston's account in Dalrymple to Hillsborough, Mar. 13, 1770, in *Documents of American Revolution*, 2:66; Thomas Hutchinson to Thomas Gage, Mar. 6, 1770, in R. G. Adams, *New Light*, 14; James Murray to Elizabeth Smith, Mar. 12, 1770, in *Letters of Murray*, 163; *Boston Evening-Post*, Mar. 12, 1770; *Boston Gazette*, Mar. 12, 1770; Maurice Carr to Thomas Gage, Mar. 7, 1770, in R. G. Adams, *New Light*, 20; William Palfrey to John Wilkes, Mar. 13, 1770, in Elsey, "Wilkes and Palfrey," 480.

46. Thomas Hutchinson to Thomas Gage, Mar. 6, 1770, in R. G. Adams, *New Light*, 14–15; Thomas Hutchinson to Earl of Hillsborough, Mar. 12, 1770, in *Documents of American Revolution*, 2:59; Thomas Hutchinson to Francis Bernard, Mar. 12, 1770, Hutchinson Correspondence, Massachusetts Archives (microfilm), vol. 25, pages 380–81; *Boston Gazette*, Mar. 12, 1770.

47. This and the following paragraphs on the deliberations over the removal of the troops are based on Thomas Hutchinson to Thomas Gage, Mar. 6, 1770, in R. G. Adams, *New Light*, 14–16; Thomas Hutchinson to Earl of Hillsborough, Mar. 12, 1770, in *Documents of American Revolution*, 2:59–60; Thomas Hutchinson to Francis Bernard, Mar. 12, 1770, Hutchinson Correspondence, Massachusetts Archives (microfilm), vol. 25, pages 380–81; William Dalrymple to Earl of Hillsborough, Mar. 13, 1770, in *Documents of American Revolution*, 2:62–63; Record of Proceedings of Council of Massachusetts by Andrew Oliver, Mar. 6, 1770, in *Documents of American Revolution*, 2:53–55; Thomas Hutchinson to William Dalrymple, Mar. 6, 1770, in R. G. Adams, *New Light*, 16–19; *Boston Gazette*, Mar. 12, 1770; William Dalrymple to Thomas Gage, Mar. 7, 1770, in R. G. Adams, *New Light*, 22–23; William Dalrymple to Thomas Gage, Mar. 8, 1770, in R. G. Adams, *New Light*, 24; *A Report of the Record Commissioners, 1770 to 1777*, Mar. 6, 1770, 3–4.

48. *Selectmen's Minutes*, Mar. 7, 1770, 57–58; *Boston Gazette*, Mar. 12, 1770; *Boston Evening-Post*, Mar. 12, 1770; Andrew Oliver Jr., to Benjamin Lynde Jr., Mar. 6, 1770, in Lynde, *Diaries*, 227–28.

CHAPTER 12

1. Rowe, *Diary*, Mar. 8, 1770, 199; *Boston Evening-Post*, Mar. 12, 19, 1770; *Boston Gazette*, Mar. 12, 19, 1770; William Palfrey to John Wilkes, Mar. 13, 1770, in Elsey, "Wilkes and Palfrey," 483; Thomas Hutchinson to Thomas Gage, Mar. 18, 1770, in R. G. Adams, *New Light*, 31.

2. Rowe, *Diary*, Mar. 16, 1770, 199; *Boston Evening-Post*, Mar. 12, 19, 1770; *Boston Gazette*, Mar. 12, 19, 1770; William Dalrymple to Thomas Gage, Mar. 8, 1770, in R. G. Adams, *New Light*, 24; Thomas Gage to William Dalrymple, Mar. 12, 14, 1770, in R. G. Adams, *New Light*, 26, 29–30.

3. Thomas Gage to Thomas Hutchinson, Mar. 12, 1770, in R. G. Adams, *New Light*, 28; Thomas Hutchinson to Thomas Gage, Mar. 18, 1770, in R. G. Adams, *New Light*, 30–31.

4. Thomas Gage to Thomas Hutchinson, Mar. 26, 1770, Hutchinson Correspondence, Massachusetts Archives (microfilm), vol. 25, pages 383–84; Thomas Gage to William Dalrymple, Mar. 26, Apr. 9, 1770, in R. G. Adams, *New Light*, 36, 45; Thomas Hutchinson to Thomas Gage, Apr. 22, 1770, Hutchinson Correspondence, Massachusetts Archives (microfilm), vol. 25, page 388; Thomas Gage to Earl of Hillsborough, Apr. 24, June 2, 1770, in *Correspondence of Gage*, 1:255, 259; *Boston Evening-Post*, May 21, 1770.

5. Rowe, *Diary*, Apr. 24, 1770, 201; *Boston Evening-Post*, Apr. 30, 1770; Christie, "British Response," 199; Miller, *Sam Adams*, 213.

6. Hoerder, *Crowd Action,* 234–35; Knollenberg, *Growth of American Revolution*, 74.

7. *Boston Evening-Post*, Apr. 30, 1770; *Boston Gazette*, Apr. 30, 1770; Henry Hulton to Robert Nicholson, May 4, 1770, in W. Brown, "Letters of Henry Hulton," 20.

8. Rowe, *Diary*, Apr. 26, 1770, 201; *Boston Gazette*, Apr. 30, 1770; *Boston Evening-Post*, May 21, 1770.

9. *Boston Evening-Post*, May 21, 28, 1770; Better Security to the Editors, *Boston Gazette*, May 7, 1770.

10. *Boston Gazette*, June 4, 1770; *Boston Evening-Post*, June 11, 1770.

11. *Boston Evening-Post*, June 25, 1770.

12. Henry Hulton to Robert Nicholson, June 12, 1770, in W. Brown, "Letters of Henry Hulton," 21; Samuel Cooper to Thomas Pownall, July 2, 1770, in Tuckerman, "Letters of Cooper to Pownall," 319.

13. *Boston Evening-Post*, July 2, 23, 1770; Samuel Adams to Peter Timothy, Nov. 21, 1770, in H. A. Cushing, *Writings of Samuel Adams*, 2:65.

14. *Boston Evening-Post*, July 23, 30, Aug. 13, Oct. 15, 22, 1770; Jensen, *Founding of a Nation*, 367.

15. Thomas Gage to Earl of Hillsborough, Apr. 10, July 7, 1770, in *Correspondence of Gage*, 1:249, 263–64; Thomas Gage to Lord Barrington, July 6, 1770, in *Correspondence of Gage*, 2:547; William Dalrymple to

Thomas Gage, Mar. 27, 1770, in R. G. Adams, *New Light*, 39; Henry Hulton to Robert Nicholson, May 4, 1770, in W. Brown, "Letters of Henry Hulton," 16–17.

16. Thomas Hutchinson to Thomas Gage, Mar. 18, 1770, in R. G. Adams, *New Light*, 31; Freiberg, "Introduction," *JHR*, 46:x–xi.

17. Thomas Hutchinson to House, Apr. 11, 17, May 31, 1770, *JHR*, 46:149–50, 166–67, 47:9; House to Thomas Hutchinson, Apr. 13, 19, 1770, *JHR*, 46:155, 170.

18. Lord and Calhoon, "Removal of the Massachusetts General Court," 736–38; Thomas Hutchinson to House, Mar. 15, 16, 22, 23, 1770, *JHR*, 46:90, 92, 97, 99; House to Thomas Hutchinson, Mar. 15, 23, July 31, 1770, *JHR*, 46:91, 98, 47:71; Draft of reasons to halt business at the House of Representatives until meeting place is returned to Boston, *JHR*, 47:27.

19. Earl of Hillsborough to Thomas Gage, Apr. 14, June 12, 1770, in *Correspondence of Gage*, 2:107, 103–4; Earl of Hillsborough to Thomas Hutchinson, June 12, 1770, in *Documents of the American Revolution*, 2:102; Thomas Gage to Earl of Hillsborough, Aug. 18, 1770, in *Correspondence of Gage*, 1:265; Hutchinson, *Diary and Letters,* 1:27; Thomas Gage to William Dalrymple, Sept. 2, 1770, in R. G. Adams, *New Light*, 74; Thomas Gage to Lord Barrington, Sept. 8, 1770, in *Correspondence of Gage*, 2:557; Thomas Gage to Earl of Hillsborough, Sept. 8, 1770, in *Correspondence of Gage,* 1:267–68.

20. Hutchinson, *Diary and Letters,* 1:28–30.

21. *Boston Evening-Post*, Sept. 17, 24, 1770; Thomas Gage to Earl of Hillsborough, Oct. 6, 1770, in *Correspondence of Gage*, 1:271; House to Thomas Hutchinson, Nov. 20, 1770, *JHR*, 47:171–72; Thomas Hutchinson to House, Nov. 20, 1770, *JHR*, 47:172, 182; Deposition of John Phillips, Nov. 8, 1770, *JHR*, 47:173; Deposition of Stephen Hall, Nov. 8, 1770, *JHR*, 47:173–74.

22. J. Adams, *Diary*, 3:292–95, Mar. 5, 1773, 2:79.

23. Ferling, *John Adams*; William Pencak, "John Adams," American National Biography Online, www.anb.org/articles/01/01.00007.html; L. H. Butterfield, introduction to J. Adams, *Diary,* 1:xli–lii.

24. Josiah Quincy to Josiah Quincy Jr., Mar. 22, 1770, in Quincy, *Memoir,* 26–27; Josiah Quincy Jr. to Josiah Quincy, Mar. 26, 1770, in *Memoir,* 27–28; Zobel, *Boston Massacre*, 220–21.

25. Zobel, *Boston Massacre*, 221; Reid, "Lawyer Acquitted," 206; P. Shaw, *American Patriots,* 123; *JHR*, June 6, 1770, 47:16; *Boston Gazette*, June 11, 1770; J. Adams, *Diary*, June 26, 1770, 1:351.

26. William Molineux to Robert Treat Paine, Mar. 9, 1770, in Riley and Hanson, *Papers of Robert Treat Paine*, 2:463–64; *Boston Town Records*, Mar. 6, 13, 1770, 1–2, 14; Committee of Boston to John Wilkes, Mar. 23, 1770, in Ford, "Wilkes and Boston," 213–14.

27. Thomas Gage to William Dalrymple, Mar. 12, 1770, in R. G. Adams, *New Light*, 27; Thomas Hutchinson to Thomas Gage, Mar. 18, Apr. 1, 1770, in R. G. Adams, *New Light*, 31, 42; Town of Boston to Thomas Hutchinson, Mar. 19, 1770, in H. A. Cushing, *Writings of Adams*, 2:8; Samuel Cooper to Thomas Pownall, Mar. 26, 1770, in Tuckerman, "Letters of Cooper to Pownall," 318; James Bowdoin to William Bollan, Mar. 27, 1770, in *Bowdoin-Cooper Papers*, 169; Council to William Bollan, Mar. 27, 1770, in R. G. Adams, *New Light*, 40–41; William Dalrymple to Thomas Gage, Apr. 2, 1770, in R. G. Adams, *New Light*, 43.

28. Wroth and Zobel, "Editorial Note" and Documents for Rex v. Richardson, *LPJA*, 2:396–430; Zobel, *Boston Massacre*, 231.

29. Rowe, *Diary*, Mar. 5, 1770, 198; William Palfrey to John Wilkes, Mar. 13, 1770, in Elsey, "Wilkes and Palfrey," 483; *Boston Gazette*, Mar. 12, 1770; William Dalrymple to Earl of Hillsborough, Mar. 13, 1770, in *Documents of American Revolution*, 2:63–66; Thomas Gage to William Dalrymple, Mar. 26, 1770, in R. G. Adams, *New Light*, 36–37.

30. Thomas Hutchinson to Thomas Gage, June 23, 1770, in R. G. Adams, *New Light*, 56–57; *Boston Evening-Post*, June 25, 1770; Samuel Cooper to Thomas Pownall, July 2, 1770, in Tuckerman, "Letters of Cooper to Pownall," 320; *Boston Town Records*, July 10, 1770, 34.

31. Boston Committee to Thomas Preston, July 11, 1770, in R. G. Adams, *New Light*, 58–61; Thomas Gage to Thomas Preston, Aug. 12, 1770, in R. G. Adams, *New Light*, 69.

32. Anonymous to Preston, July 20, 1770, in R. G. Adams, *New Light*, 62; William Dalrymple to Thomas Gage, Sept. 3, 1770, in R. G. Adams, *New Light*, 74–75; *Boston Evening-Post*, Sept. 10, 1770; Thomas Hutchinson to Thomas Gage, Sept. 11, 1770, in *Documents of American Revolution*, 2:183.

33. Wroth and Zobel, "Editorial Note" to the Boston Massacre Trials, *LPJA*, 3:16–17; Hugh White, James Hartigan, Matthew Kilroy to the Honourable Judges of the Superior Court, Oct. 24, 1770, in Noble, "Communication of original papers," 66.

34. William Palfrey to John Wilkes, Oct. 23–30, 1770, in Elsey, "Wilkes and Palfrey," 424–25; Wroth and Zobel, "Editorial Note" to Boston Massacre Trials, *LPJA*, 3:17–19; Reid, "Lawyer Acquitted," 197; Zobel, *Boston Massacre*, 246.

35. *LPJA*, 3:46–98 (Paine's quote on 92); William Palfrey to John Wilkes, Oct. 23–30, 1770, in Elsey, "Wilkes and Palfrey," 425; Zobel, *Boston Massacre*, 246–66; Reid, "Lawyer Acquitted," 198–207; *Boston Gazette*, Dec. 10, 1770.

36. Wroth and Zobel, "Editorial Note," *LPJA*, 3:24–25; *LPJA*, 3:99–100; Zobel, *Boston Massacre*, 270–71.

37. *LPJA*, 3:101–57 (Quincy quotes on 101 and 156); Zobel, *Boston Massacre*, 271–77.

38. *LPJA*, 3:157–225.

39. *LPJA*, 3:226–41.

40. *LPJA*, 3:242–70 (Adams quotes on 242 and 266).

41. Paine's closing in this and the following paragraph comes from *LPJA*, 3:270–82 (Paine quotes on 279, 281, and 282; Adams quote on 88).

42. Wroth and Zobel, "Massachusetts Bench and Bar," *LPJA*, 1:xcviii, ciii–civ, cxi–cxii; *LPJA,* 3:282–324; *Boston Gazette*, Dec. 10, 17, 1770.

43. T. Hutchinson, *History of Massachusetts Bay*, 3:237; Proclamation by Thomas Hutchinson, Dec. 13, 1770, *Boston Evening-Post*, Dec. 17, 1770; Vindex [Samuel Adams], *Boston Gazette*, Dec. 10, 17, 24, 31, 1770, Jan. 7, 14, 21, 28, 1771.

CONCLUSION

1. Shepherd and Walton, *Shipping, Maritime Trade*, 115.

2. *Boston Gazette*, Mar. 11, 1771.

3. *Boston Gazette*, Mar. 9, 1772, Mar. 14, 1774, Mar. 13, 1775, Mar. 11, 1776, Mar. 10, 1777, Mar. 10, 1783; *Boston Evening-Post*, Mar. 8, 1773, Mar. 14, 1774; *Orations . . . to commemorate the evening of the fifth of March, 1770 . . .* (Boston, 1785).

Works Cited

Adair, Douglass, and John A. Schutz, eds. *Peter Oliver's Origin and Progress of the American Rebellion*. San Marino, Calif., 1961.

Adams, John. *Diary and Autobiography of John Adams*. Ed. L. H. Butterfield. 4 vols. Cambridge, Mass., 1961.

Adams, Randolph G. *New Light on the Boston Massacre*. Worcester, Mass., 1938.

Alden, John. *General Gage in America*. Baton Rouge, 1948.

———. "John Mein: Scourge of Patriots." Colonial Society of Massachusetts, *Publications* 34 (1942): 571–99.

Allison, Robert J. *The Boston Massacre*. Beverly, Mass., 2006.

"An Alphabetical List of the Sons of Liberty who dined at Liberty Tree, Dorchester, Aug. 14, 1769." Massachusetts Historical Society, *Proceedings* 11 (1869–70): 140–42.

Anderson, Fred. *Crucible of War: The Seven Years' War and the Fate of Empire in British North America, 1754–1766*. New York, 2000.

———. *A People's Army: Massachusetts Soldiers and Society in the Seven Years' War*. New York, 1984.

Anderson, George P. "Ebenezer Mackintosh, Stamp Act Rioter and Patriot." Colonial Society of Massachusetts, *Publications* 26 (March 1924): 15–64.

———. "A Note on Ebenezer Mackintosh." Colonial Society of Massachusetts, *Publications* 26 (February 1926): 348–61.

Archer, Richard. *Fissures in the Rock: New England in the Seventeenth Century*. Hanover, N.H., 2001.

Bailyn, Bernard. *The Ordeal of Thomas Hutchinson*. Cambridge, Mass., 1975.

Barrow, Thomas C. *Trade and Empire: The British Customs Service in Colonial America, 1660–1775*. Cambridge, Mass., 1967.

Bass, Henry, to Samuel P. Savage, December 19, 1765, in Massachusetts Historical Society, *Proceedings* 44 (1910–11): 688–89.

Baxter, W. T. *The House of Hancock: Business in Boston, 1724–1775*. Cambridge, Mass., 1945.

Benton, J. H., Jr. *Early Census Making in Massachusetts, 1643–1765, with a Reproduction of the Lost Census of 1765 (Recently Found) and Documents Relating Thereto*. Boston, 1905.

Berkin, Carol. *Jonathan Sewall: Odyssey of an American Loyalist.* New York, 1974.

Berlin, Ira. *Many Thousands Gone: The First Two Centuries of Slavery in North America.* Cambridge, Mass., 1998.

Bernard, Francis. *Select Letters on the Trade and Government of America; and the Principles of Law and Polity, Applied to the American Colonies.* 2nd ed. London, 1774.

Bowdoin-Temple Papers. Massachusetts Historical Society, *Collections*, 6th ser., IX, 1897.

Boyer, Lee R. "Lobster Backs, Liberty Boys and Laborers in the Streets: New York's Golden Hill and Nassau Street Riots." *New-York Historical Society Quarterly* 62 (October 1973): 281–308.

Boyle, John. "Boyle's Journal of Occurrences in Boston, 1759–1778." *New England Historical and Genealogical Register* 84 (1930): 142–71, 248–68.

Breen, T. H. "The Covenanted Militia of Massachusetts Bay: English Background and New World Development." In *Puritans and Adventurers: Change and Persistence in Early America.* New York, 1980. 24–45.

———. *The Marketplace of Revolution: How Consumer Politics Shaped American Independence.* New York, 2004.

Bridenbaugh, Carl. *Cities in Revolt: Urban Life in America, 1743–1776.* New York, 1955.

Brown, Abrah English. *John Hancock: His Book.* Boston, 1898.

Brown, Richard D. "The Massachusetts Convention of Towns, 1768." *William and Mary Quarterly*, 3rd ser., 26 (1969): 94–104.

———. *Revolutionary Politics in Massachusetts: The Boston Committee of Correspondence and the Towns, 1772–1774.* Cambridge, Mass., 1970.

Brown, Wallace. "An Englishman Views the American Revolution: The Letters of Henry Hulton, 1769–1776." *Huntington Library Quarterly* 36 (November 1972): 1–26, and (February 1973): pt. 2, 139–51.

Bullion, John L. *A Great and Necessary Measure: George Grenville and the Genesis of the Stamp Act, 1763–1765.* Columbia, Mo., 1982.

———. "Security and Economy: The Bute Administration's Plans for the American Army and Revenue." *William and Mary Quarterly*, 3rd. ser., 45 (July 1988): 499–509.

———. "'The Ten Thousand in America': More Light on the Decision on the American Army, 1762–1763." *William and Mary Quarterly*, 3rd. ser., 43 (October 1986): 646–57.

Bullock, Steven C. *Revolutionary Brotherhood: Freemasonry and the Transformation of the American Social Order, 1730–1840.* Chapel Hill, N.C., 1996.

Calhoon, Robert McCluer. *The Loyalists in Revolutionary America, 1760–1781.* New York, 1973.

Carp, Benjamin L. *Rebels Rising: Cities and the American Revolution.* New York, 2007.

Cary, John. *Joseph Warren*. Urbana, Ill., 1961.

Channing, Edward, and A. C. Coolidge, eds. *The Barrington-Bernard Correspondence*. Cambridge, Mass., 1912.

Christie, Ian R. "British Response to American Reactions to the Townshend Acts, 1768–1770." In Walter H. Conser Jr., Ronald M. McCarthy, David J. Toscano, and Gene Sharp, eds., *Resistance, Politics, and the American Struggle for Independence, 1765–1775*. Boulder, 1986. 193–214.

Cleary, Patricia. *Elizabeth Murray: A Woman's Pursuit of Independence in Eighteenth-Century America*. Amherst, Mass., 2000.

Conser, Walter H., Jr. "The Stamp Act Resistance." In Walter H. Conser Jr., Ronald M. McCarthy, David J. Toscano, and Gene Sharp, eds., *Resistance, Politics, and the American Struggle for Independence, 1765–1775*. Boulder, 1986. 22–88.

Countryman, Edward. *A People in Revolution: The American Revolution and Political Society in New York, 1760–1790*. Baltimore, 1981.

Cushing, Harry Alonzo, ed. *The Writings of Samuel Adams*. 4 vols. New York, 1904–8.

Cushing, Thomas. "Letters of Thomas Cushing, from 1767 to 1775." Massachusetts Historical Society, *Collections*, 4th ser., 4 (1858): 347–66.

Day, Alan, and Katherine Day. "Another Look at the Boston 'Caucus.'" *Journal of American Studies* 5 (April 1971): 19–42.

Depositions of Soldiers, British National Archives, CO5/88 XC1580.

Desrochers, Robert E., Jr. "Slave-for-Sale Advertisements and Slavery in Massachusetts, 1704–1781." *William and Mary Quarterly*, 3rd. ser., 59 (July 2002): 623–64.

Dickerson, Oliver Morton, comp. *Boston under Military Rule as Revealed in a Journal of the Times*. Boston, 1936.

———. "The Commissioners of Customs and the 'Boston Massacre.'" *New England Quarterly* 27 (September 1954): 307–25.

———. *The Navigation Acts and the American Revolution*. Philadelphia, 1951.

———. "Opinion of Attorney General Sewall of Massachusetts in the Case of the Lydia." *William and Mary Quarterly*, 3rd. ser., 4 (October 1947): 499–504.

Documents of the American Revolution, 1770–1783 (Colonial Office Series), Volume II Transcripts 1770. Ed. K. G. Davies. Shannon, Ireland, 1972.

Drake, Samuel Adams. *Old Landmarks and Historic Personages of Boston*. Revised ed. Boston, 1906.

Egnal, Marc. *A Mighty Empire: The Origins of the American Revolution*. Ithaca, N.Y., 1988.

Egnal, Marc, and Joseph A. Ernst. "An Economic Interpretation of the American Revolution." *William and Mary Quarterly*, 3rd. ser., 29 (January 1972): 1–32.

Elsey, George M. "John Wilkes and William Palfrey." Colonial Society of Massachusetts, *Publications*, 34 (1943): 411–28.

Everard, H. *History of Thomas Farrington's Regiment subsequently designated the 29th (Worcestershire) Foot, 1694 to 1891.* Worcester, England, 1891.

Ferling, John. *John Adams: A Life.* New York, 1992.

Fields, Barbara. "Slavery, Race, and Ideology in the United States of America." *New Left Review* 181 (May–June 1990): 95–118.

Fischer, David Hackett. *Paul Revere's Ride.* New York, 1994.

———. *Washington's Crossing.* New York, 2004.

Ford, Worthington Chauncy. "John Wilkes and Boston." Massachusetts Historical Society, *Proceedings* 47 (1913–14): 190–215.

Fowler, William M., Jr. *The Baron of Beacon Hill: A Biography of John Hancock.* Boston, 1980.

Fredrickson, George M. *White Supremacy: A Comparative Study in American and South African History.* New York, 1981.

Frey, Sylvia. *The British Soldier in America: A Social History of Military Life in the Revolutionary Period.* Austin, Tex., 1981.

Gage, Thomas. *The Correspondence of General Thomas Gage.* Vol. 1. Ed. Clarence E. Carter. New Haven, Conn., 1931.

———. *The Correspondence of General Thomas Gage.* Vol. 2. Ed. Clarence E. Carter. New Haven, Conn., 1933.

Gilje, Paul A. *Liberty on the Waterfront: American Maritime Culture in the Age of Revolution.* Philadelphia, 2004.

———. *The Road to Mobocracy: Popular Disorder in New York City, 1763–1834.* Chapel Hill, N.C., 1987.

Gordon, Lord Adam. "Journal of an Officer who Travelled in America and the West Indies in 1764 and 1765 [Journal of Lord Adam Gordon]." In Newton D. Mereness, ed., *Travels in the American Colonies.* New York, 1916. 367–456.

Gordon, William. *The History of the Rise, Progress, and Establishment of the Independence of the United States of America . . .* 4 vols. London, 1788.

Gould, Eliga. *The Persistence of Empire: British Political Culture in the Age of the American Revolution.* Chapel Hill, N.C., 2000.

Greene, Lorenzo. *The Negro in Colonial New England, 1620–1776.* New York, 1942.

Higginbotham, A. Leon, Jr. *In the Matter of Color: Race and the American Legal Process: The Colonial Period.* New York, 1978.

Hoerder, Dirk. *Crowd Action in Revolutionary Massachusetts, 1765–1780.* New York, 1977.

Horton, James Oliver, and Lois E. Horton. *In Hope of Liberty: Culture, Community and Protest among Northern Free Blacks, 1700–1860.* New York, 1997.

Hulton, Ann. *Letters of a Loyalist Lady.* Cambridge, Mass., 1927.

Hutchinson, Peter Orlando, ed. *The Diary and Letters of His Excellency Thomas Hutchinson, Esq. . . . .* 2 vols. Boston, 1884–86.

Hutchinson Correspondence. Massachusetts Archives (microfilm), reels 25, 26.

Hutchinson, Thomas. *The History of the Colony and Province of Massachusetts-Bay.* Vol. 3. Ed. Lawrence Shaw Mayo. Cambridge, Mass., 1936.

Jasper Mauduit: Agent in London for the Province of Massachusetts-Bay, 1762–1765. Massachusetts Historical Society. *Collections* 74 (1917).

Jensen, Merrill. *The Founding of a Nation: A History of the American Revolution 1763–1776.* New York, 1968.

Johnson, Allen S. "The Passage of the Sugar Act." *William and Mary Quarterly*, 3rd ser., 16 (October 1959): 507–14.

————. *A Prologue to Revolution: The Political Career of George Grenville, 1712–1770.* Lanham, Md., 1997.

Jordan, Winthrop. *White over Black: American Attitudes toward the Negro, 1550–1812.* Chapel Hill, N.C., 1968.

Journals of the House of Representatives of Massachusetts. Vols. 37–47. Ed. Malcolm Freiberg. 1760–71; reprint, Boston, 1965–78.

Knollenberg, Bernhard. *Growth of the American Revolution, 1766–1775.* New York, 1975.

————. *Origin of the American Revolution: 1759–1766.* Revised ed. New York, 1961.

Kulikoff, Alan. "The Progress of Inequality in Revolutionary Boston." *William and Mary Quarterly*, 3rd. ser., 28 (July 1971): 375–412.

Labaree, Benjamin. *The Boston Tea Party.* New York, 1964.

Langford, Paul. "The First Rockingham Ministry and the Repeal of the Stamp Act: The Role of the Commercial Lobby and Economic Pressures." In Walter H. Conser Jr., Ronald M. McCarthy, David J. Toscano, and Gene Sharp, eds., *Resistance, Politics, and the American Struggle for Independence, 1765–1775.* Boulder, 1986. 89–118.

Lawson, Philip. *George Grenville: A Political Life.* Oxford, 1984.

Lemisch, Jesse. "Jack Tar in the Streets: Merchant Seamen in the Politics of Revolutionary America." *William and Mary Quarterly*, 3rd. ser., 25 (July 1968): 371–407.

"Letters from Andrew Eliot to Thomas Hollis." Massachusetts Historical Society, *Collections*, 4th ser., 4 (1858): 398–461.

Letters to the Ministry from Governor Bernard, General Gage, and Commodore Hood. And Also Memorials to the Lords of the Treasury from the Commissioners of the Customs, With Sundry Letters and Papers Annexed to the Said Memorials. Boston, 1769.

Lord, Donald C., and Robert M. Calhoon. "The Removal of the Massachusetts General Court from Boston, 1769–1772." *Journal of American History* 60 (March 1969): 735–55.

Lynde, Benjamin. *The Diaries of Benjamin Lynde and of Benjamin Lynde, Jr.; with an Appendix.* Boston, 1880.

Maier, Pauline. *From Resistance to Revolution: Colonial Radicals and the Development of American Opposition to Britain, 1765–1776.* New York, 1972.

———. *The Old Revolutionaries: Political Lives in the Age of Samuel Adams.* New York, 1980.

Marks, Robert B. *The Origins of the Modern World: A Global and Ecological Narrative.* Lanham, Md., 2002.

Mayo, Catherine Barton, ed. *Additions to Thomas Hutchinson's "History of Massachusetts Bay."* Worcester, Mass., 1949.

McManus, Edgar J. *Black Bondage in the North.* Syracuse, N.Y., 1973.

Melish, Joanne Pope. *Disowning Slavery: Gradual Emancipation and "Race" in New England, 1780–1860.* Ithaca, N.Y., 1998.

Middlekauff, Robert. *The Glorious Cause: The American Revolution, 1763–1789.* New York, 1982.

Miller, John C. *Sam Adams, Pioneer in Propaganda.* Boston, 1936.

Moore, George H. *Notes on the History of Slavery in Massachusetts.* 1866; reprint, New York, 1968.

Morgan, Edmund S. "The Postponement of the Stamp Act." *William and Mary Quarterly,* 3rd ser., 7 (July 1950): 353–92.

Morgan, Edmund S., and Helen M. Morgan. *The Stamp Act Crisis: Prologue to Revolution.* 1953; revised ed., New York, 1962.

Murray, James. *Letters of James Murray, Loyalist.* Ed. Nina M. Tiffany and Susan I. Lesley. 1901; reprint, Boston, 1972.

Nash, Gary B. *The Unknown American Revolution: The Unruly Birth of Democracy and the Struggle to Create America.* New York, 2005.

———. *The Urban Crucible: Social Change, Political Consciousness, and the Origins of the American Revolution.* Cambridge, Mass., 1979.

Nicolson, Colin. *The "Infamas Govener": Francis Bernard and the Origins of the American Revolution.* Boston, 2001.

———, ed. *The Papers of Francis Bernard: Governor of Colonial Massachusetts, 1760–69.* Vol. 1 (1759–63). Colonial Society of Massachusetts, *Collections* 73 (2007).

Noble, John. "Communication of Original Papers Relating the Trial of Captain Thomas Preston and the Soldiers Concerned in the Riot of the Fifth of March, 1770." Colonial Society of Massachusetts, *Publications* 5 (1897–98): 58–77.

Norton, Mary Beth. "A Cherished Spirit of Independence: The Life of an Eighteenth Century Boston Businesswoman." In Carol Ruth Berkin and Mary Beth Norton, eds., *Women of America: A History.* Boston, 1979. 48–60.

———. *Liberty's Daughters: The Revolutionary Experience of American Women, 1750–1800.* Boston, 1980.

Orations . . . to commemorate the evening of the fifth of March, 1770 . . . Boston, 1785.

Palfrey, John Gorham. *History of New England.* 5 vols. Vol. 5. Boston, 1890.

Pencak, William. *War, Politics and Revolution in Provincial Massachusetts.* Boston, 1981.

Piersen, William D. *Black Yankees: The Development of an Afro-American Sub-Culture in New England.* Amherst, Mass., 1988.

Quincy, Josiah. *Memoir of the Life of Josiah Quincy Jun.* 2nd ed. Boston, 1874.

Quincy, Josiah, Jr. *Reports of Cases Argued and Adjudged in the Superior Court of Judicature of the Province of Massachusetts Bay between 1761 and 1772.* Ed. Samuel M. Quincy. Boston, 1865.

Re-dedication of the Old State House. Boston, 1882.

Reid, John Phillip. *In Defiance of the Law: The Standing-Army Controversy, the Two Constitutions, and the Coming of the American Revolution.* Chapel Hill, N.C., 1981.

————. *In a Rebellious Spirit: The Argument of Facts, the Liberty Riot, and the Coming of the American Revolution.* University Park, Pa., 1979.

————. "A Lawyer Acquitted: John Adams and the Boston Massacre Trials." *American Journal of Legal History* 18 (1974): 189–207.

A Report of the Record Commissioners of the City of Boston, Containing the Boston Records from 1660 to 1701. Boston, 1881.

A Report of the Record Commissioners of the City of Boston, Containing the Boston Records from 1700 to 1728. Boston, 1883.

A Report of the Record Commissioners of the City of Boston, Containing the Boston Records from 1729 to 1742. Boston, 1885.

A Report of the Record Commissioners of the City of Boston, Containing the Boston Records from 1742 to 1757. Boston, 1885.

A Report of the Record Commissioners of the City of Boston, Containing the Boston Town Records, 1758 to 1769. Boston, 1886.

A Report of the Record Commissioners of the City of Boston, Containing the Boston Town Records, 1770 to 1777. Boston, 1887.

A Report of the Record Commissioners of the City of Boston, Containing the Records of Boston Selectmen, 1701 to 1715. Boston, 1884.

A Report of the Record Commissioners of the City of Boston, Containing the Selectmen's Minutes from 1764 through 1768. Boston, 1889.

A Report of the Record Commissioners of the City of Boston, Containing the Selectmen's Minutes from 1769 through April, 1775. Boston, 1893.

Riley, Stephen T., and Edward W. Hanson, eds. *The Papers of Robert Treat Paine.* Vol. 2. Boston, 1992.

Rowe, John. *Diary and Letters.* Ed. Anne R. Cunningham. Boston, 1902.

Schlesinger, Arthur M. *The Colonial Merchants and the American Revolution, 1763–1776.* New York, 1918.

Sewall, Samuel. "The Selling of Joseph: A Memorial." In M. Halsey Thomas, ed., *The Diary of Samuel Sewall.* 2 vols. New York, 1973. 2:1117–21.

Seybolt, Robert F. *Town Officials of Colonial Boston, 1634–1775*. Cambridge, Mass., 1939.

Shaw, Charles. *A Topographical and Historical Description of Boston*. Boston, 1817.

Shaw, Peter. *American Patriots and the Rituals of Revolution*. Cambridge, Mass., 1981.

Shepherd, James F., and Gary M. Walton. *Shipping, Maritime Trade, and the Economic Development of Colonial North America*. Cambridge, Mass., 1972.

Shipton, Clifford K. *Sibley's Harvard Graduates*. Vols. 7–17. Boston, 1945–75.

A Short Narrative of the Horrid Massacre in Boston, Perpetrated in the Evening of the Fifth Day of May, 1770, by Soldiers of the 29th Regiment, which with the 14th Regiment Were Then Quartered There; with some Observations on the State of Things Prior to that Catastrophe. 1770; reprint, Williamstown, Mass., 1973.

Shy, John. *Toward Lexington: The Role of the British Army in the Coming of the American Revolution*. Princeton, N.J., 1965.

Stiles, Ezra. *Extracts from Itineraries and Other Miscellanies of Ezra Stiles, 1755–1794, with a Selection from His Correspondence*. Ed. Franklin B. Dexter. New Haven, Conn., 1916.

Sweet, John Wood. *Bodies Politic: Negotiating Race in the American North, 1730–1830*. Baltimore, 2003.

Taylor, Robert J., Mary-Jo Kline, and Gregg L. Lint, eds. *Papers of John Adams, September 1755–October 1773*. Vol. 1. Cambridge, Mass., 1977.

Tiedemann, Joseph S. *Reluctant Revolutionaries: New York City and the Road to Independence, 1763–1776*. Ithaca, N.Y., 1997.

Tuckerman, Frederick. "Letters of Samuel Cooper to Thomas Pownall, 1769–1777." *American Historical Review* 8 (January 1903): 301–30.

Tudor, William. *The Life of James Otis of Massachusetts: Containing also, Notices of Some Contemporary Characters and Events from the Year 1760 to 1775*. Boston, 1823.

Twombly, Robert C., and Robert H. Moore. "Black Puritan: The Negro in Seventeenth-Century Massachusetts." *William and Mary Quarterly*, 3rd ser., 24 (April 1967): 224–42.

Tyler, John W. *Smugglers and Patriots: Boston Merchants and the Advent of the American Revolution*. Boston, 1986.

Warden, G. B. *Boston, 1689–1776*. Boston, 1970.

Warren, Mercy Otis. *History of the Rise, Progress and Termination of the American Revolution*. 3 vols. 1805; reprint, New York, 1970.

Waters, John J., Jr. *The Otis Family in Provincial and Revolutionary Massachusetts*. Chapel Hill, N.C., 1968.

Waters, John J., Jr., and John A. Schutz. "Patterns of Massachusetts Colonial Politics: The Writs of Assistance and the Rivalry between the Otis and Hutchinson Families." *William and Mary Quarterly*, 3rd ser., 24 (October 1967): 543–67.

Watson, D. H., ed. "Joseph Harrison and the Liberty Incident." *William and Mary Quarterly*, 3rd ser., 20 (October 1963): 585–95.

Winsor, Justin, ed. *Memorial History of Boston, 1630–1880*. 4 vols. Vol. 3. Boston, 1880–81.

Wolkins, G. G. "Daniel Malcom and Writs of Assistance." Massachusetts Historical Society, *Proceedings* 58 (1924–25): 5–84.

———."The Seizure of John Hancock's Sloop 'Liberty.'" Massachusetts Historical Society, *Proceedings* 55 (1921–22): 239–84.

Wood, Betty. *The Origins of American Slavery: Freedom and Bondage in the English Colonies*. New York, 1997.

Wroth, L. Kinvin, and Hiller B. Zobel, eds. *Legal Papers of John Adams*. 6 vols. Vols. 1–3. Cambridge, Mass., 1965.

Young, Alfred F. *Liberty Tree: Ordinary People and the American Revolution*. New York, 2006.

———. "The Women of Boston: 'Persons of Consequence' in the Making of the American Revolution, 1765–76." In Harriet B. Applewhite and Darline G. Levy, eds., *Women and Politics in the Age of the Democratic Revolution*. Ann Arbor, Mich., 1990. 181–226.

Zilversmit, Arthur. *The First Emancipation: The Abolition of Slavery in the North*. Chicago, 1967.

Zobel, Hiller B. *The Boston Massacre*. New York, 1970.

Index